Artificial Intelligence in Legal Systems

This book presents a comprehensive analysis of the transformative impact of artificial intelligence (AI) on legal frameworks within the European Union and beyond. It illustrates both the promising benefits of AI in improving access to justice and the significant challenges that necessitate thoughtful regulatory frameworks and interdisciplinary cooperation.

This book highlights the expansive applications of AI, ranging from case management to predictive analytics, while also scrutinizing ethical challenges and legal implications. It addresses the pressing issue of data protection in the context of Generative Pre-trained Transformer (GPT) technology, emphasizing the EU's commitment to individual privacy rights. This book also evaluates AI's role in public governance, using Albania as a case study, and examines the potential of blockchain technology in enhancing legal processes. The ethical nuances surrounding AI's integration into legal systems are critically examined, particularly regarding algorithmic bias and human oversight. This book advocates for a collaborative approach involving legal experts and data scientists to navigate these complexities effectively.

This book is a key resource for postgraduate students, researchers, and legal professionals seeking to better understand the benefits and risks of incorporating AI into legal practice.

Artificial Intelligence in Legal Systems

Bridging Law and Technology through AI

Edited by
Eriona Çela, Narasimha Rao Vajjhala,
and Behrouz Aslani

CRC Press
Taylor & Francis Group
Boca Raton London New York

CRC Press is an imprint of the
Taylor & Francis Group, an **informa** business

A CHAPMAN & HALL BOOK

Designed cover image: Shutterstock

First edition published 2026
by CRC Press
2385 NW Executive Center Drive, Suite 320, Boca Raton FL 33431

and by CRC Press
4 Park Square, Milton Park, Abingdon, Oxon, OX14 4RN

CRC Press is an imprint of Taylor & Francis Group, LLC

© 2026 selection and editorial matter, Eriona Çela, Narasimha Rao Vajjhala, and Behrouz Aslani; individual chapters, the contributors

ISBN: 978-1-032-89241-2 (hbk)
ISBN: 978-1-032-89239-9 (pbk)
ISBN: 978-1-003-54189-9 (ebk)

DOI: 10.1201/9781003541899

Typeset in Times
by codeMantra

Contents

Foreword

As an expert in emerging technologies and social computing, I have always been fascinated by how technology reshapes human interactions, knowledge-sharing, and institutions. Among these, the legal system stands out as a sector where the potential for transformation is tremendous, although it includes a lot of challenges. With the emergence of Artificial Intelligence (AI), we are witnessing a chance to redefine how justice is administered, accessed, and understood.

What fascinates me most about AI in the legal sector is its capacity to address long-standing challenges: accelerating legal research, enhancing decision-making processes, and widening access to justice for the underprivileged. These possibilities connect strongly with the ideas of social computing, using technology to increase cooperation and accessibility, and emerging technologies, where innovation fosters empowerment and understanding. AI in legal systems examines how these concepts merge to build more equitable and efficient legal systems.

This book addresses AI's potential not simply as a tool for efficiency but as a catalyst for systemic transformation. From natural language processing in document review to predictive analytics in case outcomes, the examples provided here highlight how AI may supplement the skills of legal practitioners. Yet, as someone strongly interested in understanding the social elements of technology, I am equally drawn to this book's reflections on ethics, transparency, and the risks of biases. These challenges are crucial as we work toward developing AI-driven systems that reflect and support societal standards and norms.

What is most noticeable is this book's emphasis on education and skill-building for legal practitioners. As AI becomes a cornerstone of modern legal systems, training practitioners with the skills to efficiently and ethically take advantage of these tools will be critical. This aligns with the concept of social computing and emerging technologies, where the focus is on enabling individuals to navigate and excel in an increasingly digital society.

AI in legal systems is more than a discussion of technological potential; it is a comprehensive guide to ensuring that innovation serves humanity. It bridges the gap between law and technology, demonstrating how interdisciplinary collaboration can lead to substantial advancements. For readers from the disciplines of education, technology, and law, this book offers not just insights but also a vision for how AI could enhance one of society's most fundamental institutions.

As you engage with the ideas and case studies presented in this book, I encourage you to think about how your own expertise, whether in law, technology, or education, can contribute to this transformative journey. The future of AI in legal systems is a collaborative endeavor, and this book offers an exciting foundation for making that future more just, inclusive, and impactful.

Vasileios Paliktzoglou

ABOUT THE FOREWORD AUTHOR

Dr. Vasileios Paliktzoglou is an academic and industry professional who holds a Ph.D. in Computer Science from the University of Eastern Finland. He is an active contributor to academia, serving as a guest and associate editor for prestigious journals such as the *Journal of Information Systems Education* (*JISE*) and *IAFOR Journal of Education*. He has been a keynote speaker at several academic and industry events, sharing his insights on social computing, collaborative learning, and emerging technologies in higher education. Dr. Paliktzoglou also actively participates in international research projects, highlighting his commitment to advancing knowledge and innovation as the Book Series Editor for "Emerging Technologies in Education" at Vernon Press and "AI and Education" at STAR Scholars Press. His expertise continues to shape the academic and research landscape at Bahrain Polytechnic.

Preface

Artificial Intelligence in Legal Systems is a timely exploration of how artificial intelligence (AI) is transforming the legal field in the midst of a global digital revolution. As technology continues to redefine industries and societal functions, the legal system, a cornerstone of governance and justice, faces unique challenges and opportunities brought about by AI. This book seeks to bridge the gap between technological advancements and the ethical, procedural, and practical demands of the legal profession. Through its comprehensive chapters, this book delves into AI's multifaceted impact on legal systems. It examines AI's capabilities to automate routine tasks, analyze large datasets, and streamline case management, while also addressing critical issues such as transparency, accountability, and ethical dilemmas. By presenting a balanced view of the promises and perils of AI integration, this book provides a roadmap for legal practitioners, policymakers, and scholars to navigate this complex landscape.

A significant portion of this book focuses on the European Union's approach to regulating AI in the legal domain. It provides an in-depth analysis of the EU's legal frameworks and explores the challenges posed by integrating AI tools, such as algorithmic bias, data privacy concerns, and ethical considerations in decision-making. Beyond the EU, this book incorporates perspectives from other regions, offering a global view of AI's impact on legal systems and the shared struggles to ensure fairness and justice in an era of rapid technological change. This book also advocates for a collaborative approach to AI adoption, emphasizing the importance of aligning AI tools with the needs of legal professionals and the broader goals of justice. By tailoring AI to specific legal contexts and judicial processes, contributors demonstrate how this technology can enhance efficiency and decision-making while preserving the foundational values of the legal system. Practical strategies and case studies further illustrate how AI can address complex legal challenges while maintaining integrity and accountability.

Artificial Intelligence in Legal Systems serves as both a guide and a critical resource for those at the forefront of legal innovation. It equips readers with the insights needed to harness AI responsibly, balancing its transformative potential with the ethical imperatives of justice and fairness. Legal professionals will find actionable recommendations for integrating AI into their practice, while policymakers and scholars will gain a deeper understanding of the regulatory and societal implications of AI in law. Ultimately, this book underscores the importance of thoughtful and ethical AI integration in the legal system. It seeks to empower its readers to not only embrace technological advancements but also to safeguard the principles of transparency, equity, and accountability that underpin the rule of law. As the legal field continues to evolve in the face of AI's transformative power, this book provides a vital framework for navigating its complexities and opportunities with confidence and clarity.

Behrouz Aslani
Narasimha Rao Vajjhala

Acknowledgments

The journey of editing this book *Artificial Intelligence in Legal Systems* has been both enlightening and profoundly rewarding, and we extend our heartfelt gratitude to those who contributed to this work. First and foremost, we would like to thank the authors and contributors, each of whom brought unique insights and expertise that enriched the content of this book. Your dedication to exploring the intricate intersections of artificial intelligence (AI) and law has been invaluable. We must express our sincere appreciation to the legal scholars and practitioners whose research and experiences provided a foundation for our discussions. Your willingness to engage with the ethical and practical dimensions of AI implementation in legal frameworks has illuminated the path forward. We are particularly grateful to the experts in data science and technology who shared their knowledge on emerging innovations. Your collaboration has underscored the importance of interdisciplinary approaches in addressing the complex challenges associated with AI in legal systems.

Finally, we would like to acknowledge our families and friends for their unwavering support and encouragement throughout this project. Their belief in the importance of this work motivated us to persist in navigating the multifaceted issues surrounding AI and law. This book is a testament to the collaborative spirit of those who strive to better understand the evolving dynamics of technology and justice. We hope that it serves as a resource for legal professionals, scholars, and policymakers dedicated to fostering the responsible integration of AI into legal systems worldwide.

Eriona Çela
Narasimha Rao Vajjhala
Behrouz Aslani

About the Editors

Eriona Çela is a distinguished academic currently serving as a Full-Time Professor at the University of New York Tirana, where she is a member of the Faculty of Law and Social Sciences in the Department of Psychology. She earned her Ph.D. in Teaching Methodology of English for Specific Purposes (ESP) from the University of Bari "Aldo Moro" in Italy, enhancing her extensive background in language education, which includes earlier degrees in English Language and Law from the University of Tirana and Business Academy College in Albania. Dr. Çela's research interests are broad and interdisciplinary, focusing on Business English, Teaching Methodology, ESP, Academic Writing, Higher Education, Plagiarism, and European Integration, among others. She is well versed in teaching a range of subjects including Academic Writing, ESL, Business English, and Legal English. She also has significant expertise in translating legal, business, and educational documents. Her academic experience spans several respected institutions, including previous roles as an Assistant Professor at the University of Luarasi, University of Elbasan "Aleksandër Xhuvani," University of Tirana, and University of Durrës "Aleksandër Moisiu." In addition to her academic roles, Dr. Çela has held significant administrative positions within the Albanian Ministry of Education and Sport, where she contributed to integration, coordination, and project feasibility. Dr. Çela is active in the academic community as a member and managing editor of various editorial boards, including those for the *European Journal of Arts, Humanities and Social Sciences*, and the *International Journal of Risk and Contingency Management*. Her contributions to conferences and scholarly journals are numerous, underscoring her commitment to advancing research and practice in her fields of expertise. She also brings practical insights into her teaching and research from her experiences as a trainer and higher education expert involved in quality assurance and educational reforms in Albania. This rich background informs her ongoing contributions to academic discussions and policy-making in education, both in Albania and internationally.

Narasimha Rao Vajjhala currently serves as the Dean of the Faculty of Engineering and Architecture at the University of New York Tirana in Albania. He previously held the position of Chair for the Computer Science and Software Engineering programs at the American University of Nigeria. Dr. Vajjhala is a senior member of both the ACM and IEEE. He is the Editor-in-Chief of the *International Journal of Risk and Contingency Management* (*IJRCM*) and a member of the Risk Management Society (RIMS) and the Project Management Institute (PMI). With over 23 years of experience, Dr. Vajjhala has taught programming and database-related courses across Europe and Africa at both graduate and undergraduate levels. He has also worked as a consultant for technology firms in Europe and participated in EU-funded projects. Dr. Vajjhala holds a Doctorate in Information Systems and Technology from the

United States, a Master of Science in Computer Science and Applications from India, and a Master of Business Administration specializing in Information Systems from Switzerland.

Behrouz Aslani holds a Ph.D. in Management Science and Engineering from Stanford University, where he also earned a Master's in the same field and another in Economics. With extensive global experience, Dr. Aslani has managed multinational projects in over 15 countries and provided consulting services for various sectors. He has taught a wide range of business and management courses to over 8,000 students across multiple institutions, including the American University of Nigeria and California State Polytechnic University. Dr. Aslani is also the founder and president of Integrated Renewable Energy Inc., generating significant advancements in solar energy applications.

Contributors

V. S. Anoop
Kerala University of Digital Sciences,
    Innovation and Technology
Thiruvananthapuram, India

Behrouz Aslani
University of La Verne
La Verne, California

Sonika Bhardwaj
Symbiosis International Deemed
    University
Pune, India

Eralda Methasani Çani
University of Tirana
Tirana, Albania

Eriona Çela
University of New York Tirana
Tirana, Albania

Miralda Çuka
University of New York Tirana
Tirana, Albania

Homam Reda El-Taj
Dar Al-Hekma University
Jeddah, Saudi Arabia

Rita Ghiyal
Symbiosis International Deemed
    University
Pune, India

Hysmir Idrizi
Albanian American Development
    Foundation (AADF)
Tirana, Albania

Rajiv Iyer
Amity University Maharashtra
Mumbai, India

Mohammed Fawaz J
Kerala University of Digital Sciences,
    Innovation and Technology
Thiruvananthapuram, India

Siddharth Kanojia
O.P. Jindal Global University
Sonipat, India

Reald Keta
Prime Minister's Office
Tirana, Albania

Madhavi Kilaru
VNR Vignana Jyothi Institute of
    Engineering and Technology
Hyderabad, India

Navonita Mallick
School of Law, KIIT-DU
Bhubaneswar, India

Sourav Mandal
Symbiosis International Deemed
    University
Pune, India

Vedprakash Maralapalle
Amity University Maharashtra
Mumbai, India

Andrea Mazelliu
University of New York Tirana
Tirana, Albania

Jonaid Myzyri
Public Procurement Commission
Tirana, Albania

Valbona Ndrepepaj
University of Tirana
Tirana, Albania

Vasiliki Papadouli
Vrije Universiteit Brussel, International
  Hellenic University
Brussels, Belgium

Sanghamitra Patnaik
School of Law, KIIT-DU
Bhubaneswar, India

Beata Polok
Dar Al-Hekma University
Jeddah, Saudi Arabia

Rajasekhara Mouly Potluri
Kazakh-British Technical University
Almaty, Kazakhstan

Margarita Robles-Carrillo
University of Granada
Granada, Spain

Shashwata Sahu
School of Law, KIIT-DU
Bhubaneswar, India

Saranya A
Amity University Maharashtra
Mumbai, India

Narasimha Rao Vajjhala
University of New York Tirana
Tirana, Albania

Shivali Wagle
Symbiosis International Deemed
  University
Pune, India

Bartłomiej Żyłka
Independent Researcher
Poland

1 The Impact of Artificial Intelligence (AI) in the Legal System

Eriona Çela, Behrouz Aslani, and Narasimha Rao Vajjhala

1.1 INTRODUCTION

Artificial intelligence (AI) has transformed modern society, revolutionized industries, and reshaped the way we work, innovate, and address complex challenges. Among these transformations, the legal system—a foundation of societal order—stands at the crossroads of technological revolution and ethical scrutiny. As AI continues to permeate legal practices and governance structures, its implications for efficiency, transparency, accountability, and justice demand thorough exploration.

1.2 AI IN THE LEGAL SECTOR: OPPORTUNITIES AND CHALLENGES

AI's integration into the legal system offers unprecedented opportunities to streamline operations and improve outcomes. Legal professionals now leverage AI tools to manage routine tasks, such as document review, legal research, case management, and predictive analytics. By utilizing Machine Learning (ML) and Natural Language Processing (NLP) technologies, lawyers, judges, and other legal practitioners are equipped to process complex data with remarkable accuracy and speed, enabling them to focus on nuanced legal analysis and decision-making.

Despite these advancements, the legal sector's adoption of AI is fraught with challenges. Ethical concerns about algorithmic bias, the erosion of human judgment, and data privacy issues highlight the need for regulatory and ethical oversight. These concerns are particularly critical in contexts where justice, fairness, and accountability are at stake.

1.3 SCOPE AND OBJECTIVES OF THIS BOOK

This book delves into the transformative role of AI in the legal system, balancing an exploration of its potential benefits with an analysis of the ethical and legal dilemmas it introduces. By examining case studies, regulatory frameworks, and technological innovations worldwide, this book provides a comprehensive understanding of how AI can be responsibly integrated into the legal profession.

DOI: 10.1201/9781003541899-1

The overarching objective is to foster a balanced discourse, guiding policymakers, legal practitioners, and scholars through the complexities of AI adoption in the legal system. This approach ensures that technological advancements enhance, rather than undermine, the principles of justice, fairness, and accountability.

1.4   ORGANIZATION OF THIS BOOK

This book is structured into 13 chapters, each focusing on critical aspects of AI's role in the legal system. The first chapter introduces this book and summarizes the topics discussed. Other chapters offer a holistic perspective on AI's transformative impact in modern legal practice and governance.

1.4.1   ARTIFICIAL INTELLIGENCE IN THE LEGAL SECTOR: APPLICATIONS, ETHICAL CHALLENGES, AND LEGAL CONCERNS UNDER EUROPEAN UNION LAW

Chapter 2 examines the significant transformation of the legal profession through the increasing adoption of AI systems, which range from handling administrative tasks to performing complex legal analyses. It emphasizes the dual nature of AI's impact—offering substantial efficiency gains while also raising critical ethical and legal challenges, particularly regarding transparency and liability. Ultimately, the chapter underscores the necessity for further legal analysis of these emerging issues within the context of the EU's AI Regulation 2024/1689, highlighting their importance for contemporary legal scholarship and practice.

1.4.2   EUROPEAN UNION'S PERSPECTIVE ON PROTECTION OF PERSONAL DATA IN THE ERA OF GPT TECHNOLOGY

Chapter 3 analyzes the European Union's leadership in the advancement of Generative Pre-trained Transformer (GPT) technology while emphasizing the importance of safeguarding personal data. It focuses on the complexities of the EU legal framework as it strives to balance innovation in Generative Artificial Intelligence with the protection of individual privacy rights, exploring the moral, legal, and societal implications of this technology. By examining the EU's political demands and harmonization efforts, the chapter provides a thorough assessment of the legal challenges and future developments at the intersection of law and technology regarding personal data protection.

1.4.3   THE ARTIFICIAL INTELLIGENCE STRATEGY OF THE EUROPEAN COURT OF JUSTICE: NATURE, SCOPE, AND CONSEQUENCES

Chapter 4 examines the Artificial Intelligence Strategy of the Court of Justice of the European Union, presented in 2024, to assess its scope and limitations given the Court's significant authority in the judicial realm. It situates this strategy within the broader European context, especially the implications of Regulation (EU) 2024/1689 and the Council of Europe Framework Convention on Artificial Intelligence and

Human Rights. Through a detailed examination of the strategy's structural, conceptual, and functional aspects, along with its ethical foundations and governance model, the chapter concludes with insights into the effectiveness and challenges of the strategy.

1.4.4 TRANSPARENCY AND ACCOUNTABILITY IN AI SYSTEMS: A REALISTIC APPROACH IN ALBANIA

Chapter 5 explores the challenges and potential solutions for integrating artificial intelligence into public governance, using Albania as a case study to highlight issues of AI transparency and accountability frameworks. It takes a two-fold approach by first analyzing the legal and policy frameworks that govern these aspects, referencing international standards and Albanian legislation, and then investigating the practical challenges of AI integration, such as data infrastructure limitations and regulatory gaps. Ultimately, the chapter underscores the transformative impact of AI on legal systems and advocates for an interdisciplinary collaboration among data scientists, legal experts, and ethicists to effectively navigate the complexities and ethical dilemmas associated with AI in governance.

1.4.5 FINE-TUNING A DOMAIN-SPECIFIC LARGE LANGUAGE MODEL USING LOW-RANK ADAPTATION TECHNIQUE FOR LEGAL AI APPLICATIONS: CASE OF INDIA

Chapter 6 examines the advancements in AI, specifically in natural language processing (NLP), and how they can be applied to enhance judicial decision-making processes through the development of a large legal language model, SaulLM. It focuses on fine-tuning SaulLM using the Low-Rank Adaptation Technique (LoRA) on an Indian legal dataset to create NLP systems capable of performing complex judicial tasks, such as semantic segmentation and legal statute identification. Additionally, the chapter emphasizes the importance of making this model publicly accessible via HuggingFace to support accessible justice and timely decision-making in the legal domain.

1.4.6 APPLICATION OF ARTIFICIAL INTELLIGENCE IN THE INDIAN LEGAL SYSTEM: PROS AND CONS

Chapter 7 investigates the transformative role of AI in the legal system, highlighting its ability to enhance efficiency, accuracy, and accessibility in legal practices. It emphasizes various applications of AI, such as automating routine tasks, conducting legal research, and utilizing predictive analytics, which enable legal professionals to focus on higher-value work and make more informed decisions. Additionally, the chapter addresses the significant challenges and ethical considerations accompanying AI adoption in legal systems, including algorithmic bias and privacy concerns, particularly within the context of India's legal framework.

1.4.7 An Analysis of the EU Artificial Intelligence Act

Chapter 8 provides an overview and contextual analysis of the European Union's "EU AI Act," the first comprehensive regulatory framework for artificial intelligence systems, adopted by the Council of the European Union in May 2024. It focuses on the key issues addressed by the Act, the discussions leading to its drafting and adoption, and its implications for the European Union market. Additionally, the chapter highlights the values underpinning the regulation and explores potential criticisms that may arise in response to its implementation.

1.4.8 Merging Artificial Intelligence with the Existing Legal Frameworks: A Comparative Analysis of EU's AI Act

Chapter 9 examines the regulatory and legal challenges faced by banks and Non-Banking Financial Companies (NBFCs) in India as they integrate AI technologies into their operations. It focuses on compliance and risk management issues within the existing regulatory framework, highlighting the complexities that arise from the introduction of AI in the financial sector. To provide a comprehensive analysis, the chapter draws on both qualitative and quantitative data from various stakeholders, including industry reports, regulatory papers, expert interviews, and a structured questionnaire from 200 diverse respondents.

1.4.9 Public Procurement and Artificial Intelligence: The Case of Albania

Chapter 10 explores the legal changes and applications of AI in Albania's public procurement system, established 54 years after the Turing test, marking it as a significant case study in Europe. It focuses on analyzing the new AI-based public procurement procedures using a two-stage legal research methodology while addressing concerns about the legal protection of economic operators and the role of courts in dispute resolution related to AI-driven decisions. The chapter highlights the promising potential of AI in enhancing legal processes while emphasizing the importance of upholding ethics and human rights.

1.4.10 Decentralizing the Law: Exploring the Potential of Blockchain Technology in Legal Processes

Chapter 11 explores how blockchain technology can transform the legal sector by enhancing the capabilities of traditional centralized databases. It focuses on key aspects such as decentralization, immutability, and smart contracts, which contribute to increased efficiency, transparency, and security in legal processes, including the digitization of court decisions and property conveyances. Additionally, the chapter addresses limitations concerning bias, privacy, and data protection, offering a critical evaluation of both the potential benefits and the challenges of implementing blockchain in global legal systems.

1.4.11 ETHICAL AND LEGAL IMPLICATIONS FOR ARTIFICIAL INTELLIGENCE IN LAW

Chapter 12 examines the ethical and legal considerations surrounding the integration of AI into legal frameworks, focusing on the operational effectiveness of AI alongside consequentialist and deontological ethical theories. It emphasizes the need to analyze AI's impact on critical legal principles such as fairness, accountability, and transparency, while addressing challenges like algorithmic bias, data privacy, and human rights protection. Ultimately, the chapter advocates for a balanced integration of ethics into AI systems to ensure that human oversight is maintained while enhancing the intelligence and effectiveness of AI in legal practice.

1.4.12 DEMOCRATIZING LEGAL AID: THE ROLE OF AI IN PROVIDING AFFORDABLE JUSTICE

Chapter 13 explores the role of AI in enhancing access to justice, particularly for vulnerable and marginalized communities. It focuses on evaluating how AI-powered solutions, such as chatbots and predictive analytics, can make legal services more accessible and affordable across different economic and social classes, while also addressing the ethical and practical challenges associated with bias and data privacy. By employing a doctrinal research method, the chapter seeks to demonstrate the potential of AI to streamline legal aid services and advocates for establishing ethical regulatory frameworks to support effective integration of AI into the legal system.

1.5 CONCLUSION

AI's role in the legal system represents a double-edged sword: it has the potential to revolutionize the profession, streamline processes, and enhance decision-making, but it also raises critical ethical and legal challenges. Algorithmic biases, lack of transparency, and data privacy issues underscore the need for robust regulatory frameworks and ethical guidelines.

This book provides a nuanced exploration of AI's integration into the legal system, emphasizing the importance of balancing innovation with accountability and fairness. By addressing these complex issues, it serves as a valuable resource for navigating the evolving relationship between AI and the legal profession, fostering a future where technology and justice coexist harmoniously.

2 Artificial Intelligence in the Legal Sector

Applications, Ethical Challenges, and Legal Concerns under European Union Law

Vasiliki Papadouli

2.1 INTRODUCTION

For the past 20 to 30 years, Artificial Intelligence (*AI*) has become a scientific field of primary importance on a global scale. Since its official establishment in 1956 at the Dartmouth Conference until today, it has been constantly contributing to various fields of modern life, showing exceptional achievements. Today's AI systems can execute technical tasks, such as booking appointments, and render (qualitative) judgements. This is why they have already had extended application in the legal sector: from legal searching, drafting contracts, and reviewing legal documents to the prediction of case outcomes, AI systems have become a valuable tool for modern legal practitioners (i.e., lawyers) as well as for judges or arbitrators.

However, the application of AI to the legal sector is not completely new at all. The first steps date back to the 1960s, 1970s, and 1980s, when the pioneers of legal informatics launched the first AI systems for legal professionals: the *Boolean search*, McCarthy's system *Taxman*, and Ronald Stamper's system *Legol*. The first one (*Boolean search*) facilitated—still today— (legal) search in big databases using words such as "and," "or," and "not," for matching strings (Bench-Capon et al., 2012), while *Taxman* and *Legol* were AI systems capable of modelling arguments in tax law cases and providing formal models of organisational rules and regulations, accordingly. Although quite "primitive," these AI systems highlighted the immense potential of AI in the legal sector, especially as far as the formalisation of legal texts and legal reasoning is concerned, also demonstrating the great interest of legal professionals in "adopting" automation tools in their realm of work.

The interconnection between AI and the legal profession has gained critical importance and great enthusiasm during the following decades, when autonomous AI systems and generative AI tools based on natural language processing (like ChatGPT) emerged. Although at the beginning they were considered disruptive technologies,

 DOI: 10.1201/9781003541899-2

sparking a hot debate over whether they would benefit the legal profession or pose a threat—potentially leading to the gradual displacement of jobs—today they are widely accepted by the legal community thanks to their significant advantages for modern legal practice, mainly speed, increased accuracy, and cost reductions. These same advantages have also urged official judicial authorities to implement AI tools for handling administrative tasks and supporting judges in making court decisions (or even substituting them).

Indeed, today, the implementation of AI systems is deemed essential for modern legal practitioners aiming to gain a competitive advantage in the legal services market, as well as for official judicial authorities for the efficient time and process management of pending legal cases (Siqueira et al., 2024). Nonetheless, the ever-expanding application of AI tools challenges traditional concepts of human legal expertise (Biresaw et al., 2022) and raises several concerns about the ethical and legal implications of how these systems are used today in the legal sector, i.e., about the morality and legality of their usage by legal practitioners in delivering legal services, as well as by judges when rendering court decisions.

This chapter sheds light on the most important ethical and legal challenges concerning the implementation of AI systems in the legal sector, especially under European Union law. In the first part of this chapter, some of the most important AI tools used in the modern legal sector are presented. In the second and third parts, these systems are examined from an ethical and legal perspective for legal practitioners and judges. To understand the ethical and legal concerns raised by AI tools— often called *autonomous AI systems*—their key features as well as their inherent limitations, i.e., the so-called *black-box problem* or *black-box effect*, must also be examined. Since a lot has already been written worldwide about the "nature" of these AI systems as "black boxes," emphasis is given only to those technical elements that concern the legal profession and can affect the quality of legal services and the correctness of court decisions as well. Furthermore, the scope and limitations of these systems are important for their legal treatment worldwide, especially for their categorisation under the recent European Union Regulation on AI 2024/1689 about harmonised rules on AI (*AI Act*), described in the next section. Although a thorough analysis of the AI Act cannot take place in this chapter, the most crucial elements concerning AI systems utilised in the legal sector should be highlighted in comparison to other governmental approaches from different districts. The last part of this chapter entails concluding remarks on ethical guidance for the use of AI tools in the legal sector, considering the realm of current governmental approaches to AI and the reports of international organisations as well.

2.2 AI SYSTEMS IN THE LEGAL SECTOR

AI systems already have extended applications in the legal sector, with the range of tasks undertaken growing steadily. From practical-administrative tasks to pure (qualitative) judgements, AI tools seem to be a necessity for modern legal practitioners, especially lawyers, and judges as well. For a better review of these systems, they can be divided into various categories, based on their application, as follows (Becerra, 2018; Ng, 2022; Amato et al., 2023; Villasenor, 2024):

2.2.1 AUTOMATION AND DRAFTING TOOLS

AI systems for case management are scheduling and filing tools, assisting legal practitioners and judicial authorities in handling working time and paperwork. Typical examples are: "Tyler Technologies' Odyssey," "Cogito," and "TAR."

- **AI Systems for Document Automation**: These are systems that can draft legal documents such as contracts, proxies, non-disclosure agreements, find spelling errors, and suggest rewrites. Typical examples are: "Clifford Chance Dr@ft," used not only by legal practitioners but also by clients themselves, "LegalZoom," "Desktop Lawyer," "Rocket Lawyer," and "ClickLaw."

2.2.2 RESEARCH AND ANALYTICAL TOOLS

- **AI Systems for Legal Research**: These are systems that can search legal databases for law precedents, identify similarities and differences among legal cases, and sketch arguments and counterarguments. Typical examples are: "DataLex," "Ravel," used in the USA in 2017 for scanning case law and making it accessible in visual maps with citations; "CARA," which summarises law cases and suggests legal arguments; "Casetext" and "Fastcase," which present intersections among law cases and statutes; "Luminance," which provides legal arguments; "Lexis Nexis," and "Westlaw Edge."
- **AI Systems for Contract and Legal Review**: These are systems that can identify gaps or problematic clauses in contracts and appropriately advise on legal handling, recommend legal strategies to win lawsuits, identify problematic clauses, suggest modifications/amendments, or check compliance with regulatory frameworks. Typical examples are: "Law Geex," "Thought River," "Legal Robot," and "Kira System."
- **AI Systems for Evidence Analysis**: These are systems used, e.g., for forensic predictions, defining crime scenes, or analysing DNA, like "TrueAllele."

2.2.3 ADVISORY AND COMMUNICATION TOOLS

- **AI Systems for Providing Legal Advice**: These are systems that can provide legal reasoning, i.e., form and provide answers to a specific legal question and communicate them to the client. Typical examples are: "Blue J Legal," "ROSS," "Lexis Answers," "Watson Debater," "DoNotPay," especially for consumer protection, and "Allira."

2.2.4 PREDICTION TOOLS

- **AI Systems for Predictive Legal Analysis**: These systems can predict a legal case outcome after analysing legislation and searching for legal precedents. Typical examples are: "COMPAS" (Correctional Offender Management Profiling for Alternative Sanctions), "Empirical Scotus," "Lex Machina," and "Case Cruncher Alpha." Such AI systems have already been used to predict the decisions of the European Court of Human Rights, as well as those of the Supreme Court of Justice in the USA, and similar tools are also used by Japanese judicial authorities.

- **AI Tools for Criminal Recidivism of Offenders**: These systems are used by official state judicial authorities for criminal recidivism assessment or relevant risks. Typical examples are "COMPAS" and the "Public Assessment Tool" utilised in the USA.

2.2.5 DISPUTE RESOLUTION TOOLS

- **AI Systems for Online Dispute Resolution (e-Arbitrators or e-Judges)**: These are systems that can solve disputes between contractual parties, usually in the framework of smart contracts, i.e., contracts that are self-performed and self-executed via blockchain platforms. Typical examples are: "Modria," used especially for family disputes; "eBay Resolution Center," used for handling disputes between sellers and buyers contracting through the homonymous online marketplace; as well as "China's Smart Courts" (Dan et al., 2024).

This list is not exhaustive; instead, it shows only some of the most important and widely used AI systems in the legal sector, and it will be enriched with new AI tools as AI technology evolves and new AI developments appear.

2.3 ADVANTAGES OF AI SYSTEMS USED IN THE LEGAL SECTOR

The advantages of the aforementioned AI systems for all stakeholders in the legal sector (i.e., lawyers, judges, and parties) are obvious, as analysed immediately below (Sheeba, 2023):

a. **Advantages for Lawyers (Brooks et al., 2020)**: AI systems are time-saving, cost-saving, and improve accuracy, thereby assisting lawyers in efficiently addressing legal cases and serving a wider range of clients. Indeed, a great part of lawyers' daily work involves administrative tasks, legal research, and the drafting of legal documents. By saving this labour time, lawyers can focus on more substantive, high-value legal matters, provide more sophisticated legal services, serve more clients, and better predict their cases' outcomes while reducing their professional costs. This leads to enhanced lawyers' productivity and efficiency and, in turn, to increased profits for lawyers, especially for younger ones: since the latter are more familiar with legal technologies, they can gain a competitive advantage in the legal services market by implementing AI tools in their daily work (at least until big law firms invest huge amounts of money in legal technologies and "employ' highly advanced AI systems in their daily work routine). Further, new types of legal professions have already arisen: *Legal Technologists* or *Legal Analysts*. These are lawyers with special knowledge of AI technologies, who can provide a new kind of legal service to their clients (who can also be lawyers or law firms), i.e., legal services for AI tools implementation, data management, process automation, training, and support. This new kind of legal profession challenges the ominous prediction of job losses in the future due to the implementation of AI tools.

b. **Advantages for Judicial Authorities**: Accordingly, AI tools assist judicial authorities in handling legal cases and improving their accuracy. Indeed, as in the case of lawyers, judges need to spend a lot of their time on practical tasks, such as entering data or describing facts in court decisions. These are time-consuming tasks that are significantly facilitated by AI tools. Accordingly, searching for legal precedents and statutes is another time-consuming task and a prerequisite for any court decision. Since AI tools can undertake these tasks, the judicial process is significantly shortened. Further, judges' efficiency is enhanced since they can address more complex legal matters and handle more legal cases (Adhikary et al., 2024). The same advantages apply also to arbitrators, including cost-effectiveness in this case.

c. **Advantages for Parties**: Further, advisory AI systems and AI dispute resolution mechanisms can render decisions quickly. Thereby, they can shorten the time of legal disputes, leading to a quick resolution. AI advisory and communication tools, such as chatbots and virtual assistants that provide legal advice and guidance to the public, also enhance people's access to justice, and given that many of these systems are provided pro bono, they are also cost-saving (Mowbray et al., 2020).

The advantages of AI systems for all stakeholders are of significant importance. Nonetheless, AI systems have a "negative aspect" as well, raising several ethical challenges and legal concerns, as discussed in the next section.

2.4   ETHICAL CHALLENGES AND LEGAL CONCERNS

2.4.1   ETHICAL CHALLENGES

The most significant ethical risk raised by AI systems in the legal sector concerns their potential for unfair outcomes due to their inherent opacity. Although *AI systems*—especially the autonomous ones, which are deemed the most sophisticated and advanced AI systems nowadays—can accomplish overly complex tasks on any subject matter, they are not able to "explain" their decisions, nor can their designers do so (Papadouli, 2023a; Wrbka & Fenwick, 2024). This constitutes the so-called *black-box problem* or *black-box effect*, from which all autonomous AI systems suffer (Papadouli, 2023a). There are several reasons for this phenomenon, among which the most significant are the systems' internal *complexity* (Burrel, 2016; Carabantes, 2020), the *lack of visibility into training data sets* or *into the methods of data selection* (Burrel, 2016), as well as the *inherent biases* from which the training datasets may "suffer," i.e., previous wrong human decisions that the autonomous AI system uses to train its algorithm (Hull, 2023).

A lot of human rights violation incidents, during—and due to—the operation of autonomous AI systems, have already been noticed worldwide due to the black-box effect, especially due to *algorithmic biases* (Papadouli, 2023a). As far as the legal sector is concerned, a typical example is that of the robot-judges. More specifically, autonomous AI systems have been "employed" in the USA for predicting the criminal recidivism of offenders by the official judicial authorities in several US states (COMPAS). These systems were able to estimate the risk of recidivism based, inter alia, on interviews with the offenders, on information originating from public registries, and on publicly available data, such as age, sex/gender, family status, education, income, and antisocial behaviours (Eaglin, 2016). Given that these AI systems are black boxes, they cannot explain their outcomes, which may be affected by gender and racial biases (e.g., against women, people of different nationalities, minorities). This was already noticed in the USA in 2016, where it was found that thousands of AI algorithms used in criminal justice were biased against specific groups of people (Afro-Americans). Accordingly, China introduced in 2017 AI systems for assisting judges in handling e-commerce and intellectual property disputes in specialised internet courts (Hangzhou), but it was soon found that they exhibited biases based on prior rulings. Similar incidents have also been reported in the Netherlands (AI systems for sentencing recommendations and predictive policing), Canada (AI tools for predicting the likelihood of reoffending), South Africa (AI tools for predicting case outcomes), India, etc.

The aforementioned examples raise several ethical concerns regarding human rights. Algorithmic biases can result in infringements on the right to fair justice, human dignity, the right to personality, and the principle of equality. They also undermine the presumption of innocence and deny access to justice for marginalised groups of people, minorities, or lower-income social classes. Further, by adopting discriminatory decisions, AI systems perpetuate social inequalities, affecting people worldwide in a massive way and undermining trust in both AI technology and the justice system (Koplin, 2023).

2.4.2 Legal Challenges

The unfairness of AI systems, particularly of autonomous ones, raises in turn several legal concerns, some of the most important of which are the following (Guillermin et al., 2021; British Institute of International and Comparative Law, 2023):

a. **Lack of Explainability**: AI systems' inherent opacity and lack of explainability, as already described in the previous section (2.4.1), contradict the duty of judicial authorities to justify court decisions, leading, in turn, to violations of the right to a fair trial, according, inter alia, to Article 6 of the European Convention on Human Rights. They also adversely impact lawyers' contractual obligation arising from the contract concluded with their clients to provide legal services *lege artis*, i.e., reasonably and with sufficient justification for any legal handling. In both cases, liability issues arise—namely, state responsibility for judicial authorities (without prejudice to the right to appeal) and contractual liability for lawyers towards their clients.

b. **Liability Issues in Case of Wrong AI Decisions**: Another question raised regarding AI systems utilised in the legal sector is whether legal practitioners using AI systems in their workflow should be held liable in the case of incorrect AI decisions—for example, when they miss an important deadline due to AI system bugs.

Although a lot has been written in legal doctrine on this topic—with some legal scholars even providing *de lege ferenda* arguments for the necessity of attributing legal personality to autonomous AI systems, or for treating them as modern slaves or hybrid persons (Papadouli, 2023b; Wrbka & Fenwick, 2024)—the most well-grounded opinion considers AI systems as mere tools in the hands of their users, who are accountable for any erroneous outcomes produced by these systems. Therefore, when legal practitioners decide to "employ" one of the aforementioned AI systems in their daily work, any incorrect decision rendered is attributed to the lawyers, who are thereby accountable for failing to deliver, or for delivering incorrect, legal advice to their clients.

The situation is like what occurs when lawyers delegate tasks to several physical persons, legal or paralegal staff, between whom and the client, there is no contractual connection for the provision of legal services. The lawyer is the one who has concluded the contract for the provision of legal services with the client, and he/she is the one who should supervise the legal or paralegal staff, check their deliverables, oversee and direct the work delegation; thus, the lawyer remains responsible for the work produced by his/her staff, legal or paralegal, on his/her behalf. Lawyers' responsibility has already been confirmed by jurisprudence in the USA, accepting that "the duty of competent representation includes the duty of adequately supervising non-attorney employees," in Hessinger & Assocs. case (192 B.R. 211, 223, Bankr. N.D. Cal. Jan. 22, 1996), or that "delegation of activities which ordinarily comprise the practice of law is proper only if the lawyer maintains a direct relationship with the client involved, supervises and directs the work delegated to the paralegal, and assumes complete ultimate responsibility for the work product produced by the paralegal," in the Stegemann case (206 B.R. 176, 179, Bankr. C.D. Ill. Mar. 3, 1997).

The same applies in the case of AI systems "employed" by lawyers to execute administrative tasks or conduct more qualitative ones, like legal research As was recently confirmed by the Southern District of New York, the court decided that an attorney at law who relied upon ChatGPT to handle legal cases is liable to their client if a deadline is missed because of a wrong AI system suggestion or decision (Neumeister, 2023). Despite the exceptional outcomes of autonomous AI systems and large language models, like ChatGPT, lawyers should not over-rely on them but should always be aware of their inherent limitations and check their results (Ceva & Jiménez, 2022).

This standpoint is also well supported by most codes of professional conduct for lawyers worldwide. These codes require that legal services be provided by lawyers *lege artis*, i.e., with integrity, in compliance with professional standards and best practices, and with respect for the ethical

rules of the legal profession. Taking into account the new reality shaped by disruptive technologies and their dynamic intervention in the legal sector, as analysed above (Section 2.2), delivering legal services *lege artis* today "acquires" new dimensions that reshape the legal profession in a different way (Infantino & Di Matteo, 2024). Today's lawyers should be appropriately educated not only on legal matters but also on new disruptive technologies if they want to utilise them in their work and enjoy their advantages. This means that modern lawyers should be educated on AI tools prior to their implementation in their work, be aware of the ethical and legal concerns they may raise (Koessler, 2024), and maintain competence in utilising them in the field of their practice, including their competence to review their outcomes, and even recall or reject them if needed (Garingan & Pickard, 2021). Otherwise, lawyers can be held liable to their clients for non *lege artis* performance of legal advice (malpractice).

Similar concerns also arise for arbitrators and state judicial authorities that have implemented AI systems in their work. As far as the latter is concerned, in cases where AI systems render wrong decisions (e.g., because of insufficient, inaccurate, or biased data), and these decisions are adopted by judicial authorities, state responsibility may also come into question due to unfair trial. This has already happened in the USA after the disclosure that the AI system COMPAS, utilised by state judicial authorities, rendered biased decisions (Engel et al., 2024). Many motions were filed against states by offenders, arguing that the use of algorithms in criminal justice violates their right to due process and the right to an individual sentence based on accurate information, while the use of data related to gender and race is unconstitutional. However, the *Wisconsin Supreme Court of Justice* rejected such a motion in 2016, claiming that the claimant did not provide sufficient evidence of racial discrimination, and that the court decision was not based solely on the algorithm' s outcomes, but rather on other elements that explained the sentence imposed (Loomis v. Wisconsin, 881 N.W.2d 749 (Wisc. 2016)). The *Indiana Supreme Court* reached the same conclusion some years earlier (2010) (Malenchik v. State, 928 N.E.2d 564 (Ind. 2010)), by overturning an earlier decision of the *Indiana Court of Appeals* in the Rhodes case (Rhodes v. State 896 N.E.2d 1193 (Ind. Ct. Appeal 2008)), where the infringement of the right to an individual sentence because of algorithm use was confirmed. Subsequently, the *Court of Appeal of Michigan,* aligned with the *Loomis* and *Malenchic* court decisions, rejected motions in 2019, claiming lack of evidence of any discriminatory treatment of the claimants by the algorithm (People v. Younglove, N. 341901, 2019 WL 846117 (Mich. Ct. Appeal Feb. 21, 2019)).

However, this standpoint seems anachronistic, as it does not consider the black-box effect from which all autonomous AI systems suffer. In addition, it underestimates the importance of data quality and their complex editing process (Freeman, 2016; Washington, 2018), ignores the factual and objective lack of evidence from the claimants' side, and endorses the extended use of AI systems by judges without the appropriate

knowledge to explain judicial reasoning influenced by algorithmic predictions. These concerns have been taken into consideration by the *Supreme Court of Western Australia*, which recently pointed out that "the research data and methods underlying the assessment tools are assumed to be correct, but this has not been established by the evidence" (Director of Public Prosecutions for Western Australia v. Mangolamara (2007) 169 A. Crim. R. 379 [2007] WASC 71, [165]).

Similarly, the recent proposal of the European Commission on AI (COM (2022) 496 final – *AI Liability Directive*) takes into account, inter alia, the inability of claimants who suffered damages due to AI systems to prove the causal link between their damage and the AI systems' proper operation, and provides several rebuttable presumptions of the burden of proof in favour of the claimants. This proposal concerns any case of non-contractual, fault-based liability regime. It does not establish a new legal basis for the claimants; rather it introduces procedural evidence rules in favour of claimants and at the expense of AI providers or deployers. Although it has been heavily criticised (Hacker, 2024), it is expected that it will significantly assist claimants in combating autonomous AI systems' black-box effect.

c. **Risk of Confidentiality Violation**: The particularity of the lawyer-client relationship, which is characterised by a deep sense of trust, empathy, and high-level confidentiality (based not only on the grounds of General Data Protection Regulation (GDPR) but also on the "traditional" attorney-client privilege), highlights another dangerous aspect of AI systems utilised in the legal sector. AI systems may demand access to sensitive data to provide an output; accordingly, lawyers may be "obliged" to release such data, as well as important evidence or crucial facts, to an AI platform—especially those based on generative AI models (such as ChatGPT)—to receive legal assistance. In this way, such information may become accessible to the public. Thus, the use of AI systems may undermine the confidential relationship between lawyers and clients, leading to confidentiality violations.

This is a typical situation that gives rise to a lawyer's contractual and extra-contractual liability toward their clients for breach of confidentiality, while lawyers may also face disciplinary penalties. To mitigate this risk, lawyers should be trained in the proper use of AI systems, especially those offered to the public and based on language learning models, such as ChatGPT, to be aware of the ethical and legal challenges they may raise and to effectively protect their clients' data.

Further, they should inform their clients of the potential use of AI systems in legal services and the possible ramifications, and ask for their prior consent. This is an obligation provided for in the European Union under both the GDPR (Article 6) and the AI Act (Article 13, especially for high-risk AI systems, and Article 50).

d. **Unauthorised Practice of Law (?)**: Another controversial point regarding the use of AI systems in the legal sector is that advisory and communication AI tools can provide legal services directly to the public, sometimes even pro bono. For instance, the AI system DoNotPay overturned 160,000

of 250,000 parking tickets and, since its launch, has scored a success rate of 64%, appealing over $4 million. On one hand, this is considered an advantage of AI technology, as already mentioned above, since it ensures access to legal advice, especially for people who cannot afford traditional legal services (Greenleaf et al., 2018). On the other hand, it can be argued that when such AI tools operate without human oversight by lawyers, they unlawfully provide legal services because they do not have a licence to practice law, as required in some districts.

The licence to practice law guarantees the lawful provision of legal advice, usually after exams; it ensures completeness, specialised knowledge, and professional accountability, safeguards the legal system and public interest, and promotes ethical legal practice. The unauthorised practice of law is illegal and punished with severe penalties in many districts. It constitutes anti-competitive behaviour towards authorised lawyers, while it may also jeopardise the public interest in cases where correct legal advice is provided. Indeed, the first case regarding the unauthorised practice of law by AI systems has already been brought before US courts: the AI provider of the aforementioned AI system DoNotPay is currently facing a class action lawsuit before California courts on the grounds of unauthorised practice of law (Allyn, 2024).

Apart from administrative (or even criminal) penalties related to the unauthorised practice of law, AI providers of such systems will also be held liable to the individuals who received legal advice from the system if the advice was incorrect and led to damages. To mitigate this risk, this kind of AI system should be permitted only when it is "adopted" and overseen by licensed lawyers, who are authorised to practice law and will be held accountable for its use.

The risks and legal concerns mentioned in this section are only some of the most important ethical and legal challenges raised by the utilisation of AI systems in the legal sector. The aforementioned concerns highlight that, apart from astonishing achievements, AI systems can also cause harm to human rights as well as severe damages. This constitutes an inherent limitation of such systems, which challenges AI's further evolution and public acceptance, thereby urging the need for legal regulation of AI.

2.5 GOVERNMENTAL APPROACHES FOR AI SYSTEMS UTILISED IN THE LEGAL SECTOR, ESPECIALLY UNDER THE AI ACT

Many states worldwide have already undertaken legislative initiatives to regulate trustworthy AI, i.e., to promote AI technology in an ethical way. For instance, the UK released a policy paper on AI governance in 2023 following its previous policy paper on AI regulation published in 2022. Based on these policy papers, several guiding principles for AI—including safety, security, transparency, explainability, fairness, accountability, and governance—are introduced as soft-law guidance for businesses' best practices in the UK. Furthermore, the USA has recently adopted a sector-specific approach to AI by delegating responsibilities to various federal

agencies in cases of AI malpractice. Given that there is no federal legal enactment for AI in the USA to date, President Biden's executive order is supplemented by several federal and state pieces of legislation, especially regarding data use and consumer protection. In 2023, China put into force the Interim Measures for the Management of Generative Artificial Intelligence Services, establishing a more coherent legal framework for generative AI providers. The Interim Measures impose several obligations on AI providers, primarily concerning AI system security assessments, data use, labelling of AI-generated content, provision of guidance for lawful AI use by users, and the introduction of internal mechanisms to handle complaints and reports.

While important for the further development of AI and its public acceptance worldwide, the aforementioned governmental policies do not introduce a comprehensive approach to AI; that is, they do not establish a coherent legal framework for the use of all kinds of AI systems and for the accountability of AI developers and users. The most consistent legislative initiative regarding AI to date appears to be the European Union Regulation 2024/1689 on harmonised rules on AI (henceforth *AI Act*), which has been legally enacted. With this act, the European Union aspires to establish a uniform legal framework for the development, placing on the market/ putting into service, and use of AI systems within the internal EU market, in accordance with the core ethical principles and values of the EU.

The AI Act adopts a risk-based approach and categorises AI systems into several categories based on the risk of harm they may pose to human rights, as provided in the *Charter of Fundamental Rights of the European Union*. Under this approach, AI systems fall into one of the following categories: (a) *Prohibited AI systems (Article 5)*: These are systems that may cause unacceptable risks to human rights and, therefore, are not permitted in the EU market; (b) *high-risk AI systems (Article 6 et seq.)*: these are systems that may cause significant harm to human rights, and, therefore, they are permittable within the EU only if specific (strict) requirements are met. These requirements, detailed in the AI Act for various AI system operators (primarily providers and deployers, as defined in the AI Act), include prior system risk management assessment, training, validation and testing data sets based on specific standards; technical documentation for the entire "life cycle" of the system; record-keeping; system transparency (i.e., informing users that they are interacting with, or that their data are being processed by, an AI system); and human oversight over the AI system; (c) *Low-risk AI systems*: these systems may pose limited harm to human rights and are permitted within the EU under less stringent requirements than high-risk systems. They must comply with transparency rules (Article 50), and AI providers and deployers are encouraged to adopt codes of conduct for their use (Article 95); and (d) *Minimal-risk AI systems*: These systems pose minimal risk to human rights and are permitted within the EU. Operators are encouraged to adopt codes of conduct for their use (Article 50).

An autonomous AI system—or, according to the terminology adopted by the AI Act, *a general-purpose AI model* (Article 51 et seq.)—which requires a vast amount of data and employs several techniques to train its algorithm, can be implemented in one of the aforementioned types of AI systems (i.e., prohibited, high risk, low risk, minimal risk), thus imposing further obligations on the operators of *general-purpose AI systems.*

The European legislator has already assessed some AI systems as prohibited or high-risk AI systems *a priori*. Some of these systems specifically concern the legal

sector and the legal profession. More specifically, Article 5(1)(b) provides that prohibited AI systems are those that make

> risk assessments of natural persons in order to assess or predict the risk of a natural person committing a criminal offence, based solely on the profiling of a natural person or on assessing their personality traits and characteristics,

While in Annex III, paragraph 8, high-risk AI systems are, inter alia, those that are…

> used by a judicial authority or on their behalf to assist a judicial authority in researching and interpreting facts and the law and in applying the law to a concrete set of facts, or to be used in a similar way in alternative dispute resolution

The distinction between prohibited and high-risk AI systems is crucial for judicial authorities, since they can use only the second category (high-risk AI systems), while the first is totally prohibited. Nonetheless, this distinction may be difficult in practice: the "borderline" between prohibited and high-risk AI systems is whether they are used as a *substitute for the judge* or *as an assisting tool for the judge*. In other words, when the AI system is used to substitute human assessment—like an AI system that assesses natural persons' criminal behaviour based solely on their profiling, personality traits, and/or characteristics, without any objectively verifiable facts—this is prohibited because it violates the human right to a fair trial. In contrast, when the AI system is used to assess natural persons' criminal behaviour based not on profiling and personal traits, but on verifiable facts, such as previous suspicious transactions, it is acceptable as a high-risk AI system, according to Recital 42. Such systems may assist judges in interpreting facts and/or applying the law to the concrete set of facts. Accordingly, AI systems used by alternative dispute resolution bodies for the same purposes are also high-risk, according to Recital 63.

In contrast, when an AI system is used for performing mere procedural tasks, improving the result of human activity, detecting decision-making patterns without any influence on the result, or fulfilling a merely preparatory task for a human judgement, it is not categorised as high-risk, except when it involves "profiling." For instance, AI systems that execute mere administrative tasks, such as summarisation (cf. Deroy et al., 2024; Khalid et al., 2024), anonymisation (Păiş et al., 2024), pseudonymisation of court decisions, data entry, translations, or communications with the parties, are not high-risk AI systems, but rather low or minimal risk.

In case of damages caused by AI systems, AI providers and AI deployers may be held liable. Although the AI Act does not include any liability provisions—it provides only for a "human right to explanation" of individual decision-making in Article 86 (Infantino & Di Matteo, 2024)—AI providers' liability can be based on contracts they may have concluded for the provision of AI systems as tools or services with their clients, i.e., lawyers, judicial authorities, or the public (e.g., contracts for the supply of digital content or digital services, according to EU Directive 2019/770) (Markou, 2024). They may also be held liable as producers of defective products (Ren & Du, 2024; Novelli et al., 2024), under the recent EU Directive 2024/2853 on liability for defective products (*Product Liability Directive*, or *PLD*), which replaces the previous EU Directive 85/274/EEC, provided the necessary requirements are met. Considering the inherent complexity of autonomous AI systems (Recitals 3, 28, and 42), the no-fault liability regime of

the PLD is now enhanced by several alleviations of the burden of proof with regard to the existence of a system's defectiveness and the causal link, in favour of the claimants (Recitals 6, 13, and 17). Under the "new" PLD recently adopted by the European institutions, claimants are entitled to compensation for damages caused by defective products, which now explicitly include software, such as standalone AI systems (Recital 13). Accordingly, developers or producers of AI systems can be treated as manufacturers under the directive and may be held liable for damages caused by their systems (subject to the exceptions provided in Article 6). Therefore, in the case of AI systems utilised in the legal sector, AI providers may be held liable to individuals who used the AI system and suffered damages, even in the absence of a contractual relationship.

Further, AI deployers—i.e., lawyers implementing AI tools in their daily work—may also be held liable to their clients, usually based on the contract concluded between them, as mentioned above.

2.6 CONCLUDING REMARKS

The above analysis aspired to shed light on the main ethical risks and legal concerns raised when AI systems are "employed" in the legal sector by legal practitioners and judicial authorities. It revealed that, although AI systems may have significant advantages for all stakeholders in the legal sector, they may also pose significant risks. To mitigate these concerns and, in turn, eliminate the risk of liability, AI users (i.e., lawyers, judges, arbitrators) should be equipped with clear ethical guidance when utilising AI systems in their realm of work, while public authorities should consider these risks when regulating AI. More specifically:

- **AI Literacy**: First and foremost, lawyers and judicial authorities must become AI literate before they decide to implement AI tools in their course of work. This means that they should be appropriately educated on disruptive technologies to be able to oversee their operation and recall or reject their outcomes. This cannot result in the exclusion of their liability in case of damages caused to the parties or clients by their "employed" AI systems, but it can significantly limit the risk of harm that the AI systems can pose to third parties, while it also justifies their accountability from both a legal and an ethical perspective.
- **Transparency**: AI literacy is the basis for human (lawyers' and judges') oversight of AI systems, which, in turn, presupposes the transparency of those systems. Transparency constitutes a specific subfield of AI, called *explainable AI* (also known as *XAI*), which has recently emerged, aiming to create appropriate techniques that allow autonomous AI systems to be explicable while maintaining high levels of autonomy (Papadouli, 2022). Transparency is a pivotal point for trustworthy AI worldwide, and for this reason, it is included in all governmental policies on AI, including the AI Act (Article 50).
- **Building Trust with Stakeholders**: The risks raised by the use of AI systems may have adverse effects on public acceptance of AI: public trust in AI systems utilised by judges may be jeopardised due to algorithmic biases,

while lawyers may be reluctant to use AI systems that are considered black boxes. To mitigate these risks public authorities should work together with lawyers and bar associations to develop a clear framework for the trustworthy and responsible use of AI by legal professionals, as the UK has already begun to do. The same consultation should also be conducted with judicial authorities to ensure the trustworthy use of AI systems by the courts.

- **International Collaboration**: Considering the international dimensions of the modern economy as well as the use of AI, confirming the responsible use of AI is not merely a matter for each legal order, but rather an international concern that demands close collaboration among states. Key international stakeholders, such as the United Nations (Governing AI for Humanity final report), UNESCO (Report on GenAI), and the Council of Europe (The Framework Convention on AI), can play a pivotal role: their published reports on trustworthy AI can serve as the basis for a global consensus on the responsible use of AI worldwide.

REFERENCES

Adhikary, S. et al. (2024) "A case study for automated attribute extraction from legal documents using large language models." *Artificial Intelligence and Law*, 7, 1–22. https://doi.org/10.1007/s10506-024-09425-7.

Allyn, B. (2024) "A Robot was Scheduled to Argue in Court, Then Came the Jail Threats." Available online at https://www.npr.org/2023/01/25/1151435033/a-robot-was-schedule d-to-argue-in-court-then-came-the-jail-threat, last access 25 Jan 2025.

Amato, F. et al. (2023) "Evolving justice sector: An innovative proposal for introducing AI-based techniques in court offices." In Gerhard, G., Juris, H. (eds.) *Electronic Government and the Information Systems Perspective*, Springer Nature, Cham, pp. 75–88. https://doi.org/10.1007/978-3-031-39841-4.

Becerra, S.D. (2018) "The rise of artificial intelligence in the legal field: Where we are and where we are going." *Journal of Business, Entrepreneurship & the Law*, 11(1), 27–52.

Bench-Capon, T. et al. (2012) "Conceptual organization of case law knowledge bases. Commentary by Adam Z. Wyner." In *A History of AI and Law in 50 Papers: 25 Years of the International Conference on AI and Law*. https://doi.org/10.1007/S10506-012-9131-X.

Biresaw, S.M. et al. (2022) "The impacts of artificial intelligence on research in the legal profession." *International Journal of Law and Society*, 5, 53–65.

British Institute of International and Comparative Law (2023) "Use of Artificial Intelligence in Legal Practice." Available online at https://www.biicl.org/documents/170_use_of_artificial_intelligence_in_legal_practice_final.pdf, last access 7 Dec 2024.

Brooks, C. et al. (2020) "Artificial intelligence in the legal sector: Pressures and challenges of transformation." *Cambridge Journal of Regions, Economy and Society*, 13, 135–152. https://doi.org/10.1093/cjres/rsz026.

Burrel, J. (2016) "How the machine "thinks": Understanding opacity in machine learning." *Algorithms Big Data & Society*, 3, 1–12. https://doi.org/10.1177/2053951715622512.

Carabantes, M. (2020) "Black-box artificial intelligence: An epistemological and critical analysis." *AI & Society*, 35, 309–317. https://doi.org/10.1007/s00146-019-00888-w.

Ceva, E., Jiménez, M.C. (2022) "Automating anticorruption?" *Ethics and Information Technology*, 24, 48. https://doi.org/10.1007/s10676-022-09670-x.

Dan, J. et al. (2024) "Integrating legal event and context information for Chinese similar case analysis." *AI & The Law*, 33, 1. https://doi.org/10.1007/s10506-023-09377-4.

Department of Commerce Announces New Actions to Implement President Biden's Executive Order on AI. Available online at https://www.commerce.gov/news/press-releases/2024/04/department-commerce-announces-new-actions-implement-president-bidens, last access 24 Dec 2024.

Deroy, A. et al. (2024) "Applicability of large language models and generative models for legal case judgement summarization." *AI & The Law*, 2, 12848. https://doi.org/10.1007/s10506-024-09411-z.

Directive (EU) 2019/770 of the European Parliament and of the Council of 20 May 2019 on certain aspects concerning contracts for the supply of digital content and digital services. Available online at https://eur-lex.europa.eu/legal-content/EN/TXT/HTML/?uri=CELEX:32019L0770, last access 24 Nov 2024.

Directive (EU) 2024/2853 of the European Parliament and of the Council of 23 October 2024 on liability for defective products and repealing Council Directive 85/374/EEC. Available online at https://eur-lex.europa.eu/legal-content/EN/TXT/HTML/?uri=OJ:L_202402853, last access 13 Dec 2024.

Eaglin, J. (2016) "Population-based sentencing." *Cornell Law Review*, 106, 353–408.

Engel, C. et al. (2024) "Code is law: How COMPAS affects the way the judiciary handles the risk of recidivism." *AI & The Law*, 8, 1572. https://doi.org/10.1007/s10506-024-09389-8.

European Union Regulation (EU) 2024/1689 of the European Parliament and of the Council of 2024 laying down harmonised rules on artificial intelligence and amending Regulations (EC) No. 300/2008, (EU) No. 167/2013, (EU) No. 168/2013, (EU) 2018/858, (EU) 2018/1139 and (EU) 2019/2144 and Directives 2014/90/EU, (EU) 2016/797 and (EU) 2020/1828 (Artificial Intelligence Act). Available online at https://eur-lex.europa.eu/legal-content/EN/TXT/HTML/?uri=OJ:L_202401689, last access 15 Nov 2024.

Freeman, K. (2016) "Algorithmic injustice: How the Wisconsin Supreme Court failed to protect due process rights in State v. Loomis." *North Carolina Journal of Law and Technology*, 75, 76–105.

Garingan, D., Pickard, A.J. (2021) "AI, algorithms and the legal information world. Artificial intelligence in legal practice: Exploring theoretical frameworks for algorithmic literacy in the legal information profession." *Legal Information Management*, 21, 97–117. https://doi.org/10.1017/S1472669621000190.

Greenleaf, G. et al. (2018) "Building sustainable free legal advisory systems: Experiences from the history of AI & law." *Computer Law & Security Review*, 34(2), 314–326. https://doi.org/10.1016/j.clsr.2018.02.007.

Guillermin, M. et al. (2021) "Ethical digital lawyering. From technical to philosophical insights." In Keith, F., Ramsey, W.M. (eds.) *The Cambridge Handbook of Artificial Intelligence*, Cambridge University Press, Cambridge, UK, pp. 298–311. https://doi.org/10.1017/9781108936040.023.

Hacker, P. (2024) "The European AI liability directives – Critique of a half-hearted approach and lessons for the future." *Computer Law & Security Review*, 52, 105871. https://doi.org/10.1016/j.clsr.2023.105871.

Hull, G. (2023) "Dirty data labeled dirt cheap: Epistemic injustice in machine learning systems." *Ethics and Information Technology*, 25, 38. https://doi.org/10.1007/s10676-023-09712-y.

Infantino, M., Di Matteo, L.A. (2024) "AI, lawyers and consumers." In DiMatteo, L.A., Poncibó, C., Howells, G. (eds.) *The Cambridge Handbook of AI and Consumer Law*, Cambridge University Press, Cambridge, UK, pp. 252–272. https://doi.org/10.1017/9781009483599.024.

Khalid, R., Naeem, A., Deepak, S. (eds.) (2024) *Extractive Summarization of Indian Legal Judgments: Bridging NLP and Generative AI for Socially Responsible Content Generation*, Springer, Singapore. https://doi.org/10.1007/978-981-97-8460-8.

Koessler, L. (2024) "Fiduciary requirements for virtual assistants." *Ethics and Information Technology*, 26, 21. https://doi.org/10.1007/s10676-023-09741-7.

Koplin, J.J. (2023) "Dual-use implications of AI text generation." *Ethics and Information Technology*, 25, 32. https://doi.org/10.1007/s10676-023-09703-z.

Markou, C. (2024) "Substituted consumers." In DiMatteo, L.A., Poncibó, C.,Howells, G. (eds.) *The Cambridge Handbook of AI and Consumer Law*, Cambridge University Press, Cambridge, UK, pp. 19–36. https://doi.org/10.1017/9781009483599.006.

Mowbray, A. et al. (2020) "Utilising AI in the legal assistance sector—Testing a role for legal information institutes." *Computer Law & Security Review*, 38, 105407. https://doi.org/10.2139/ssrn.3379441.

Neumeister, L. (2023) "Lawyers submitted bogus case law created by ChatGPT. A judge fined them $5,000" AP NEWS. Available online at https://apnews.com/article/artificial-intelligence-chatgpt-fake-case-lawyers-d6ae9fa79d0542db9e1455397aef381c, last access 19 Jan 2025.

Ng, C. (2022) "AI in the legal profession." In DiMatteo, L.A., Poncibó, C.,Howells, G. (eds.) *The Cambridge Handbook on Artificial Intelligence*, Cambridge University Press, Cambridge, UK, pp. 35–42. https://doi.org/10.1017/9781009072168.006.

Novelli, C. et al. (2024) "Generative AI in EU law: Liability, privacy, intellectual property, and cybersecurity." *Computer Law & Security Review*, 55, 106066. https://doi.org/10.1016/j.clsr.2024.106066.

Păiş, V. et al. (2024) "System for the anonymization of Romanian jurisprudence." *AI & The Law*, 1572, 8382. https://doi.org/10.1007/s10506-024-09420-y.

Papadouli, V. (2022) "Transparency in artificial intelligence: A legal perspective." *Journal of Ethics and Legal Technologies*, 4(31), 25–40.

Papadouli, V. (2023a) "Artificial intelligence's black box: Posing new ethical and legal challenges on modern societies." In Kornilakis, A., Nouskalis, G., Pergantis, V., Tzimas, T. (eds.) *Artificial Intelligence and Normative Challenges: International and Comparative Legal Perspectives*, Cambridge University Press, Cambridge, UK, pp. 39–62. https://doi.org/10.1007/978-3-031-41081-9.

Papadouli, V. (2023b) "The role of the autonomous machines at the conclusion of a contract: Contractual responsibility according to current rules of private law and prospects." In Kornilakis, A., Nouskalis, G., Pergantis, V., Tzimas, T. (eds.) *Artificial Intelligence and Normative Challenges: International and Comparative Legal Perspectives*, Cambridge University Press, Cambridge, UK, pp. 65–84. https://doi.org/10.1007/978-3-031-41081-9.

Ren, G., Du, J. (2024) "Harmonizing innovation and regulation: The EU Artificial Intelligence Act in the international trade context." *Computer Law & Security Review*, 54, 106028. https://doi.org/10.1016/j.clsr.2024.106028.

Singapore's Approach to AI Governance. Available online at https://www.pdpc.gov.sg/help-and-resources/2020/01/model-ai-governance-framework, last access 24 Dec 2024.

Siqueira, F.A. et al. (2024) "Segmenting Brazilian legislative text using weak supervision and active learning." *AI & The Law*, 2024, 5. https://doi.org/10.1007/s10506-024-09419-5.

UK Policy paper "Establishing a pro-innovation approach to regulating AI" (2022) Available online at https://www.gov.uk/government/publications/establishing-a-pro-innovation-approach-to-regulating-ai/establishing-a-pro-innovation-approach-to-regulating-ai-policy-statement, last access 24 Dec 2024.

Villasenor, J. (2024) "Generative artificial intelligence and the practice of law: Impact, opportunities, and risks." *Minnesota Journal of Law, Science & Technology*, 5(2), 25–48.

Washington, A. (2018) "How to argue with an algorithm: Lessons from the COMPAS-Propublica Debate." *Colorado Technology Law Journal*, 17, 133–159.

Wrbka, S., Fenwick, M. (2024) "Liability for autonomous systems." In DiMatteo, L.A., Poncibó, C.,Howells, G. (eds.) *The Cambridge Handbook of AI and Consumer Law*, Cambridge University Press, Cambridge, UK, pp. 129–146. https://doi.org/10.1017/9781009483599.015.

3 European Union's Perspective on Protection of Personal Data in the Era of GPT Technology

Bartłomiej Żyłka, Siddharth Kanojia,
Homam Reda El-Taj, and Beata Polok

3.1 INTRODUCTION

In the realm of AI development worldwide, safeguarding personal data remains a crucial concern. This is particularly relevant for systems based on Generative Pre-trained Transformer (GPT) models, which represent a significant evolution in artificial intelligence, especially within the field of natural language processing (NLP). GPT technology relies on deep neural networks and large-scale data processing to generate coherent text across diverse context. The primary architecture behind GPT models is the transformer, which revolutionized NLP through its attention mechanism. This mechanism allows the model to dynamically assess the importance of various parts of the input data, enabling GPT to efficiently handle complex tasks such as text generation, translation, summarization, and conversational interaction.

GPT models operate through two core processes: pre-training and fine-tuning. Pre-training involves training the model on vast datasets sourced from the internet, enabling it to predict and generate text based on patterns recognized in the data (Sheng 2022). During this phase, the model learns grammar, semantics, and factual knowledge. Fine-tuning, on the other hand, refines the pre-trained model using specific, often smaller datasets tailored to its intended application, such as customer service chatbots or legal text generation.

As a machine learning model, GPT is designed to effectively understand and generate human-like language using both unsupervised and supervised learning techniques. However, the training process raises significant concerns regarding the security of individual users and the data used in it (Lund and Wang 2023). These concerns have emerged alongside the increasing efficiency and popularity of widely accessible tools such as ChatGPT, developed by OpenAI. ChatGPT, along with models such as BERT, RoBERTa, and XLNet, represents the forefront of AI developed by OpenAI (GPT), Google (BERT), and Microsoft (XLNet) (Hadi et al. 2023). These models rely on processing enormous amounts of data through self-learning techniques.

DOI: 10.1201/9781003541899-3

Current trends indicate a rapidly growing adoption of this technology, which is proving effective across various fields. The benefits of GPT are undeniable, offering significant advantages for society and the economy, as recognized by international organizations, including the United Nations, the Council of Europe, and the Organization for Economic Cooperation and Development (OECD). Among these, the European Union (EU) has positioned itself as a global leader in both AI development and data protection. The EU's dual approach reflects a commitment to nurturing innovation while safeguarding fundamental rights such as privacy.

In its approach to AI development, the EU seeks to create an environment that fosters innovation while adhering to European values such as transparency, fairness, and accountability. This vision is encapsulated in initiatives like the White Chapter on Artificial Intelligence, which guarantees a human-centered approach to AI, ensuring that technology serves society. Furthermore, the European Union funds research projects and establishes regulatory frameworks to encourage ethical AI development and set global standards for responsible innovation.

In terms of data protection, the EU has established itself as a global leader by developing a regulatory framework that includes the General Data Protection Regulation (GDPR), one of the most significant data protection laws worldwide (Bradford 2020). Enforced in 2018, the GDPR set a new standard for data privacy by granting individuals more control over their personal data and imposing strict obligations on data controllers. Its extraterritorial scope ensures that any entity processing data related to EU citizens must comply with the GDPR, regardless of its location. This transparency-focused approach reinforces the EU's commitment to privacy as a fundamental right.

To further guide the EU's digital transformation, the European Commission introduced the "Europe's Digital Decade" policy program (Hernandez et al. 2023). This initiative outlines specific targets for 2030 in areas such as skill development, secure digital infrastructure, business digitalization, and the digitalization of public service. In May 2020, the Commission also released a report titled "Shaping the Digital Future of Europe," which highlights its focus on creating a Europe fit for the digital age from 2020 to 2025. The report emphasizes the importance of the digital single market, the use of AI, and support for digital innovation and skills (Carver 2023).

While the EU has made substantial efforts to integrate AI into its legislative and regulatory frameworks, these measures often struggle to keep pace with the multidimensional and dynamic nature of AI. Therefore, this article aims to present a concise overview of the key issues related to the development of AI, particularly GPT-based language models, in the context of personal data protection within the EU. It also examines relevant EU regulations that directly or indirectly impact AI development.

3.2 IMPORTANCE OF PROTECTING PERSONAL DATA

Data protection encompasses a set of measures and practices aimed at safeguarding personal data, ensuring its privacy and security. Its primary objective is to prevent unauthorized access, use, disclosure, alteration, or destruction of personal information. In the context of electronic signatures, data protection plays a critical role in upholding the confidentiality and integrity of both transmitted and stored information. In today's digital economy, data has become a commodity, traded and sold in exchange for services or financial gain. The core principles of data protection revolve around privacy, security, and ethical duties upheld by state and non-state actors. Data privacy is an individual's absolute rights-based interest in maintaining control over their personal information and how it is used. On the other hand, security focuses on protecting data from leakage, unauthorized access, or misuse through the implementation of appropriate technical and organizational measures. Ethical responsibilities require governments and private actors to handle data transparently, accountably, and fairly. Consequently, the state actors should strike a balance between the need to collect data and the right to privacy so as not to exercise excessive surveillance against citizens. Similarly, non-state actors, particularly corporate actors, should ensure user consent, data minimization, and the ethical use of data for commercial purposes. Therefore, these principles should set the framework while showing respect for the autonomy of all parties concerned and engendering trust within the digital ecosystem (Anand and Brass 2021).

The OECD highlights the significance of safeguarding privacy and personal data in national cryptography policies and the use of cryptographic methods. Furthermore, concerning digital signatures, entities such as certification authorities and registration authorities are responsible for handling personal data in accordance with applicable jurisdictional requirements. Transactional privacy also constitutes a crucial element of data protection, ensuring that personal data obtained during transactions is treated with confidentiality and accuracy, even when the subscribing party is unaware of its collection (Betkier 2018). Data protection is a topic of paramount importance in the realms of scientific research and technology. The importance of protecting personal information stems from the need to prevent its misuse by malicious entities in fraudulent activities, including phishing and identity theft (Alkhalil et al. 2021).

Meanwhile, various nations have experienced instances of malicious actors continuously seeking opportunities to exploit weaknesses in data security systems, aiming to steal personal information for financial gain and other illicit activities. Accordingly, protecting personal data is not just about individual safety; it is also about maintaining the trust and security of the entire digital ecosystem. Likewise, in the context of business and commerce, personal data is the cornerstone of personalized services and targeted marketing. Hence, mistrust among consumers caused by misuse or data breaches can obliterate the reputation of a company. Subsequently, businesses have both a legal and moral responsibility to safeguard consumer information, as data breaches can have serious repercussions. Protecting personal information holds utmost importance in sectors such as healthcare. To ensure patient privacy and the precision of medical diagnoses and treatments, medical records, treatment histories, and other sensitive health information must be securely maintained. Unauthorized access to such personal information can cause psychological and emotional harm. The sense of vulnerability and betrayal of trust can be devastating. Consequently, protecting personal data is not a question of choice or preference. Rather, it is an ethical, legal, and practical obligation for both state and non-state actors.

3.2.1 Data Handling in GPT Models

The efficiency of GPT models stems from their ability to process and learn from massive amounts of data. However, this advantage also poses challenges regarding data protection. Because GPT models require massive and diverse datasets, which often contain personal data, concerns have been raised about privacy and data security (Kanojia 2024). The GDPR emphasizes the need for data minimization, ensuring that only necessary data is collected and processed for a specific purpose (Li et al. 2024a). In contrast, GPT models thrive on massive amounts of unstructured data, making compliance with such regulations difficult (Buddiga 2023).

Furthermore, the transparency of data processing is often compromised due to the "black-box" nature of AI models like GPT. These models operate through extraordinarily complex internal mechanisms, making it difficult for developers and users to track how decisions or outputs are derived (Ruiz Sarrias et al. 2024). This lack of transparency hinders the ability to explain how specific data are used during the model's learning process, raising concerns about potential misuse or accidental exposure of sensitive data (Masao et al. 2024).

3.2.2 Challenges in Data Protection

Data protection is one of the most important challenges associated with GPT models. Since these models rely on publicly available datasets obtained from the web, they may unwittingly include non-consented personal data. The GDPR and similar data protection frameworks require individuals to give explicit consent for their data to be used in any processing activity. In the case of GPT, where data collection is automated and involves massive datasets, it is impractical to obtain consent from every data subject (Binhammad et al. 2024).

Moreover, the concept of data minimization—a cornerstone of the GDPR—poses another major challenge. Data minimization involves collecting and processing only the data necessary to achieve a specific purpose. However, GPT models benefit from exposure to as much data as possible, including duplicate or irrelevant data, to generate accurate and contextually relevant outputs (Al-kfairy et al. 2024). Balancing the need for intensive data inputs with the principle of minimization is a fundamental dilemma in the development of AI.

3.3 ETHICAL CONSIDERATIONS

Beyond data protection, ethical considerations play a critical role in developing and deploying GPT models. A major concern is the expansion of inherent biases in training data. GPT models, by design, reflect patterns in their training datasets, meaning that any bias—whether racial, gender-based, or socioeconomic—can be perpetuated through the model's output. This has serious implications, especially in high-stakes applications such as law enforcement, healthcare, and employment, where biased decisions can reinforce existing inequalities (Sheng 2022).

Another ethical challenge is the model's potential to generate harmful or misleading content. Given the complexity of GPT models, they can produce texts that appear very plausible but may be factually incorrect or intentionally harmful (Ruiz Sarrias et al. 2024). The use of AI to generate fake news, fake content, and other forms of misinformation has raised alarms among policymakers, who are increasingly concerned about the potential for AI to be used in disinformation campaigns (Fan et al. 2024).

Furthermore, when considering the ethical use of GPT models, the question of accountability arises. It remains unclear who should be held responsible. If an AI system produces harmful or misleading content—the developers, the users, or the AI itself? This question becomes even more complicated when considering the increasing autonomy of AI systems in generating outputs without human intervention (Binhammad et al. 2024).

3.4　OPERATIONALITY OF GENERATIVE ARTIFICIAL INTELLIGENCE

AI is a field dedicated to developing computer systems and models with the capability to perform tasks that would normally require human intelligence. Within the realm of AI, models like GPT (Generative Pre-trained Transformer) have emerged as prominent examples. These models are known for their remarkable aptitude in comprehending and generating human-like text. To comprehend the technical intricacies of GPT-based AI models, it is essential to delve into their operational intricacies. The process initiates with data collection and preprocessing. GPT models undergo a pre-training phase during which they process a vast corpus of text data gathered from the internet. This process is instrumental in the model's acquisition of linguistic patterns, grammar, and contextual understanding. OpenAI's GPT-3 model, for instance, is trained on a colossal dataset encompassing over 570GB of text.

At the core of GPT models is the transformer architecture, an intricate neural network framework celebrated for its ability to capture long-range dependencies within data (Vaswani et al. 2017). To facilitate text analysis, data is tokenized, breaking it down into smaller units, typically words or subwords. Each token is associated with an embedding vector that encapsulates its meaning within the model's framework. The subsequent step involves pre-training, wherein the model forecasts the next word in a sentence. During this phase, the model acquires the proficiency to discern syntax, semantics, and exercise common sense reasoning. This is achieved by fine-tuning the model's parameters to align with the linguistic patterns observed in the training data (Devlin et al. 2018). Following pre-training, GPT models can be fine-tuned to cater to specific tasks, rendering them versatile for a multitude of applications such as text generation, translation, summarization, and more (Radford et al. 2019). When users input a prompt or query, GPT generates text by predicting the next token given the context of the input. This is achieved through a process known as autoregressive text generation. Text generation transpires by predicting one token at a time, with each token influencing the next based on probability distributions. GPT models come in a range of sizes, with larger models containing more parameters. Larger models tend to exhibit superior performance but demand more extensive computational resources (Brown et al. 2020). Additionally, it is imperative to acknowledge the ethical considerations associated with AI models like GPT. Concerns encompass bias in generated content, the propagation of misinformation, and the potential for misuse. Addressing these concerns forms an integral part of the operational process. Attempts to normatively capture the entirety of the complex processes referred to as AI remain a significant challenge, to the present moment, there is no lack of universally accepted definition—largely due to the dynamic and multifaceted evolution of AI systems. The intricate nature and rapid advancements of AI make it difficult to stay abreast of its progress and effectively regulate it. The complexity and accelerating growth of AI contribute to the difficulty of keeping pace with its rapid developments and implementing appropriate regulation. Despite these challenges, the necessity of developing a legal definition of what is meant by the concise term AI or AI systems has prompted many international organizations to undertake this effort, with varying degrees of success. Among the definitions of AI systems, it is worth mentioning the one created by the OECD, which defines an AI system as:

> (...) a machine-based system that can, for a given set of human-defined objectives, make predictions, recommendations, or decisions influencing real or virtual environments. AI systems are designed to operate with varying levels of autonomy.

On the other hand, the Committee on Artificial Intelligence of the Council of Europe adopted a significantly more elaborate definition in the Draft Framework Convention on Artificial Intelligence, Human Rights, Democracy, and the Rule of Law.

> Artificial intelligence system means any algorithmic system or a combination of such systems that, as defined herein and in the domestic law of each Party, uses computational methods derived from statistics or other mathematical techniques to carry out functions that are commonly associated with, or would otherwise require, human intelligence and that either assists or replaces the judgment of human decision-makers in carrying out those functions. Such functions include, but are not limited to, prediction, planning, classification, pattern recognition, organization, perception, speech/sound/ image recognition, text/sound/image generation, language translation, communication, learning, representation, and problem solving.

The examples of definitions can be numerous; however, from the perspective of the EU, which views artificial intelligence as a central element of the digital transformation of society and one of its key priorities, the situation is remarkably similar. One of the more comprehensive definitions of AI can be found in the Communication from the European Commission on AI, which defines it as follows:

> AI refers to systems that display intelligent behaviour by analyzing their environment and taking actions – with some degree of autonomy – to achieve specific goals. AI-based systems can be purely software-based, acting in the virtual world (e.g., voice assistants, image analysis software, search engines, speech, and face recognition systems) or AI can be embedded in hardware devices (e.g., advanced robots, autonomous cars, drones, or Internet of Things applications).

> (Palladino 2021)

As a result of over two years of work on the AI Act project, which aims to become the world's first comprehensive regulatory framework governing the functioning of artificial intelligence, the EU will also establish a unified definition of artificial intelligence:

'artificial intelligence system' (AI system) means software that is developed with one or more of the techniques and approaches listed in Annex I and can, for a given set of human-defined objectives, generate outputs such as content, predictions, recommendations, or decisions influencing the environments they interact with.

The definition adopted in the AI Act refers to Annex I, which lists the following artificial intelligence techniques and approaches:

a. Machine learning approaches, including supervised, unsupervised, and reinforcement learning, using a wide variety of methods, including deep learning.
b. Logic- and knowledge-based approaches, including knowledge representation, inductive (logic) programming, knowledge bases, inference and deductive engines, (symbolic) reasoning, and expert systems.
c. Statistical approaches, Bayesian estimation, search, and optimization methods.

The EU legislator, in its definition, did not limit itself to a specific technology, aiming to capture a broad scope. This approach can be considered fully justified from the perspective of the effectiveness of the AI Act and the protection of data processed by AI.

3.5 GDPR REGULATION IN THE CONTEXT OF THE DEVELOPMENT OF ARTIFICIAL INTELLIGENCE

The issue of data protection has long been a concern within the EU, which is actively working to align AI developments with high-quality data protection standards. One of the earliest significant documents addressing this matter was the European Data Protection Directive, also known as Directive 95/46/EC. This directive played a crucial role in establishing the legal framework for privacy and human rights in the EU regarding the processing and free movement of personal data. The Treaty of Lisbon added Article 16(1) to the TFEU, stating that everyone has the right to the protection of personal data concerning them. The EU's efforts to establish a unified approach to data protection are exemplified by the GDPR. Introduced in 2016, the GDPR marked a significant advancement in safeguarding personal data. Although it was adopted in 2016, it became enforceable in 2018 due to the extensive preparations and adjustments required for compliance. The GDPR replaced the previously applicable Directive 95/46/EC on the protection of personal data. The GDPR, as a secondary act of European law, has a direct effect on national law in the form in which it was published in the Official Journal of the EU. The EU legislator aimed to strengthen the protection of personal data, including its processing by artificial intelligence systems, although the regulation does not contain direct references to AI. Instead, it focuses on the general context of personal data protection, introducing a set of principles and requirements that impact the application of AI in the EU. As a result, the adoption of the GDPR by the European Parliament and the Council was based on Article 16 of the TFEU (Hijmans 2016), emphasizing the need to prioritize individual rights over any other objective. One of the fundamental issues of the GDPR in relation to AI, including technologies like GPT, is the presence of numerous general clauses and vague formulations. These can be interpreted broadly, thereby undermining the basic principles of data protection.

According to Article 5(1)(a), alternative 3, of the GDPR, personal data must be processed transparently in relation to the data subject. This requirement is particularly relevant in the context of issues related to artificial intelligence. Furthermore, Article 39 of the GDPR establishes the principle of transparency, which requires that all information and communication regarding the processing of personal data must be easily accessible and understandable, using clear and plain language. This principle specifically applies to the information provided to individuals whose data is being processed, including the identity of the data controller, the purposes of processing, and additional information to ensure fair and transparent processing in relation to these individuals and their rights to confirmation and access to personal data concerning them. The requirements of transparency are further elaborated in Articles 12–15 of the GDPR, which impose obligations on data controllers to provide information and ensure access to personal data. These obligations are supported by the requirement to implement appropriate technical and organizational measures. However, in the case of AI, especially self-learning technologies such as GPT, data controllers face many challenges in transparently demonstrating the potential impacts of AI in each individual case. At this point, a fundamental problem arises: the blatant misalignment between EU regulations on personal data protection and the specific nature of self-learning AI systems. This misalignment results in significant limitations to achieving complete transparency in data processing. According to the fundamental provision of the GDPR, processing of personal data is permitted only with the explicit consent of the data subjects. However, the contemporary AI applications use large datasets, some of which can contain sensitive personal information. Correspondingly, it might be exhausting to verify that consent is attained and monitored for all data used in AI applications. The regulation also reinforces the principle of data minimization, which entails the limitation of collecting and storing personal data for specific purposes. Meanwhile, collecting humongous datasets is a very natural trait of AI. Apparently, ensuring the harmonious coexistence of the GDPR and the operationality of AI applications can be formidable and challenging. Other practical implications of the regulation are the implementation of the GDPR's "right to explanation," which is complex and challenging with sophisticated AI models, since many AI systems, especially deep learning models, are regarded as "black boxes". Thus, it can be challenging to provide accurate justifications for the choices they make. Similarly, the AI models may be trained with prejudiced data, which might provide biased results. Algorithmic discrimination can lead to discriminatory practices, since current legislation does not offer explicit guidance on how to adequately address it. Striking an equilibrium between data security, privacy, and the application of AI can be complicated. The GDPR's emphasis on data protection may need stringent security measures, which could make AI applications less beneficial.

The weakness of the GDPR regulation and the lack of uniformity in its application became evident with the global success of Chat-GPT, which relies on processing vast amounts of data. Doubts regarding the compliance of the chatbot's operations with European regulations on personal data protection started to arise in individual EU member states. Italy was the first European country where the functioning of Chat-GPT was temporarily restricted. By a decision dated March 30, 2023, based on Article 58(2)(f) of the Regulation (EU) 2016/679 of the European Parliament and of the Council of April 27, 2016, the Italian data protection authority (Garante per la protezione dei dati personali) imposed a temporary limitation on the processing of all personal data of Chat-GPT users within the territory of Italy (Chiara 2023). The Italian authority cited the lack of a proper legal basis for the functioning of AI, which is necessary for the lawful collection and processing of personal data used to train the algorithms. The authority pointed out that the actions of OpenAI L.L.C. violated Articles 5, 6, 8, 13, and 25 of the GDPR.

According to the Italian data protection authority, Chat-GPT unlawfully collects personal data of users due to the lack of information provided to users and all concerned parties regarding the data collected by OpenAI LLC and processed by the Chat-GPT service. Also, there is no adequate legal basis justifying the mass collection and storage of personal data to "train" the algorithms underlying the functioning of Chat- GPT. Furthermore, the information provided by Chat-GPT does not always correspond to real data, indicating improper handling of personal data. It was also pointed out that, despite the terms published by OpenAI stating that the service is reserved for users above 13 years of age, there is a lack of age verification systems for Chat-GPT users, thereby exposing children under the age of 13 to responses that are completely inappropriate for their level of development and self-awareness.

Similar concerns were expressed by national data protection authorities in Germany, Spain, and France. The European Data Protection Board (EDPB) has established a new task force specifically dedicated to addressing privacy issues related to Chat-GPT and similar artificial intelligence technologies. The task force will focus on assessing the compliance of these technologies with the GDPR and ensuring the protection of individuals' personal data. Its goal is to ensure that the development and deployment of Chat-GPT are aligned with European privacy standards and respect individuals' right to privacy. The task force will collaborate with relevant stakeholders, including artificial intelligence developers and privacy experts, to gather knowledge and formulate recommendations regarding privacy protection in the context of AI-based chat systems.

The functioning of AI and potential violations of data processing principles outlined in the GDPR can be considered one of the main challenges for the EU in the context of AI system development. For many years, there has been awareness of the numerous and often unpredictable consequences arising from AI processing vast amounts of data. Despite these acknowledged risks, it is difficult to argue that the GDPR provisions concerning data protection have been fully effective, as practice suggests otherwise. Despite the existence of artificial intelligence systems in various forms for several decades, the EU legislator did not adequately anticipate technological advancements when drafting the GDPR (Kesa and Tanel 2020). Therefore, in recent years, it has become entirely justified to question whether, and to what extent, practical problems related to artificial intelligence, particularly technologies based on self-learning GPT models that process massive amounts of data, can be resolved within the existing legal framework.

3.6 POLITICAL DEMANDS AND HARMONIZATION EFFORTS OF THE EU REGARDING NEW TECHNOLOGIES AND DATA PROTECTION

The growing significance and proliferation of AI technology have influenced the formulation of specific demands within the EU, which were expressed, among others, in the political guidelines for the European Commission for the years 2019–2024. In response to these demands, President Ursula von der Leyen announced that the Commission would propose regulations establishing a coordinated European approach to the social and ethical implications of artificial intelligence. In line with this announcement, on February 19, 2020, the Commission published a White Paper on Artificial Intelligence—*A European Approach to Excellence and Trust*. The White Paper outlined strategic options for achieving the dual objective of promoting the use of artificial intelligence while addressing the risks associated with certain applications of this innovative technology. The document emphasized the need for the EU to define its own path, based on European values, to promote the development and deployment of artificial intelligence.

On February 19, 2020, the European Commission issued a communication to the European Parliament, the Council, the European Economic and Social Committee, and the Committee of the Regions titled *European Strategy for Data*. In this document, the Commission set an ambitious goal of making the EU a model society where data enables better decision-making, both in businesses and the public sector. It also emphasized the need to create appropriate legal foundations for regulating the functioning of artificial intelligence while respecting fundamental rights, such as data protection, as enshrined in the Charter of Fundamental Rights of the EU and the Treaty on the Functioning of the EU. The European Commission highlighted interoperability and data quality, as well as their structure, authenticity, and integrity, as crucial factors for harnessing the value represented by data, especially in the context of implementing AI. It also emphasized the importance for encouraging the use of standardized and commonly compatible formats and protocols for collecting and processing data from various sources in a coherent and interoperable manner across all sectors and vertical markets, through a progressive plan for ICT standardization (Wallace 2020). Furthermore, concerning public services, the European Commission highlighted the need to strengthen European interoperability frameworks. The European Commission's proposal dated April 21, 2021, regarding the establishment of harmonized rules on AI (the AI Act), aimed to implement these postulates. The rationale behind the proposal clearly indicated that promoting AI-based innovation is linked to the Data Governance Act, the Directive on Open Data, and other initiatives that are part of the European Data Strategy.

The AI Act, whose goal is to comprehensively regulate the functioning of AI within the EU, was adopted in 2024. The Act classifies AI applications into three risk categories. The first category includes systems that pose an unacceptable risk, high risks, and low or minimal risks. Unacceptable risks, such as state-run social scoring like that implemented in China, are prohibited. The second category encompasses high-risk applications, like CV-scanning tools that evaluate job candidates, which must adhere to certain legal standards. Finally, applications that are not specifically banned or categorized as high-risk remain mostly unregulated. The adoption of the regulation aligns with the EU's ongoing policy of digital transformation, aimed at integrating digital technologies used by businesses and addressing their impact on society. AI is recognized as one of the technologies with the greatest influence.

On June 14, 2023, the European Parliament adopted a series of amendments with a majority of 499 votes, some of which relate to the relationship between data protection and AI. The adoption of these amendments was influenced, among others, by the opinions of the European Central Bank, the European Data Protection Board, and the European Data Protection Supervisor. Amendment No. 3 significantly expanded the objectives of the regulation, defining them as follows:

> The purpose of this Regulation is to promote the uptake of human centric and trustworthy artificial intelligence and to ensure a prominent level of protection of health, safety, fundamental rights, democracy and rule of law and the environment from harmful effects of artificial intelligence systems in the Union while supporting innovation and improving the functioning of the internal market. This Regulation lays down a uniform legal framework in particular for the development, the placing on the market, the putting into service and the use of artificial intelligence in conformity with Union values and ensures the free movement of AI-based goods and services cross-border, thus preventing Member States from imposing restrictions on the development, marketing and use of Artificial Intelligence systems (AI systems), unless explicitly authorized by this Regulation. Certain AI systems can also have an impact on democracy and rule of law and the environment. These concerns are specifically addressed in the critical sectors and use cases listed in the annexes to this Regulation.

> (De Almeida et al. 2021)

The reference to the use of AI in line with the values of the Union also relates to the fundamental value of data protection. This provision was reinforced by Amendment No. 4, which introduced a completely new Article 1a. It explicitly states that the regulation should protect the values of the Union, facilitate the distribution of benefits from artificial intelligence in society, and safeguard individuals, businesses, democracy, the rule of law, and the environment from threats, while also stimulating innovation and employment and establishing the Union as a leader in this field. Amendment directly related to the training methods of GPT-like technologies is introduced in Article 2a of the draft, which specifically highlights the frequent reliance of AI on processing large amounts of data, including personal data. This necessitates the grounding the AI Act on Article 16 of the Treaty on the Functioning of the European Union (TFEU). Article 16 of the TFEU guarantees the right to the protection of personal data and envisages the adoption of provisions concerning the protection of individuals regarding the processing of personal data. The EU legislator has also emphasized the risks and material and non-material physical, psychological, social, and economic harm that AI can pose to the public or private interest and to the fundamental rights of individuals protected by EU law, depending on the specific circumstances of its application and use, as well as the level of technological development. The draft regulation sets forth the requirement for artificial intelligence systems to make their utmost efforts to comply with high-level general principles that promote a cohesive, human-centric approach to ethical and trustworthy artificial intelligence, in accordance with the Charter and the values upon which the Union is founded. These include the protection of fundamental rights, the guiding and supervisory role of humans, technical robustness and safety, privacy and data management, transparency, non-discrimination and fairness, as well as social and environmental well-being.

According to the newly added Article 28a in the draft regulation, when classifying an artificial intelligence system as a high-risk system, the scale of its harmful impact on fundamental rights protected by the Charter is of paramount importance. Among these rights is the right to the protection of personal data, among others. The draft regulation acknowledges the risks associated with AI systems, which can arise from both their design and their use. Operators of high-risk AI systems play a crucial role in safeguarding fundamental rights, including the right to the protection of personal data, complementing to the obligations of the provider during the development of AI systems. According to the EU legislator, operators of AI systems have a better understanding of how a high-risk AI system will be specifically applied and can therefore identify potential serious risks that were not anticipated during the development stage, thanks to more precise knowledge of the context of use and the individuals or groups of individuals that the system may impact, including marginalized and particularly vulnerable groups. The draft regulation states that operators should establish appropriate management structures in this specific usage context, such as provisions for human oversight and procedures for handling complaints and claims, as choices in the management structures can be crucial in mitigating threats to fundamental rights in specific use cases. To effectively ensure the protection of fundamental rights, an operator of a high-risk AI system should conduct an impact assessment of the system on fundamental rights before deploying it. The impact assessment should be accompanied by a detailed plan describing the measures or tools that will help mitigate the identified risks to fundamental rights, to be completed no later than the time of deployment. If such a plan cannot be identified, the operator should refrain from deploying the system. When conducting the impact assessment, the operator of the AI system should notify the national supervisory authority and, to the greatest extent possible, the relevant stakeholders, as well as representatives of groups that may be affected by the AI system, in order to gather the necessary information for the impact assessment. They should also be encouraged to provide a summary of the impact assessment regarding fundamental rights for public knowledge on a website. These obligations should not apply to small and medium-sized enterprises (SMEs) that may have difficulty conducting such consultations due to a lack of resources. However, SMEs should also make efforts to engage with such representatives when conducting the impact assessment on fundamental rights. Additionally, considering the potential impact and the need for democratic oversight and control, operators of high-risk AI systems who are public authorities or institutions, bodies, offices, and agencies of the Union, as well as operators designated as access providers under Regulation (EU) 2022/1925, are required to register the deployment of each high-risk AI system in a public database.

On a similar front, the EU has also started preparing to put into force the ePrivacy Regulation, an ambitious legislative plan geared to encompass electronic communications, cookies, and their interplay with future technologies, especially AI.

In line with the GDPR's consent-driven approach, this regulation stresses the necessity for explicit, unequivocal user consent for the processing of electronic communications data. Consequently, data subjects will have more control and choice over how their data is utilized, particularly in the case of AI systems that depend on user-generated data. The Regulation also intends to preserve the confidential nature of electronic communications as a fundamental principle, forbidding the interception or surveillance of communications without the subject's express consent. This is vital for AI systems like chatbots or voice assistants that assess communications data. As a result, applications of AI that rely on data obtained through cookies or electronic communications may face challenges conforming to these stringent regulations. The ePrivacy Regulation aims to promote a unified approach to data protection and privacy in the EU as a supplement to the GDPR. These regulations may operate together to provide an integrated data protection structure, which will affect how AI is developed and used across different industries.

Also, to cope with the evolving challenges posed by cyber threats, the EU has been developing a comprehensive cybersecurity framework. This framework is directly applicable to the integration of AI into numerous industries. The Network and Information Systems Directive, implemented in 2018, outlines criteria for the security of network and information systems in sectors essential to the public, such as healthcare, transport, finance, energy, and others. The operations of these sectors are increasingly adopting the AI models. Hence, operators of such critical and digital service providers are mandated under these guidelines to maintain the accountability and robustness of their systems. Later, in 2019, a framework for the cybersecurity certification of goods, services, and procedures was developed by the EU through the Cybersecurity Act. The certification and trust-building protocols of this Act can be implemented within AI systems to ensure their security and reliability. Meanwhile, many cybersecurity competence centers have been established throughout the EU to encourage cooperation and knowledge exchange among member states, businesses, and academia. These centers are vital for strengthening the resilience of digital infrastructures and boosting research and innovation in AI and cybersecurity.

3.7 CONCLUSION

This chapter has provided an in-depth analysis of the European Union's position on the protection of personal data within the rapidly advancing domain of generative pre-trained transformer (GPT) technology. By exploring both the operational facets of GPT and its profound impact on privacy and personal data, this chapter has highlighted the pressing challenges posed by the massive datasets required for AI models, such as the conflict between data minimization principles and the operational needs of GPT models. It further emphasized how the European Union, through its robust legal frameworks such as the GDPR, has taken proactive steps to address these challenges.

Moreover, the European Union has demonstrated a clear commitment to navigating the moral, legal, and societal complexities surrounding GPT technology. This commitment is reflected in its ability to balance the promotion of technological innovation with the safeguarding of citizens' fundamental rights. The political guidelines for the European Commission (2019–2024), along with the White Paper on Artificial Intelligence, underscore the EU's focus on creating an ethical and human-centered

AI ecosystem. These initiatives aim not only to harness the economic benefits of AI but also to mitigate the risks associated with issues such as privacy violations, bias, and the misuse of personal data.

The European Strategy for Data further reinforces the EU's goal of becoming a global leader in responsible data-driven innovation. It aims to create a society where data enhances decision-making while upholding citizens' fundamental rights, including privacy and data protection. By establishing stringent regulations and promoting ethical AI practices, the EU seeks to prevent the unintended consequences of GPT technology, such as the propagation of bias, the lack of transparency in data processing, and the risk of disinformation. The "black-box" nature of GPT models and the challenges in achieving transparency and accountability are being actively addressed by the EU to ensure that AI development aligns with European values of fairness, transparency, and accountability.

The two-year legislative process has resulted in critical changes, emphasizing a trustworthy, human-centered approach to AI that aligns with European values while ensuring the free flow of AI-based goods and services across national borders. As the legislative process advances, it is evident that the EU remains at the forefront of global efforts to encourage innovation, protect fundamental rights, and establish itself as a leader in the field of artificial intelligence. By skillfully navigating the complexities of generative AI, the EU is setting an example of how to foster technological progress while upholding the privacy, security, and ethical principles that underpin a fair and just digital society.

3.8 KEY TERMS AND CONCEPTS

AI (Artificial Intelligence): The simulation of human intelligence in machines designed to perform tasks that typically require human intelligence, such as language understanding, problem-solving, and decision-making.

Data Minimization: A GDPR principle that emphasizes collecting only the minimum amount of personal data necessary for a specific purpose, limiting the overcollection of sensitive data.

GDPR (General Data Protection Regulation): A comprehensive EU law enacted to protect personal data of individuals within the EU. It outlines how organizations should handle and protect personal data, with provisions for transparency, data minimization, and explicit consent.

Generative Pre-trained Transformer (GPT) Technology: GPT is a type of artificial intelligence model designed to understand and generate human-like text. It uses large datasets and self-learning techniques to analyze linguistic patterns and generate contextually relevant responses.

Machine Learning: A branch of AI that involves training algorithms on data so they can learn patterns and make predictions or decisions without being explicitly programmed for specific tasks.

Personal Data: Information related to an identifiable individual, including names, addresses, IP addresses, or even online behaviors, which must be protected to ensure privacy and prevent misuse.

Transformer Architecture: The neural network architecture used in models like GPT excels at capturing relationships between words or tokens in long-range sequences, making it effective for text processing.

REFERENCES

Al-kfairy, M., Mustafa, D., Kshetri, N., Insiew, M., & Alfandi, O. 2024. "Ethical Challenges in Generative AI: An Interdisciplinary Perspective." *Journal of Informatics*, 5, 200–220, https://doi.org/10.3390/informatics11030058.

Alkhalil, Z., Chaminda, H., Liqaa, N., & Imtiaz, K. 2021. "Phishing Attacks: A Recent Comprehensive Study and a New Anatomy." *Frontiers in Computer Science*, 3, 563060, https://doi.org/10.3389/fcomp.2021.563060.

De Almeida, P. G. R., dos Santos, C. D., & Farias, J. S. (2021). Artificial intelligence regulation: a framework for governance. *Ethics and Information Technology*, 23(3), 505–525.

Anand, N. & Brass, I. 2021. "Responsible Innovation for Digital Identity Systems." *Data & Policy*, 3, e35, https://doi.org/10.1017/dap.2021.35.

Betkier, M. 2018. "Moving Beyond Consent in Data Privacy Law. An Effective Privacy Management System for Internet Services." PhD diss., Open Access Te Herenga Waka-Victoria University of Wellington, Available at: https://openaccess.wgtn.ac.nz/articles/thesis/Moving_beyond_consent_in_data_privacy_law_An_effective_privacy_management_system_for_Internet_services/17068490.

Binhammad, M.H.Y., Othman, A., & Abuljadayel, L. 2024. "Advanced Generative Dialogue Systems for Educational Chatbots." *Creative Education*, 15, 123–135, https://doi.org/10.4236/ce.2024.158096.

Bradford, A. 2020. *The Brussels Effect: How the European Union Rules the World*. Oxford University Press, New York.

Buddiga, S.K.P. 2023. "Harnessing Natural Language Processing for Conversational AI: Evolution, Challenges, and Future Directions." *Journal of Artificial Intelligence, Machine Learning and Data Science*, 1(3), 382–385, https://doi.org/10.51219/JAIMLD/sai-kalyana-pranitha-buddiga/102.

Carver, J. 2023. "More Bark than Bite? European Digital Sovereignty Discourse and Changes to the European Union's External Relations Policy." *Journal of European Public Policy*, 31, 1–37, https://doi.org/10.1080/13501763.2023.2295523.

Devlin, J., Chang, M.-W., Lee, K., & Toutanova, K. 2018. "BERT: Pre-training of Deep Bidirectional Transformers for Language Understanding." In: Proceedings of the 2019 Conference of the North American Chapter of the Association for Computational Linguistics: Human Language Technologies, Volume 1 (Long and Short Papers) (pp. 4171–4186), https://doi.org/10.48550/arXiv.1810.04805.

Fan, S., Zheng, Y., Sun, X., Zhao, A., & Wu, Y. 2024. "Integration of GPT-4 into Multimodal Bioinformatics for Surgical Specimens." *International Journal of Surgery*, 110(9), 5854–5856, https://doi.org/10.1097/JS9.0000000000001617.

Hadi, M.U., Qureshi, R., Shah, A., Irfan, M., Zafar, A., Shaikh, M.B., Akhtar, N., Wu, J., & Mirjalili, S. 2023. "Large Language Models: A Comprehensive Survey of its Applications, Challenges, Limitations, and Future Prospects." Authorea Preprints, https://doi.org/10.36227/techrxiv.23589741.v4.

Hernandez, Q., Lorena, R.S.S., & Sven, S. 2023. *Identifying Opportunities for Streamlining European Monitoring of Digital Policies*. Publications Office of the European Union, Luxembourg, https://doi.org/10.2760/163337.

Kanojia, S. 2024. "Digitalization in Corporations: Integrating Utility of Digital Technology with Accessibility and Privacy of Data." In: M. Pucelj (eds) *Balancing Human Rights, Social Responsibility, and Digital Ethics* (pp. 227–245). IGI Global, New York, https://doi.org/10.4018/979-8-3693-3334-1.ch008.

Li, B., Beaton, D., Lee, D.S., Aljabri, B., Al-Omran, L., Wijeysundera, D.N., Hussain, M.A., Rotstein, O.D., de Mestral, C., Mamdani, M., & Al-Omran, M. 2024a. "Comprehensive Review of Virtual Assistants in Vascular Surgery." *Seminars in Vascular Surgery*, 37(3), 342–349, https://doi.org/10.1053/j.semvascsurg.2024.07.001.

Li, B., Zhang, L., & Wang, Q. 2024b. "Comprehensive Review of Virtual Assistants in Healthcare." *Healthcare AI Research Journal*, 8, 65–85.

Lund, B.D. & Wang, T. 2023. "Chatting About ChatGPT: How May AI and GPT Impact Academia and Libraries?" *Library Hi Tech News*, 40(3), 26–29, Available at: https://papers.ssrn.com/sol3/papers.cfm?abstract_id=4333415.

Palladino, N. (2021). The role of epistemic communities in the "constitutionalization" of internet governance: The example of the European Commission High-Level Expert Group on Artificial Intelligence. Telecommunications policy, 45(6), 102149.

Radford, A., Wu, J., Child, R., Luan, D., Amodei, D., & Sutskever, I. 2019. "Language Models are Unsupervised Multitask Learners." *OpenAI Blog*, 1(8), 9, Available at: Chrome-extension://efaidnbmnnnibpcajpcglclefindmkaj/https://cdn.openai.com/better-language-models/language_models_are_unsupervised_multitask_learners.pdf.

Ruiz Sarrias, O., Martínez del Prado, M.P., & González, L. 2024. "Leveraging Large Language Models for Precision Monitoring of Chemotherapy-Induced Toxicities: A Pilot Study with Expert Comparisons and Future Directions." *Cancers*, 16, 2830, Available at: https://www.mdpi.com/journal/cancers.

Zaki, M.Z. 2023. "Transforming Worlds: The Intersection of Translation Technology and Transformers." *Journal of Language and AI Technologies*, 4, 112–128, https://doi.org/10.5121/cseij.2024.14301.

4 The Artificial Intelligence Strategy of the European Court of Justice
Nature, Scope, and Consequences

Margarita Robles-Carrillo

4.1 INTRODUCTION

For some time now, artificial intelligence has been a growing topic of discussion in various forums and from several perspectives, including the administration of justice. In this area, AI can perform a wide spectrum of functions, from offering technical assistance or developing purely administrative tasks to supporting judges in the decision-making process (Re and Solow-Niederman, 2019, p. 242; Spyropoulos and Androulaki, 2023, pp. 1–8). In some cases, such as in China or India, the possibility of replacing human judgement with decisions made by a programme, a device, or robotic judge (Elsie, 2024, pp. 107–109). Without going that far, the goal of becoming a "smart court" is a declared and shared objective (Tahura and Selvadurai, 2022, pp. 3–21. In contrast to other areas, the crucial point here is that this concerns the administration of "justice" (Chronowski et al., 2021, p. 169; Tamosiuniene et al., 2024, p. 207), which is a fundamental principle and the ultimate safeguard for the respect of the law. The regulation and application of AI in the judicial sphere, therefore, raise issues that are absent, irrelevant, less serious or of lower importance in other sectors (Shevchuk et al., 2023, pp. 346–362; Garg and Chandra, 2021, p. 5).

In 2024, the Court of Justice of the European Union (CJEU) presented its *Artificial Intelligence Strategy* (Court of Justice of the European Union, 2024). According to the strategy, AI holds significant potential for the Court from a twofold perspective: it enables the automation of simple tasks in judicial and administrative areas, and it offers new possibilities in legal research, translation, and interpretation.

The analysis of the CJEU Strategy is necessary, useful, and relevant for two main reasons: (a) The potential range of functions that might be assigned to AI, according to the description of its potential; and (b) The unique nature and authority of the CJEU, which will necessarily impact the judicial practice in Member States. The debate on AI and justice is currently effervescent. The CJEU's position on the issue matters and it matters significantly.

DOI: 10.1201/9781003541899-4

Moreover, the CJEU Strategy's presentation raised expectations that might be developments in the judicial field within the general context of the European digitalization process. The 2019–2023 European e-Justice Action Plan paid specific attention to AI in some respects. Interlinking legal data, promoting semantic interoperability, and developing AI tools for the analysis of court decisions are specific areas of interest, although the primary proposed action is to define the role of AI in the field of justice (Ontanu, 2023, pp. 93–110). However, the European e-Justice Strategy 2024–2028, approved by the Council in November 2023 with the aim of guiding the ongoing digital transformation in the justice domain across the EU, makes little reference to AI (Council of the European UnionCouncil, 2023, p. 1). The then ongoing negotiations on the European regulation on AI might have advised prudence in this respect.

In the meantime, within the Council of Europe, the European Commission for the Efficiency of Justice (CEPEJ) has been actively working on the use of AI in the field of justice (Kharitonashvili, 2023, pp. 1–2; Spyropoulos & Androulaki, 2023, p. 1). In December 2018, it adopted the European Ethical Charter on the Use of Artificial Intelligence in Judicial Systems and Their Environment (European Commission for the Efficiency of Justice of the Council of Europe, 2018). In 2020, CEPEJ published a feasibility study focused on the possible introduction of mechanisms for certifying AI tools and services in the sphere of justice (European Commission for the Efficiency of Justice of the Council of Europe, 2020).

In 2020, the European Commission published a report entitled "Study on the use of innovative technologies in the justice field." The assessment of ongoing projects in terms of categories of problems and solutions, the results of consultations between Member States and institutions, and the review of existing literature led to a comprehensive and rigorous analysis of the situation (European Commission, 2020). In October 2020, the Council of the EU also published the Presidency Conclusions on the Charter of Fundamental Rights in the Context of Artificial Intelligence and Digital Change. According to them, "Access to justice, transparency and explicability of judicial processes and decision-making, an independent judiciary and legal certainty are essential to the proper functioning of the justice system in accordance with the rule of law." It defends a "fundamental rights-based approach to AI" (Council of the European UnionCouncil, 2020, pp. 11 and 7). The European approach is quite different from that of the United States and China (Chun et al., 2024).

After this introduction, the context in which the strategy emerges can be better appreciated. The European approach to AI is relevant for framing the Court's strategy. Building on this strategy, this chapter analyses the general framework, objectives and principles, issues and challenges, and the governance model designed in the CJEU Strategy.

4.2   THE EUROPEAN APPROACH TO AI

The EU's progressive approach to AI has been paradigmatic. Firstly, the debate focused on ethical values and principles in various forums with meaningful results (Nikolinakos, 2023), particularly the Ethics Guidelines for Trustworthy adopted by the High-Level Expert Group on Artificial Intelligence (Smuha, 2019). Secondly, the regulatory process was developed to address the most relevant AI-related issues, resulting in the adoption of a regulation. Finally, the need for an overarching legal framework became evident and is now under discussion.

In 2024, Regulation (EU) 2024/1689, known as the Artificial Intelligence Act, has entered into force (Regulation 2024, p. 1), while the Council of Europe Framework Convention on Artificial Intelligence and Human Rights, Democracy, and the Rule of Law was opened for signature (Council of Europe, 2024). Although they differ in scope and reflect the specificities of their respective organizations, both legal instruments are a human-centric foundation and common principles and values. According to Regulation (EU) 2024/1689, "certain AI systems intended for the administration of justice and democratic processes should be classified as high-risk, considering their potentially significant impact on democracy, the rule of law, individual freedoms as well as the right to an effective remedy and to a fair trial." Following this norm, it is appropriate to qualify the following as high-risk systems: (a) AI systems intended to be used by a judicial authority or on its behalf to assist in researching and interpreting facts and the law, and in applying the law to a concrete set of facts; (b) systems used to address the risks of potential biases, errors, and opacity; and (c) AI systems intended to be used by alternative dispute resolution bodies when the outcomes of such proceedings produce legal effects for the parties involved (Gstrein et al., 2024). Annex III lists the high-risk AI systems referred to in Article 6.2, including, in the field of administration of justice, "AI systems intended to be used by a judicial authority or on their behalf to assist a judicial authority in researching and interpreting facts and the law and in applying the law to a concrete set of facts, or to be used in a similar way in alternative dispute resolution" (Regulation, 2024, p. 128). In contrast, AI systems intended for administrative activities that do not affect the administration of justice in individual cases, such as anonymization or pseudonymization of judicial decisions, documents or data, communication between personnel, and administrative tasks, are not considered high-risk systems. Regulation (EU) 2024/1689 is clear: while the use of AI tools can support the decision-making power of judges or judicial independence, it should not replace it. Final decisions must remain a human-driven activity.

The EU has been among the first signatories of the Council of Europe Framework Convention on Artificial Intelligence and Human Rights, Democracy, and the Rule of Law, which recognizes that AI "may offer unprecedented opportunities to protect and promote human rights, democracy and the rule of law." However, it may also "undermine human dignity and individual autonomy, human rights, democracy and the rule of law." According to Article 3, the Convention covers activities "within the lifecycle of artificial intelligence systems that have the potential to interfere with human rights, democracy and the rule of law." The administration of justice is a main concern. In fact, Article 5 establishes that each Party shall adopt or maintain measures to ensure that artificial intelligence systems are not used to undermine respect for judicial independence and access to justice.

The Strategy of the CJEU has been adopted within a context in which the regulation and management of AI has become a priority at both the European and international levels. This background provides the basis for analysing the strategy from a broader and more comprehensive perspective, starting with an explanation of its general framework.

4.3 GENERAL OVERVIEW

In accordance with the terms of the strategy, the CJEU began exploring the possibilities of AI around 2019, when the Innovation Lab was established with the aim of investigating emerging technologies and how they must be addressed by the Court. In 2020, the AI+ Network was constituted, bringing together representative users from different departments, offices, and chambers of the Court.

The basic guidelines supporting this process include promoting collective intelligence, fostering multidisciplinary initiatives, and sharing experiences with other EU institutions. The concept of a "smart court" is explicitly invoked as a model of e-justice aimed at improving efficiency, transparency, and accessibility. This idea constitutes the objective of the CJEU and represents the path it has begun to follow through digitization and introduction of emerging technologies. In this regard, following its strategy, the CJEU may explore the use of AI "to analyze large amounts of legal data, provide insights into cases, improve the efficiency of legal research, or automate administrative activities" (Court of Justice of the European Union, 2024, p. 9). However, an analysis of this strategy reveals some of its shortcomings and limitations in structural, conceptual, and functional aspects.

From a *structural* perspective, the strategy does not facilitate comprehension of its content. On the one hand, Sections 4 and 5, on "risks" and "readiness," respectively, should preferably be linked, as both identify the issues posed by this technology from different perspectives. On the other hand, Sections 6–8 might be better understood as forming the governance model, articulated in different sub-sections dedicated to each aspect or component. As they are, these sections do not clearly express the effective connection and interaction between them. Finally, although Section 4 is focused on risks, some of them are detailed in the introduction but not reproduced in this specific section. The result is neither systematic nor coherent.

From a *conceptual* point of view, the CJEU's strategy raises several problems. Firstly, it recognizes that there are many definitions of AI (Emmert-Streib et al., 2020, pp. 2–3) but fails to clearly point out that there is no normative definition (Malhotra, 2017, p. 2), which is a major problem for its proper legal understanding and comprehension. Secondly, it refers to European Regulation 2024/1689 for the definition of AI when, in fact, this norm defines an "AI system," not "AI" as the CJEU's strategy seems to imply (Court of Justice of the European Union, 2024, p. 6). Thirdly, the strategy classifies AI into two types: narrow and general. Neither the definitions of these types are correct, nor is this typology the only or the most relevant one in this matter. The reference to other subfields or specialized branches—computer vision and robotics—only aggravates the problem, as those are techniques, instruments, achievements, or results, but not types of AI in a precise sense.

From a *functional* approach, the explanation of the technical performance of AI is neither clear nor minimally accurate. The comparison with classical programming does not help in improving understanding. The description fails to capture the process's basic technical nature relevant for a minimal understanding of its methodology (Emmert-Streib et al., 2020, pp. 4–5). However, the benefits of this technology are clearly identified: improving the efficiency of the Court; reducing its workload; making better use of its resources; and "lead to a more transparent, effective and efficient judicial system, benefiting both the Court and the people it serves" (Court of Justice of the European Union, 2024, p. 10).

In its conclusions, the CJEU Strategy considers that the experience acquired can enable and support the transition from the "exploration phase" to the "industrialization phase." According to the strategy, "the foundations are already in place and we have several strengths." These include an innovative organization with talented people, the catalyst function of the Innovation Lab, and the modernization of the IT landscape (Court of Justice of the European Union, 2024, p. 23). These statements imply a tone of overconfidence or optimism. In addition, when determining the steps to be taken, the strategy once again fails by offering a list of measures that lack substance, systematics, or hierarchy. This problem permeates much of the strategy and becomes evident in the definition of its objectives and principles.

4.3.1 Axiological and Teleological Background

Principles and objectives, which are a core ingredient of any European action in the digital field, do not hold this value and status in the CJEU Strategy. There is a significant imbalance between the attention given to the objectives and the much lesser emphasis placed on the principles, which are even listed later rather than earlier, as is usually the case for their nature and relevance. The principles receive scarce and inconsistent attention.

4.3.1.1 Objectives and Goals

The overall purpose of the CJEU Strategy is to harness the capabilities of responsible, equitable, traceable, reliable, and governable AI to become a smart court. The strategy focuses on three main objectives: (a) improve the efficiency and effectiveness of the administrative and judicial processes, (b) enhance the quality and consistency of judicial decisions, and (c) increase access to justice and transparency for EU citizens.

The objective of *achieving efficiency and effectiveness* entails different measures, although it does not clearly and sufficiently distinguish between the CJEU's administrative and judicial activities, as required by their different scope and nature. It envisages identifying and integrating AI solutions with several proposals that do not account for the differentiated treatment needed by each of these activities. The same applies to the following specific goals: enabling data-driven transformation, optimizing work processes, and leveraging AI benefits; creating a transformative ecosystem; and adopting a governable AI.

The goal of enhancing the quality and consistency of judicial decisions involves exploiting automation and standardization, as well as improving legal research. The main emphasis is placed on the automation of processes such as searches, translations, document correlation, legal research, and checking the consistency and quality of documents. There is only a brief reference to the need to develop the principle of explicability, despite it being a basic issue in the digital legal world.

The objective of *increasing access to justice and transparency* for European citizens includes some relevant measures for people with disabilities. Otherwise, it merely refers to tools such as chatbots, avatars, virtual assistants, or augmented reality for informational purposes. A concrete goal is collaboration with national courts, institutions, and academia, particularly for digital databases and interoperable AI solutions. The specific measures included in this section are generic and basic, and, in any case, do neither provide nor suggest the required specific discourse for judicial activities.

4.3.1.2 Principles

The principles of the CJEU Strategy have received less attention than the goals. This section of the document deserves two main critiques. On one hand, legal and ethical principles are mixed even though distinguishing them seems elemental and logical in a strategy issued by a judicial entity. On the other hand, the analysis of the strategy's statement of principles reveals three problems: (a) it does not prioritize or hierarchize them (for instance, privacy cannot be treated the same way as continuous improvement); (b) it does not distinguish between pre-existing and newly created principles or rights, which require different treatment; and (c) it ignores basic principles such as dignity and equality, or even the explicability of decisions with legal effects. This is a genuine issue. Legal principles concerning the use of AI are complex and specifically relevant in the judicial field (Tahura & Selvadurai, 2022, pp. 9–10), particularly in human rights (Corhaneanu, 2022, p. 91) and the rule of law (Greenstein, 2023, p. 287).

By contrast, the European Ethical Charter on the Use of Artificial Intelligence in Judicial Systems and Their Environment, adopted in 2018 by the European Commission for the Efficiency of Justice of the Council of Europe, clearly and precisely identifies the core principles to be respected in the processing of judicial decisions and data by algorithms: respect for fundamental rights; non-discrimination; quality and security; transparency, impartiality, and fairness; and the principle "under user control" (European Commission for the Efficiency of Justice of the Council of Europe, 2018, pp. 7–12). Although not all of them, such as the last one, are legal principles, there is a clear priority and order in the selection of these principles that is absent in the CJEU's strategy.

4.3.1.3 Issues and Challenges

The CJEU Strategy includes a specific section 4 entitled "Risks and possible mitigation strategies." However, risks and solutions are not identified and explained clearly and consistently. On the one hand, references to the risks can be found both in the introduction and in section 4 without a clear correlation between them. On the other hand, the introduction makes a distinction between two types of risks—the risk of using AI ourselves and the risk of AI being used by others—although this distinction is not exported to the rest of the strategy or specifically in section 4. Not all the risks enumerated in the introduction are considered in section 4, nor do they follow the same typology. Despite their relevance, for instance, "False or inaccurate (or irrelevant) information" and "Disinformation, censorship and control" are risks that appear only in the introduction.

4.3.1.4 General Risks

Section 4 of the Strategy focuses on the risks and mitigation measures, which are presented in a table that tries to systematize and describe each of them. Nevertheless, this exposition of risks and measures is neither systematic, comprehensive, nor coherent, and it does not address the issues or their solutions for many reasons.

Firstly, the reference to ethical concerns together with and even before mentioning the disclosure of sensitive data—which is a violation of law—makes it clear once again that the CJEU Strategy has not been able to distinguish between law and ethics (Rességuier & Rodrigues, 2020, p. 1). The description of this issue is particularly troubling. According to the strategy, the use of AI "in the judicial system could raise ethical concerns about the role of machines in the decision-making process and its impact on people's lives" (Court of Justice of the European Union, 2024, p. 17). Although there are obviously ethical concerns, as Hagendorff points out, sometimes "ethics can also simply serve the purpose of calming critical voices from the public, while simultaneously the criticized practices are maintained within the organization" (Hagendorff, 2020, p. 2). European values and principles, with their ethical dimension, are part of the EU normative framework and are applied as such. In the judicial sphere, there are many relevant and serious legal problems that a high court must be able to identify and properly address, as the solution to these legal problems is its primary function.

Secondly, concerning the identification of risks, the CJEU Strategy mixes vulnerability to cyber-attacks with explainability or resources, among others, offering a potentially confusing picture in which risks are neither properly defined nor prioritized or systematized. Not all risks are the same, and not all concepts identified as risks are actual risks. Resilience is not one. The strategy does not identify the risks clearly and precisely: the risk is not resilience or explainability, but the lack thereof. Bias is different from discrimination (Montañez et al., 2019, p. 1). Although they are related phenomena, they require different treatment because the latter is a clear infringement of a fundamental right (Corhaneanu, 2022, p. 98). Any discrimination can "undermine the credibility and fairness of the legal system" (Court of Justice of the European Union, 2024, p. 17), but it is also a breach of a fundamental right.

Thirdly, the so-called "Relevance" risk overlaps in some way with the "Bias and Discrimination" risk (European Union Agency for Fundamental Rights, 2019). They both appeal to the need for data quality and offer similar solutions. A single risk category concerning the lack of data quality might have been more coherent and comprehensive. A similar overlap happens with "Over-relying on technology" and "Hyper abuse." Although they are different phenomena, they are clearly interconnected: the former usually leads to the latter, and the latter is frequently a consequence of the former. The mitigation measures set out in each case could certainly be interchangeable and cumulative.

Fourthly, in cases of discrimination or personal data breaches, for instance, the risk mitigation strategies cannot simply consist of awareness-raising, training, testing, or red-lining. These options may be valid in other contexts but not in the working environment of a judicial entity. Establishing "red lines" at the strategic level is the mitigation measure proposed in the CJEU Strategy for both "Ethical concerns" and "Disclosure of sensitive data – Data security and data privacy," which is a clear violation of the law. While such an option may be comprehensible in other contexts, it is not understandable in the judicial domain and even less coming from a court with the status and competences of the CJEU.

Finally, some of the mitigation measures proposed in response to the risks are difficult to sustain in practical or realistic terms, or are simply not highly effective by their nature. This is the case with measures such as "Ensure end-users are aware" or "Create and communicate the appropriate policies to the end users."

There seems to be a lack of clear conviction and willingness to adopt the necessary legal measures for prevention, protection, and sanction. To begin with, the ethical aspect must be clearly differentiated from the legal aspect. Furthermore, it is necessary to identify and distinguish potential risks to fundamental rights from other types of infringements. Finally, risks must be clearly and precisely defined in terms of their scope and consequences, with solutions adapted to the nature of the threats. As Suresh and Guttag indicate, "risk assessment tools in the criminal justice system predict a risk score, but a judge may interpret this in unexpected ways before making his or her final decision" (Suresh and Guttag, 2019, p. 4). Risk assessment tools in the justice domain, can and should, function differently (Berk et al., 2021, p. 10).

4.3.1.5 Specific Risks

Readiness for adopting and using AI tools has been recognized as one of the main challenges posed by this technology. The CJEU Strategy has identified different, although connected, aspects of this problem. On the one hand, technology readiness is a basic need that requires investment in infrastructure and staff. According to the strategy, there is a need to balance the adoption of solutions for judicial activity "with the use of cloud solutions for public information" (Court of Justice of the European Union, 2024, p. 18). The distinction between judicial activity and other activities is to be welcomed; however, the reference to the use of the cloud in this context for public information is not entirely clear or appropriate. On the other hand, human resources readiness is vital to leverage the benefits of AI. To this end, the strategy identifies the measures that must be taken to train IT technicians, managers, and staff in the different departments for the adoption and correct usage of AI tools. Finally, cooperation and/or pooling resources with academia and interinstitutional partners is also an important requirement, considering the singularity of this technology and its level of development. The Interinstitutional Committee for Digital Transformation (ICDT), created in 2021, has been working on different studies concerning the readiness of European institutions and agencies for emerging technologies, to propose measures to upskill existing resources with a focus on AI.

Paradoxically and contradictorily, however, the conclusion reached by the CJEU's strategy on this point is that, although there is a high level of interest in this issue at the institutional level, the institutions have other priorities and cannot allocate resources to joint projects (Court of Justice of the European Union, 2024, p. 20), which is precisely the opposite of what is really required.

4.4 GOVERNANCE MODEL

Section 6 of the CJEU Strategy focuses on the governance model, which is further developed in Sections 7 and 8. This model, designed to support the detection, adoption, and use of AI tools, has different components: one is new, while the others are pre-existing ones that have been assigned new functions.

Firstly, the newly established AI Management Board has the mission "to ensure that the acquisition or the creation of any AI tool respects the principles stated in this chapter (Chapter 3), and especially ethics and fundamental rights." To that end, this board will have to issue an ethics and fundamental rights charter, which will serve as the basis for assessment. Once again, the absence of a clear distinction between ethical values and legal norms is inexplicable and unjustifiable, even more so when it comes from a judicial entity whose primary mission is to guarantee respect for the law, which must not be confused with ethical values.

Secondly, the AI+ Network created in February 2020 will be used to identify the areas in which AI tools will benefit current activities, as well as the prototypes and pilots designed to test the envisaged capabilities and advantages.

Thirdly, the current Informatics Steering Committee will be integrated into this governance model. The Architecture Board, an existing technical body composed of specialists, will ensure that proposals align with the high-level capabilities map described in Chapter 8. The Data Governance Board will be responsible for ensuring the consistency and coherence of data across the institution, as well as the correctness and quality of the data used in machine-learning processes.

Finally, the Innovation Lab, created in 2019, is not formally integrated into the AI governance model. However, according to the strategy, it is "the glue" that ensures that different components of the model are fed with the right information in time and the mechanism works correctly (CJEU, 2024, p. 21). It is defined as a cross-cutting capability with the mission to foster innovation and serve as a platform for exchanging ideas and creating prototypes. According to the strategy, the Innovation Lab will serve as the forum in which ideas are discussed and tested by the AI+ Network. It may also issue guidelines and contribute to the assessment of AI tools.

The logic behind this governance model and the relationship between its various components is not clear enough. Nevertheless, Section 8, which concerns the architecture and AI capabilities map, contains some interesting contributions. On the one hand, it identifies a threefold need: to prevent the adoption of solutions in an uncontrolled manner or in ways that do not comply with the organization's rules; to avoid use by individual users without appropriate control, which could lead to security, data, or other regulatory breaches; and to avoid the overuse or abuse of AI tools. However, it refers to the high-level capability map for AI developed by the Information Technology Directorate in 2019 to include this technology into the IT landscape. According to the AI strategy, the Court will integrate into its architecture "AI capabilities that will be created or adopted only once and that will be reused each time a business need is expressed" (CJEU, 2024, p. 22). These capabilities have been clustered in five AI domains: Natural Language Processing (NLP), Advanced Data Analytics, Chatbot Technologies, Speech Technologies, and Computer Vision.

4.5 CONCLUSIONS

The CJEU Strategy does not appear to be in line with the European context and approach to this issue, nor can it be easily explained or understood in accordance with either. From the precedents in the field of e-justice and ethical guidelines to the remarkable normative developments introduced by Regulation (EU) 2024/1689 and the Council of Europe Framework Convention on Artificial Intelligence, European action on AI stands out from many perspectives, particularly for its human-centric basis and its high-level, consistent, and well-defined principles. As Dignum highlights, "both the EU AI Act and the Council of Europe Framework Convention provide strong foundations for regulating AI" (Dignum, 2024). The strategy neither reaches that level nor seems to be aligned with this axiological and normative development.

The Strategy of the CJEU does not seem to be one coming from a judicial body that has to face the challenge of the emergence of technologies such as AI. A close analysis reveals its lack of substance, inconsistency, and limitations. There is no conceptual approach that unites the ideas behind a clear and precise framework. From the basic notions to the definition of objectives, principles, risks, or the governance framework, there is an asystematic and descriptive approach that neglects the technical bases and confuses the ethical with the legal. Such a phenomenon, which became widespread a few years ago and persists in some cases, is neither conceivable nor admissible in a strategy emanating from a judicial body whose primary function is the application and interpretation of the law.

Many reasons justify the need to distinguish between ethics and law, especially in the judicial sphere. On the one hand, as Hagendorff explains, "the generality and superficiality of ethical guidelines in many cases not only prevents actors from bringing their own practice into line with them, but rather encourages the devolution of ethical responsibility to others" (Hagendorff, 2020, p. 14). On the other hand, Floridi has precisely identified the underlying problem of the recurrent use of ethics with the so-called five gerunds: ethics shopping; ethics bluewashing; ethics lobbying; ethics dumping; and ethics shirking (Floridi, 2019, p. 186). Finally, the importance of distinguishing between the two is highlighted by Rességuier and Rodrigues, who state that "while we recognize that the legalistic approach to ethics is not completely off the mark, we argue that it is the end of ethics, not its teeth, not the most precious and critical aspects that ethics has to offer" (Rességuier & Rodrigues, 2020, p. 1). Ethics is a critical reflection on society and reality, voluntary and subjective. Law is an instrument for the organization of social life, collective and obligatory. Mixing or confusing them will only lead to a loss of their value in an area where both are particularly necessary, such as AI (Robles-Carrillo, 2020, pp. 5–6). Actually, and despite its title, the European Ethical Charter on the Use of Artificial Intelligence in Judicial Systems and their environment, adopted in 2018 by CEPEJ, includes a much more comprehensive and precise analysis of the "legal" problems and solutions related to the use of AI in justice (European Commission for the Efficiency of Justice of the Council of Europe, 2018).

The publication of the CJEU Strategy has been a lost opportunity from a threefold perspective: firstly, to open a substantive debate on the use of AI in the judicial sphere; secondly, to highlight the need to distinguish judicial activities from other matters in this respect; and thirdly, to advance towards the definition of a framework model by establishing essential principles such as the need for a basic technical understanding, the clear distinction between the ethical and the legal aspects of AI, and the transfer of the EU's digital model of principles and values to the judicial sphere.

ACKNOWLEDGEMENTS

This chapter has been published under the research project PID2020-114495RB-I00 funded by MCIN/AEI/10.13039/501100011033.

REFERENCES

Berk, R., Heidari, H., Jabbari, S., Kearns, M., & Roth, A. (2021). Fairness in criminal justice risk assessments: The state of the art. *Sociological Methods & Research*, 50(1), 3–44. https://doi.org/10.1177/0049124118782533

Chronowski, N., Kalman, K., & Szentgali-Toth, B. (2021). Artificial intelligence, justice, and certain aspects of right to fair trial. *Acta Universitatis Sapientiae, Legal Studies*, 10(2), 169–189.

Chun, J., Schroeder de Witt, S., & Elkins, K. (2024). Comparative Global AI Regulation: Policy Perspectives from the EU, China, and the US. Available at: https://arxiv.org/abs/2410.21279

Corhaneanu, B.-L. (2022). Artificial intelligence in the judicial system a threat to human rights? *Law Review*, 12(Special 2022), 91–101.

Council of Europe. (2024). Council of Europe Framework Convention on Artificial Intelligence and Human Rights, Democracy, and the Rule of Law, CETS No. 225. Available at: https://www.coe.int/en/web/conventions/full-list?module=treaty-detail&treatynum=225.

Council of the European Union. (2020). Conclusions on The Charter of Fundamental Rights in the context of Artificial Intelligence and Digital Change. Available at: https://www.consilium.europa.eu/media/46496/st11481-en20.pdf

Council of the European Union. (2023). European e-Justice Strategy 2024–2028. Available at: https://data.consilium.europa.eu/doc/document/ST-15509-2023-INIT/en/pdf.

Court of Justice of the European Union. (2024). Artificial Intelligence Strategy. Available at: https://curia.europa.eu/jcms/upload/docs/application/pdf/2023-11/cjeu_ai_strategy.pdf.

Dignum, V. (2024). How Europe is Shaping AI for Human rights. AI Policy Lab. Available at: https://aipolicylab.se/2024/09/05/how-europe-is-shaping-ai-for-human-rights/.

Elsie, I.C. (2024). Judges, technology, and artificial intelligence: The artificial judge. *Law, Technology and Humans*, 6(2), 107–109.

Emmert-Streib, F., Yli-Harja, O., & Dehmer, M. (2020). A clarification of misconceptions, myths, and desired status of artificial intelligence. *Machine Learning and Artificial Intelligence*, 3, 524339. https://doi.org/10.3389/frai.2020.524339

European Commission. (2020). Study on the Use of Innovative Technologies in the Justice Field. Available at: https://op.europa.eu/en/publication-detail/-/publication/4fb8e194-f634-11ea-991b-01aa75ed71a1

European Commission for the Efficiency of Justice of the Council of Europe. (2018). Ethical Charter on the Use of Artificial Intelligence in Judicial Systems and their environment. Available at: https://rm.coe.int/ethical-charter-en-for-publication-4-december-2018/16808f699c

European Commission for the Efficiency of Justice of the Council of Europe. (2020). Introduction of a Mechanism for Certifying Artificial Intelligence Tools and Services in the Sphere of Justice and the Judiciary: Feasibility Study. Available at: https://rm.coe.int/feasability-study-en-cepej-2020-15/1680a0adf4

European Union Agency for Fundamental Rights. (2019). Data Quality and Artificial Intelligence—Mitigating Bias and Error to Protect Fundamental Rights. Available at: https://fra.europa.eu/en/publication/2019/data-quality-and-artificial-intelligence-mitigating-bias-and-error-protect

Floridi, L. (2019). Translating principles into practices of digital ethics: Five risks of being unethical. *Philosophy & Technology*, 32, 185–193. https://doi.org/10.1007/s13347-019-00354-x

Garg, A. & Chandra, P. (2021). Judiciary in technological paradigm: An overview. *Indian Journal of Law and Legal Research*, 3(2), 1–7.

Greenstein, S. (2023). Artificial intelligence destroyed the rule of law? *Scandinavian Studies in Law*, 69, 287–312.

Gstrein, O.J., Haleem, N., & Zwitter, A. (2024). General-purpose AI regulation and the European Union AI act. *Internet Policy Review*, 13(3), 1–26. https://doi.org/10.14763/2024.3.1790

Hagendorff, T. (2020). The ethics of AI ethics: An evaluation of guidelines. *Minds and Machines*, 30, 99–120. https://doi.org/10.1007/s11023-020-09517-8

Kharitonashvili, N. (2023). Expediency and scope of using AI in civil justice. *European Journal of Economics, Law and Politics (ELP)*, 10(1), 1–7.

Malhotra, H. (2017). Artificial intelligence: (Semi-intelligent) overview. *International In-House Counsel Journal*, 11(41), 1–9.

Montañez, G.D., Hayase, J., Lauw, J., Macias, D., Trikha, A., & Vendemiatti, J. (2019). *The Futility of Bias-Free Learning and Search*. Springer, Cham. https://doi.org/10.48550/arXiv.1907.06010

Nikolinakos, N.T. (2023). Ethical principles for trustworthy AI. In: *EU Policy and Legal Framework for Artificial Intelligence, Robotics and Related Technologies - The AI Act. Law, Governance and Technology Series*, vol 53. Springer, Cham.

Ontanu, E.A. (2023). The digitalisation of European Union procedures: New impetus following time of prolonged crisis. *Law, Technology and Humans*, 5(1), 93–110.

Re, R.M. & Solow-Niederman, A. (2019). Developing artificially intelligent justice. *Stanford Technology Law Review*, 22(2), 242–289.

Regulation (EU) 2024/1689 of the European Parliament and of the Council of 13 June 2024 laying down harmonized rules on artificial intelligence and amending Regulations (EC) No 300/2008, (EU) No 167/2013, (EU) No 168/2013, (EU) 2018/858, (EU) 2018/1139 and (EU) 2019/2144 and Directives 2014/90/EU, (EU) 2016/797 and (EU) 2020/1828 (Artificial Intelligence Act). OJ L, 12.7.2024, 1. Available at: https://eur-lex.europa.eu/legal-content/EN/TXT/PDF/?uri=OJ:L_202401689&qid=1726487371698

Rességuier, A. & Rodrigues, R. (2020). AI ethics should not remain toothless! A call to bring back the teeth of ethics. *Data & Society*, 7(2), 1–5. https://doi.org/10.1177/2053951720942541

Robles-Carrillo, M. (2020). Artificial intelligence: From ethics to law. *Telecommunications Policy*, 44(6), 1–16. https://doi.org/10.1016/j.telpol.2020.101937

Shevchuk, O., Martynovskyi, V., Volianska, O., Kompaniiets, I., & Bululukov, O. (2023). Problems of legal regulation of artificial intelligence in administrative judicial procedure. *Juridical Tribune*, 13(3), 346–362.

Smuha, N. (2019). The EU approach to ethics guidelines for trustworthy artificial intelligence. *Computer Law Review International*, 20(4), 97–106. https://doi.org/10.9785/cri-2019-200402

Spyropoulos, F. & Androulaki, E. (2023). Aspects of artificial intelligence on e-justice and personal data limitations. *Journal of Legal, Ethical and Regulatory Issues*, 26(3), 1–8.

Suresh, H. & Guttag, J. (2019). A framework for understanding unintended consequences of machine learning. In: *EAAMO '21: Proceedings of the 1st ACM Conference on Equity and Access in Algorithms, Mechanisms, and Optimization*, vol. 17, pp. 1–9. https://doi.org/10.1145/3465416.3483305

Tahura, U.S. & Selvadurai, N. (2022). The use of artificial intelligence in judicial decision-making: The example of China. *International Journal of Law, Ethics, and Technology*, 2022(3), 1–20. https://doi.org/10.55574/PYEB5374

Tamosiuniene, E., Terebeiza, Z., & Dorzinkevic, A. (2024). The possibility of applying artificial intelligence in the delivery of justice by courts. *Baltic Journal of Law and Politics*, 17(1), 207–222.

5 Transparency and Accountability in AI Systems

A Realistic Approach in Albania

Eralda Methasani Çani, Miralda Çuka,
and Andrea Mazelliu

5.1 OVERVIEW OF ARTIFICIAL INTELLIGENCE AND ITS IMPACT

One of the most significant developments that will determine the future of humanity is the digital transformation of everyday life, including the digitalization of public and private services. Internet access, technology, digital skills, and digital services are increasingly becoming prerequisites for daily life and access to public services. The digital world of the 21st century, including "artificial intelligence" (AI) is a tangible reality, alongside its challenges. The term "artificial intelligence" does not have a universally accepted definition but generally refers to a wide range of systems that use algorithms to enable computers to perform tasks that normally require human cognition, such as perception, reasoning, learning, problem-solving, and natural language understanding.

AI systems can range from rule-based systems to more complex learning models, such as Machine Learning (ML) and Deep Learning (DL), where systems improve and adapt based on the data they are fed (Sarker, 2021). ML is a subset of AI that allows computers to learn from data and make decisions or predictions without being explicitly programmed to do so. Its algorithms are designed to learn from examples, identify patterns, cluster objects with similar attributes, and improve over time through experience. While ML can be used on structured data for predictive analysis, DL performs complex data analysis on vast amounts of data. Despite the advantages of using DL for complex tasks, the large volume of data these systems rely on can perpetuate bias if the training data contains biased patterns.

The advantages of the digitalization of services, aimed at easier and more efficient access, include increased efficiency in public administration performance, reduced costs, and a lower margin of human error. More optimized and harmonized administrative processes help avoid unnecessary bureaucracy, promote sustainability and environmental protection, and reduce corruption. However, the protection

DOI: 10.1201/9781003541899-5

and effective exercise of fundamental human rights and freedoms may be at risk due to such systems. Under the non-delegation principle in the legal context, public administrations are restricted, meaning they cannot fully delegate decision-making duties to automated systems. These principles guarantee that human monitoring and control are applied to decision-making (Langer, 2024).

The United Nations, Council of Europe, OECD, and European Union have addressed the use of digital as well as AI systems in both the public and private spheres by setting minimum protection standards to humankind. The Council of Europe's body of rules on AI began to be developed in 2019, and the use of AI systems received swift attention considering the dilemma whether it is a friend or foe to human rights and freedoms. In 2024, the EU adopted the AI Act to prioritize human decision-making. The Act, considered a unique regulation, provides the following definition of an AI system: "... a machine-based system that is designed to operate with varying levels of autonomy and that may exhibit adaptiveness after deployment, and that, for explicit or implicit objectives, infers, from the input it receives, how to generate outputs such as predictions, content, recommendations, or decisions that can influence physical or virtual environments" (Regulation (EU) 2024/1689, 2024). Values and ethics to be embedded in AI systems are at the core of international norms. The OECD highlighted the need to perform AIAs as necessary to evaluate potential risks and safeguard the accountability of AI systems when and if public administrations experiment with them (OECD.AI, n.d.). These guidelines focus on transparency and accountability by emphasizing that the designation of AI usage should be understandable and trackable. OECD.AI (n.d.) provides principles to guide the responsible use of AI that shall serve as a foundational framework for governments to implement a robust system for the AI that aligns with human values and establishes responsibility in its usage. Albania is not yet a state that has adhered to the AI principles established by the OECD.

The digitization of services and the inclusion of AI is already a reality in Albania. The country has undertaken policies related to digitization across all fields. While the Albanian Constitution obliges public bodies to ensure the respect and implementation of human rights and freedoms in all activities and sectors of life, thereby setting boundaries to digitization. Over the last 10 years, access to public services in Albania has been radically transformed, from a system of direct physical interaction between the state and citizen or business to a diversified approach that links elements of direct and digital interaction through a unique government platform. As of 2020, the government has implemented a fully digitized approach to public services through the "e-Albania" platform (Order of the Prime Minister of the Republic of Albania No. 158, 2019). The digitization of public services is highly praised, even though it is associated with problems, especially for vulnerable groups.

5.2 THE NEED FOR TRANSPARENCY, EXPLAINABILITY, AND ACCOUNTABILITY IN ARTIFICIAL INTELLIGENCE SYSTEMS

AI has become an important part of our lives across various sectors with the purpose of automating processes and enhancing efficiency. However, as AI systems have become more advanced and autonomous, their positive impact on improving efficiency, driving innovation, automating processes, and solving complex problems can be overshadowed by issues stemming from a lack of AI literacy. The latter implies a deeper understanding and awareness of how personal data is used, how models are trained, how specific outcomes are generated by these systems, and an understanding of the risks of bias and the need to critically assess the output. The success of ML and DL learning methods in different domains, including biology, medicine, law, economics, and education, is accompanied by the complexity of understanding how these models work, why they make certain decisions, which features most affect the model's output, and the degree of certainty the model has in the outcome it generates such success (Salih et al., 2024).

Balasubramaniam et al. (2023) discuss how to develop responsible AI systems and address the ethical issues associated with AI. Various interest groups around the world have defined guidelines and principles to ensure responsible AI usage (pp. 331–346). To ensure this, transparency refers to the degree to which processes, decisions, and data within AI systems are understandable and open, how the inner workings of AI algorithms, decision-making processes, and data usage, are clear to various stakeholders, including developers, users, policymakers, and the public. Another term used interchangeably with transparency in AI usage, is explainability. Most users of AI systems are not aware of how specific outputs are generated. The lack of interpretability in AI models means that users have to accept the outcome of a decision-making system without being aware of the intricacies that led to that decision. However, there are several models that operate differently from each other based on the mathematical models they rely on and the quality of data they are fed. In such cases, the outcome might differ across models. Due to this, explainable AI (XAI) is an emerging field that focuses on developing techniques to make AI models more interpretable (Ali et al., 2023).

The ML and DL models often function as "black boxes," where the internal workings are unknown to most users. The black-box nature of these systems raises several ethical concerns. XAI aims to demystify "black-box" models into a more comprehensible form to increase the model's transparency and build trust among end users in the model's outcomes. Such additional reassurances are essential for the widespread implementation of these models, particularly in high-risk fields. Nwakanma et al. (2023) compare SHAP (SHapley Additive exPlanations) and LIME (Local Interpretable Model-agnostic Explanations) in the context of explainable activity detection and classification. These two methods work by providing insights into the factors that influence individual predictions, making it easier to understand how specific outputs are derived.

Figure 5.1 provides a comparative analysis of three types of AI systems with varying levels of transparency, accuracy, and interpretability. The black-box model offers the highest level of accuracy but lacks transparency, meaning that the decision-making process cannot be understood or explained. For critical applications that handle extremely sensitive data, the use of black-box models may be problematic, as they might be prone to unethical and biased outputs. One example would be the case of using AI in recruitment tools; in the case of Amazon, it was discovered that the system had gender bias, as it consistently downgraded resumes from female applicants (O'Neil, 2016). The gray box, on the other hand, balances accuracy and

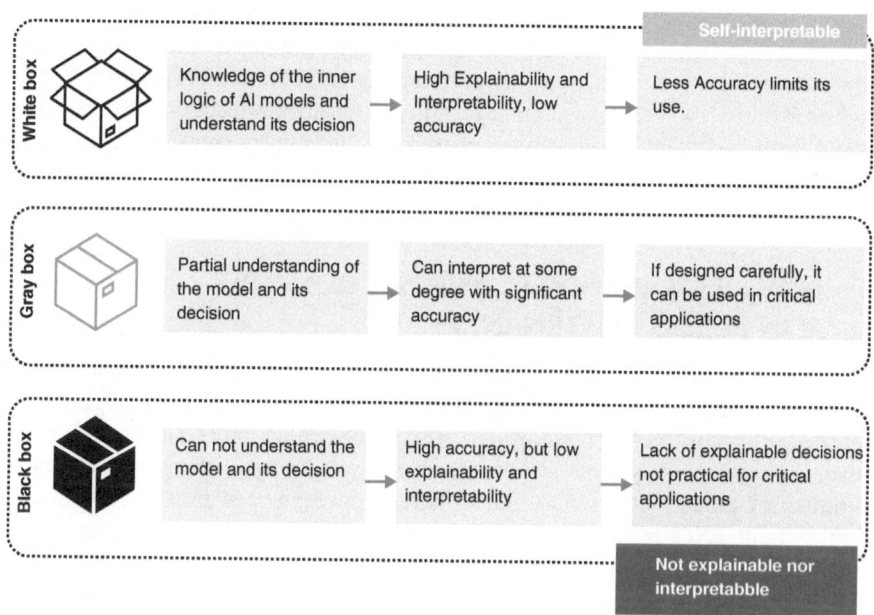

FIGURE 5.1 A comparison of white-box, gray-box, and black-box models for model transparency and interpretability.

interpretability by offering partial understanding of how decisions are made, making it more suitable for critical applications. On the other hand, the white-box model provides full insight into how it operates and makes decisions; however, due to low accuracy, it is not used in practical complex applications. Accuracy is desirable, but if it comes at the cost of reduced transparency, it should not be the choice for applications of a sensitive nature.

5.2.1 Understanding Bias in AI

The dangers of bias in AI systems cannot be overstated. As artificial intelligence becomes increasingly integrated into society, it is important to recognize the potential harm that biased AI can inflict (Buolamwini & Gebru, 2018). Bias in AI refers to the unfair or unjust treatment of certain groups based on race, gender, or other protected characteristics. This bias can manifest in many ways, such as discriminatory hiring practices, biased loan approvals, or even deadly decisions made by autonomous vehicles. Mensah (2023) offers a detailed review of strategies for bias mitigation by emphasizing that: "Transparency and accountability are vital when it comes to the ethical considerations of AI systems." In terms of accountability, a concern emerged in 2020, when the Dutch tax authority's AI-driven fraud detection system flagged thousands of low-income families as potential welfare fraudsters (Cath & Jansen, 2021). The system targeted families with dual citizenship or ethnic backgrounds. This led to wrongful accusations and unfair demands for repayment of childcare benefits. The incident highlighted not only flaws in AI's design, particularly bias in these algorithms, but also the need for accountability in public administration when using AI systems. This example highlights the importance of testing, transparent practices, and ethical standards in AI systems, especially in public administration, where errors can have a direct, harmful impact on citizens' lives. In the Albanian context, and given the challenges the country faces, considering AI regulatory frameworks are less established, the risks associated with unmonitored AI systems could be even more pronounced.

5.3   TOWARD TRANSPARENT AND ACCOUNTABLE AI IN PUBLIC GOVERNANCE

Governments must ensure that AI and automated systems remain transparent and accountable to the public at large. Engstrom and Ho (2020) analyze the Algorithmic Impact Assessment (AIA) as required to preside the evaluation of biases and ensure fairness in automated systems. To ensure these systems serve the public responsibly, universal guidelines for AI (UGAI) have been developed by scientific societies, think tanks, NGOs, and international organizations, which include elements of human rights, data protection, and ethical standards (AI Now Institute, 2021). The guidelines include several well-established principles for AI governance, and put forward new principles, echoing obligations of institutions and the rights of individuals. Elements of transparency, the right to a human determination, obligations of identification, fairness, assessment and accountability, accuracy, reliability and validity, data quality principle, public safety and cybersecurity obligations, the prohibition on secret profiling and on unitary scoring, as well as the termination obligation, are all considered universal AI standards, recognizing that human interest is at the core of such systems and that human control remains ultimate (CAIDP, n.d.).

In Europe, AI is used in public services, education, and welfare programs. For example, Denmark has experimented with using AI to manage the hiring of school staff, and Italy has used it to determine welfare eligibility (European Commission, n.d.). However, these systems have faced challenges, such as errors leading to unfair benefit cuts or unreasonable job assignments (Holm & Lorenz, 2022). Alon-Barkat and Busuioc (2023) analyze the challenges of automation bias and selective adherence to algorithmic advice in public sector decision-making such as in the case of implementing chatbots to assist with employment services in Austria, which have been criticized for reinforcing gender stereotypes.

In Albania, algorithmic automation is utilized in various sections of the government portal. This includes state data from the National Register of Civil Status, managed by the General Directorate of Civil Status; data from the Commercial Register, administered by the National Center of Business; data from Electronic Taxation, overseen by the General Directorate of Taxation; and other data that interacts with the e-Albania portal and is registered in the National Register of State Databases (CoM Decision No. 1147, 2020). Even though AI in governance is increasingly applied, there remains a gap in stakeholder engagement, which is important for refining Albania's legal framework in electronic governance. There is a notable lack of engagement from experts in the field and other interested parties, resulting in an absence of clear and constructive proposals aimed at enhancing the legal framework.

For example, during the consultation phase for the Law on Electronic Governance, only a few minor proposals were submitted by the involved stakeholders (Government of Albania, n.d.). Stakeholder participation is crucial for developing comprehensive and effective legislation that addresses the evolving challenges in electronic governance, data protection, and cybersecurity. Notwithstanding the limited interest by stakeholders, the electronic governance law outlines the principle of equal access to public services for all users and promotes the development of digital platforms for private and public entities. To ensure compliance with existing and sensitive legal frameworks, such as the EU General Data Protection Regulation (GDPR) regulatory framework (Regulation (EU) 2016/679, 2016), governments can test automation systems through the use of sandboxes (Jenkins, 2021).

5.3.1 INTERNATIONAL LEGAL AND POLITICAL INSTRUMENTS ON AI SYSTEMS: THE EU AND CoE FRAMEWORK

Kossow, Windwehr, and Jenkins (2021) analyze the importance of transparency in the use of algorithmic decision-making systems, identifying transparency as the most fundamental principle in all democratic systems, such as holding open meetings, establishing provisions for information, and ensuring the right to access documents (pp. 9–11). For instance, the Treaty of Lisbon of 2007 provides several articles that call for the application of transparency principles, requiring access to any information and communication related to processes or personal data, and ensuring ease of communication and accessible, clear language. This principle specifically pertains to providing information to data subjects regarding the controller's identity and the purposes underlying the processing. Additionally, it encompasses the dissemination of further information to guarantee equitable and transparent processing with respect to the natural persons involved, along with their entitlement to receive confirmation and communication concerning the personal data related to them that is undergoing processing (Treaty of Lisbon, 2027). In the context of algorithmic decision-making processes, GDPR Recital 39 (European Union, 2016) states that:

> "... any information and communication relating to the processing of... personal data be easily accessible and easy to understand, and that clear and plain language be used..." Also, it requires that "... information to the data subjects on the identity of the controller and the purposes of the processing and further information to ensure fair and transparent processing ..."

Williams et al. (2022) argue that transparency is considered a vital component of the EU's acquis to trace information (e7-5). The European Commission's Independent High-Level Expert Group on Artificial Intelligence (2019) characterizes traceability as a crucial facet of transparency, defining it as "...the capability to keep track of the system's data, development, and deployment processes, typically by means of documented recorded identification" (pp. 37–38). The EU Regulation laying down harmonized rules on Artificial Intelligence (AI) Act of 2024 sets standards to ensure that the lifecycle of AI systems is human-centered, sustainable, safe, secure, inclusive, and trustworthy, and that they guarantee respect for fundamental rights, democracy, the rule of law, and environmental sustainability (Regulation (EU) 2024/1689, 2024).

The AI Act is of key importance for Albania as well, due to the European integration process the country is pursuing.

The Council of Europe (CoE) body of rules on AI began to be developed in 2019. The topic has received swift attention from the CoE, mainly due to the dilemma of whether AI is a friend to foe or human rights and freedoms (CoE, 2020a, 2020b, 2020c, 2020d, 2020e, 2020f, 2020g, 2020h), drawing attention to the growing threat to the right of humans to form opinions and make decisions independently of automated systems. Principles of increased fairness, transparency, and accountability, in line with the responsibility to respect human rights and fundamental freedoms, are enshrined in CoE Resolution 2341/2020 and Recommendation 2181/2020. The latter requires that public governments implement a legal framework for the use of AI systems that ensures explainable, traceable, and understandable usage of such systems. The Council of Europe (2024) introduced a framework convention focusing on the interplay of AI with human rights, democracy, and the rule of law by requiring that AI systems be designed and operated transparently to facilitate accountability in governance structures. The 2024 CoE Framework Convention on Artificial Intelligence and Human Rights, Democracy, and the Rule of Law is considered the *first international legally binding treaty for the member states of the CoE* in the field of AI.

The Convention aims to ensure that activities within the lifecycle of AI systems are fully consistent with human rights, democracy, and the rule of law, while also being conducive to technological progress and innovation. It provides a set of general obligations and fundamental principles, including the protection of human dignity and individual autonomy, as well as the promotion of equality and non-discrimination, respect for privacy and personal data protection, along with transparency and oversight to ensure accountability and responsibility, as well as safe innovation and experimentation in controlled environments. The public sector that applies AI systems is required to respect the principles and obligations envisaged in the Convention, while the private sector may choose to apply the Convention's obligations or take other appropriate measures to comply with them. The Convention excludes from its scope national security, national defense, and research and development activities involving AI systems not yet made available for use, unless testing or similar activities have the potential to interfere with human rights, democracy, and the rule of law. This means that some areas still present risks to humankind and its rights and freedoms. Albania is a party to the CoE but has not yet advanced toward ratifying the Convention. No discussions have been made public to this end.

5.4   POLITICAL AND LEGAL INSTRUMENTS THAT REGULATE THE AI SYSTEMS IN ALBANIA

AI development in Albania is progressing but remains in its initial stages compared to other European countries. There is low government and private funding dedicated to AI initiatives, which hinders large-scale innovation and the widespread adoption of AI technologies. While the country has a growing pool of tech talent in the fields of data science and software engineering which are essential for AI development, there is still a shortage of experts specialized in AI, ML, or related fields, which can not only build these systems but also understand them and the implications of their use in sensitive sectors, such as public administration. An extremely critical part of AI adaptation and development is access to high-quality data. Albania faces challenges in data collection, management, and digital infrastructure, making it exceedingly difficult to implement wide-scale AI solutions. In a country that is still building its digital infrastructure, there is a lack of public and private datasets that can be used.

Despite the lack of large-scale implementation of AI systems, there are some concrete initiatives in Albania that rely on RPA (Robotic Process Automation) for the automation of administrative tasks. When combined with ML or natural language processing (NLP), these systems make process automation more intelligent by enabling decision-making processes based on historical data or real-time input. An example of such AI-powered tool is Bleta (Klei1, n.d.), which uses RPA to automate the transposition of the Acquis for European Integration. This tool streamlines governmental processes that involve substantial amounts of documentation and legal compliance, reducing the need for human intervention.

One of the major breakthroughs of AI systems is equipping them with the ability to understand and process input in human language. These NLP-based systems support both spoken and written data, which, when integrated into public portals, connect backend databases and services to pull or push citizen information (e.g., retrieving documents, verifying user identities, etc.). These systems rely on large amounts of textual data to train models that allow them to recognize patterns in language. The better the data, the better the system's ability to understand human language and generate human-like responses. One example of the use of this technology in the Albanian context is the e-Albania platform, which includes a chatbot system that leverages NLP to allow citizens to interact with various public services through a conversational interface (e-Albania, n.d.). With platforms such as these, which handle massive amounts of sensitive data, including personal identification information, financial transactions, and healthcare records, data privacy becomes a critical issue. If this data is not managed properly, there is a risk of data breaches or misuse of personal information. Albania, like many countries, will need to comply with GDPR or adopt similar frameworks to ensure data protection and privacy for its citizens.

The Government of Albania (2022) established the Digital Agenda for 2022–2026 to guide the country's approach to AI. Adopted by government decision, the agenda aims to boost investments in advanced computing, data processing, AI, cybersecurity, and essential digital skills. It seeks to integrate AI technologies to enhance service quality, positioning AI as a priority in the country's strategy for digital transformation while ensuring inclusivity. The Digital Agenda 2022–2026 declares that the ethical use of AI in public administration is fundamental. Nonetheless, the Strategy and Action Plan do not include any indicators or actions to vitalize the political goals and declared objectives. Its content and Action Plan lack specific measures to support these goals. The government acknowledges the ethical and legal challenges raised by AI, such as reliability and potential-based decision-making. It refers to respecting fundamental values and rights, but it only enumerates accountability and transparency, while several principles already elaborated in the international arena do not appear to be elevated to the needed level, considering that AI is highly controversial at the legislation level. The strategy recognizes that another strategy will follow on AI systems. Despite its ambiguity, the strategy is declarative and lacks detailed regulations for implementing AI services, particularly in threat detection and response. While it mentions fundamental values, it falls short of addressing established international principles. The strategy indicates that a subsequent plan will follow regarding AI systems.

Digital legislation preceded the use of technology in Albania, and important legislation has been promulgated for the usage of intelligent systems, as well as the offering of public services digitally (Law No. 13/2016; Law No. 33/2022; Law No. 9880, 2008; Law No. 107/2015). The Albanian Code of Administrative Procedures (2015) introduces electronic administrative decision-making, although it primarily focuses on human involvement in the decision-making process. Based on how the code has been promulgated, it appears that this code regulates the provision of public services primarily in an offline mode, requiring public bodies and administrative institutions to be actively interoperable with interested parties. However, it leaves a gap in future regulations regarding the provision of services through AI systems. Despite that, the principles of this code as enshrined in Chapter II, shall be applicable also in the digital world of providing services (Albanian Code of Administrative Procedures, 2015, Ch. II). The public organ is accountable even in cases when there is no physical communication between the interested subject for the services and the former. In this regard, the way the usage of AI systems will be implemented is left to the discretion of the lawmaker or the government, but the principles of the CAP and EU regulations shall be the basis of these systems. In cases when the principles or provisions provided by the CAP are ignored and not considered, the acts delivered by these systems are not based on rights and fundamental freedoms and can be grounds for future contestation based on illegality. Law No. 43/2023 on Electronic Governance is a crucial legal achievement in the strategy for digitalizing public administration services (Law No. 43/2023, 2023). Along with other legal frameworks for regulating electronic governance, it serves as the primary legal framework for ensuring an effective and secure electronic government, increasing citizen access to public services, and enhancing institutional transparency.

The most important document that provides for the usage of AI systems in Albania is the Council of Ministers Decision of 2024 on the approval of the document of methodology and technical standards in the usage of AI in Albania, promulgated by the CoM in a fast-track process without being consulted with the interested parties (Council of Ministers of the Republic of Albania, 2024). This document provides public institutions with several standards and principles on processes and procedures regarding the definition, measurement, and management of AI risks. This decision enshrines the principle of transparency as one of the fundamental principles for individuals, requiring that subjects be informed if the system they are using has implemented AI. It also implies that public organs should inform individuals in cases where data gathering or changes related to people, objects, or other entities appear real and authentic but are artificially generated or processed. This decision vaguely provides the standards that are used for the lifecycle of AI systems in Albania, such as transparency and explainability, by emphasizing that the ethical development of

AI systems depends on transparency and explainability, and that their level should be adaptable to the context. It vests the institution with the obligation to provide transparency at the stage in the AI lifecycle of a public service when the subjects are interacting with the AI system. This decision lacks clarity on how the transparency of these AI systems is achieved and allows for discretion by the public institutions using these systems. Transparency must be considered through human–AI interaction. The language used in the decision does not provide a clear overview of AI usage by public administration and instead leads to an unclear regulatory framework that would ensure transparency and accountability in AI usage.

5.5 CONCLUSIONS

The development and application of AI in Albania are still at an early stage, with several critical factors posing obstacles to adoption on a larger scale. The lack of AI experts, limited government and private sector investments, and issues relating to data infrastructure have all slowed the integration of AI in the Albanian public and private sectors. These limitations, along with the fast and steady pace at which other European countries are merging their services with AI systems, highlight the urgent need for robust transparency, ethical standards, and accountability as the country tries to keep up with global AI implementation.

The existing legal frameworks, while reflecting Albania's commitment to digital transformation, still fall short in addressing the specific complexities of AI systems. The Digital Agenda 2022–2026 outlines broad goals, such as the ethical use of AI and the promotion of transparency and accountability. However, the strategy remains declarative, without specifying detailed policies and mechanisms for the practical implementation of these principles. Without concrete legal instruments, it will be difficult to ensure that AI systems are transparent, auditable, and accountable to both the public and regulatory bodies.

Another overly critical area that requires attention as Albania tries to align its legal framework with the GDPR is data privacy. Platforms like e-Albania, which integrate AI for public services, process massive amounts of sensitive data. Ensuring that these systems operate transparently and in full compliance with privacy laws is especially important to maintain public trust. However, current regulations may not yet be sufficient to prevent data breaches or the misuse of personal information.

Some initiatives, such as Robotic Process Automation (RPA) in government processes, show promise as Albania tries to build a more inclusive AI ecosystem. This will involve fostering interdisciplinary collaboration between legal experts, technologists, and policymakers to create AI systems that are not only innovative but also ethical and legally compliant. Transparent AI systems, clear accountability structures, and adherence to international ethical standards are critical for Albania's continued integration of AI in both the public and private sectors. The issues that AI systems are and will be facing are not limited to Albania. The AI EU Act does not specify who bears responsibility in scenarios where AI systems cause harm or violate human rights. Knowing that AI systems involve multiple stakeholders, the AI Act does not state how responsibility will be shared if something goes wrong.

In conclusion, Albania's approach to AI still lacks declarative frameworks for detailed, actionable policies that enforce transparency, accountability, and ethical standards. A stronger focus on this will ensure that the country can fully harness the potential of AI systems while safeguarding the rights and freedoms of its citizens.

REFERENCES

AI Now Institute. (2021). *Algorithmic Impact Assessments: Toward Accountable Automation in Public Agencies*. https://ainowinstitute.org/publication/algorithmic-impact-assessments-toward-accountable-automation-in-public-agencies

Albanian Code of Administrative Procedures. (2015). *Code of Administrative Procedures of the Republic of Albania*. https://coilink.org/20.500.12592/hnxbf7 on 06 Apr 2025.

Ali, S., Abuhmed, T., El-Sappagh, S., Muhammad, K., Alonso-Moral, J.M., Confalonieri, R., Guidotti, R., Del Ser, J., Díaz-Rodríguez, N., & Herrera, F. (2023). Explainable artificial intelligence (XAI): What we know and what is left to attain trustworthy artificial intelligence. *Information Fusion*, 99, 101805. https://doi.org/10.1016/j.inffus.2023.101805

Alon-Barkat, S., & Busuioc, M. (2023). Human–AI interactions in public sector decision making: "Automation bias" and "selective adherence" to algorithmic advice. *Journal of Public Administration Research and Theory*, 33(1), 153–169. https://doi.org/10.1093/jopart/muac007

Balasubramaniam, N., Kauppinen, M., Rannisto, A., Hiekkanen, K., & Kujala, S. (2023). Transparency and explainability of AI systems: From ethical guidelines to requirements. *Information and Software Technology*, 159, 107197. https://doi.org/10.1016/j.infsof.2023.107197

Buolamwini, J., & Gebru, T. (2018). Gender shades: Intersectional accuracy disparities in commercial gender classification. In *Conference on Fairness, Accountability and Transparency* (pp. 77–91). PMLR.

Cath, C., & Jansen, F. (2021). Dutch Comfort: The limits of AI governance through municipal registers. *arXiv preprint arXiv:2109.02944.*

Center for AI and Digital Policy (CAIDP). (n.d.). *Universal guidelines for AI*. https://www.caidp.org/universal-guidelines-for-ai/

Constitution of the Republic of Albania. (1998/2022). https://qbz.gov.al/preview/635d44bd-96ee-4bc5-8d93-d928cf6f2abd

Council of Europe. (2020a). *Recommendation of the Committee of Ministers of the Council of Europe to Member States on the Human Rights Impacts of Algorithmic Systems, Adopted on 8 April 2020.*

Council of Europe. (2020b). *Resolution 2341 (2020) and Recommendation 2181 (2020) - The need for democratic governance of artificial intelligence.*

Council of Europe. (2020c). *Resolution 2343 (2020) and Recommendation 2183 (2020) - Preventing discrimination caused using artificial intelligence.*

Council of Europe. (2020d). *Resolution 2342 (2020) and Recommendation 2182 (2020) - Justice by algorithm: The role of artificial intelligence in police and criminal justice systems.*

Council of Europe. (2020e). *Recommendation 2185 (2020) - Artificial intelligence in health care: Medical, legal, and ethical challenges ahead.*

Council of Europe. (2020f). *Resolution 2345 (2020) and Recommendation 2186 (2020) - Artificial intelligence and labour markets: Friend or foe?.*

Council of Europe. (2020g). *Resolution 2346 (2020) and Recommendation 2187 (2020) - Legal aspects of "autonomous" vehicles.*

Council of Europe. (2020h). *Resolution 2344 (2020) and Recommendation 2184 (2020) - The brain-computer interface: New rights or new threats to fundamental freedoms?.*

Council of Europe. (2024). *Council of Europe Framework Convention on Artificial Intelligence and Human Rights, Democracy and the Rule of Law, Vilnius, 5.IX.2024.* Council of Europe Treaty Series - No. 225. https://rm.coe.int/1680afae67

Council of Ministers of the Republic of Albania. (2024). Vendim Nr. 479, datë 24.7.2024: *Për miratimin e dokumentit të metodologjisë dhe standardet teknike për përdorimin e inteligjencës artificiale në Republikën e Shqipërisë. QBZ.* [No. 479 On the Approval of the Methodological Document and techninal standards for the use of artificial intelligence in the Republic of Albania].

Declaration of the Committee of Ministers of the Council of Europe on the manipulative capabilities of algorithmic processes, Adopted on 13 February 2019. https://search.coe.int/cm#{%22CoEIdentifier%22:[%22090000168092dd4b%22],%22sort%22:[%22CoEValidationDate%20Descending%22]}

e-Albania. (n.d.). *Document Processing and Public Services.* https://e-albania.al

Engstrom, D. F., & Ho, D. E. (2020). Algorithmic accountability in the administrative state: The challenges of AI and machine learning to administrative law. In *Administrative Conference of the United States.* https://law.stanford.edu/wp-content/uploads/2020/02/ACUS-AI-Report.pdf

European Commission. (2020). *White Paper on Artificial Intelligence: A European Approach to Excellence and Trust.* European Union, Brussels. https://commission.europa.eu/publications/white-paper-artificial-intelligence-european-approach-excellence-and-trust_en

European Commission. (n.d.). *How the Italian Social Security and Welfare Administration (INPS) Used Artificial Intelligence to Streamline Services.* https://joinup.ec.europa.eu/collection/public-sector-tech-watch/how-italian-social-security-and-welfare-administration-inps-used-artificial-intelligence-streamline

European Union. (2016). General data protection regulation (GDPR), Recital 39. *Official Journal of the European Union,* 119, 1–88. https://eur-lex.europa.eu/legal-content/EN/TXT/?uri=CELEX:32016R0679

Government of Albania. (2022). *Strategjia Ndërsektoriale 'Axhenda Digjitale e Shqipërisë 2022–2026'* [Intersectoral Strategy 'Digital Agenda of Albania 2022–2026'].

Government of Albania. (n.d.). *Consultation process for Decision No. 413.* https://konsultimi-publik.gov.al/Konsultime/Detaje/413

Holm, J.R., & Lorenz, E. (2022). The impact of artificial intelligence on skills at work in Denmark. *New Technology, Work and Employment,* 37(1), 79–101. https://doi.org/10.1111/ntwe.12215

Jenkins, M. (2021, October 6). Algorithms in public administration: How do we ensure they serve the common good, not abuses of power. *Transparency International.* https://www.transparency.org/en/blog/algorithms-artificial-intelligence-public-administration-transparency-accountability

Jobin, A., Ienca, M., & Vayena, E. (2019). The global landscape of AI ethics guidelines. *Nature Machine Intelligence,* 1(9), 389–399.

Klei1. (n.d.). *Bleta 8B* [AI model]. Hugging Face. https://huggingface.co/klei1/bleta-8b

Kossow, N., Windwehr, S., & Jenkins, M. (2021). *Algorithmic Transparency and Accountability (Anti-Corruption Helpdesk Answer).* Transparency International. Reviewed by D. Eriksson, J. Vrushi, & L. Millar. https://www.transparency.org/

Langer, C. (2024). Decision-making power and responsibility in an automated administration. *Discover Artificial Intelligence,* 4(1), 59.

Law No. 107/2015 "On electronic identification and trusted services" [Ligj nr. 107/2015 *"Për identifikimin elektronik dhe shërbimet e besuara"*].

Law No. 13/2016 "On the manner of providing public services at the counter in the Republic of Albania" [Ligj nr. 13/2016 *"Për mënyrën e ofrimit të shërbimeve publike në sportel në Republikën e Shqipërisë"*].

Law No. 33/2022 "On open data and reuse of public sector information" [Ligj nr. 33/2022 *"Për të dhënat e hapura dhe ripërdorimin e informacionit të sektorit publik"*].

Law No. 43/2023 "On electronic governance" [Ligj nr. 43/2023 *"për qeverisjen elektronike"*]

Law No. 9880, date 25.2.2008 "On electronic signature" [Ligji nr.9880, datë 25.2.2008 *"Për nënshkrimin elektronik'].*

Mensah, G.B. (2023). Artificial intelligence and ethics: A comprehensive review of bias mitigation, transparency, and accountability in AI systems. *Preprint, November,* 10. DOI:10.13140/RG.2.2.23381.19685/1

Nwakanma, C.I., Nkoro, E.C., Ahakonye, L.A.C., Anyanwu, G.O., Njoku, J.N., & Kim, D.-S. (2023). Explainable activity detection and classification: SHAP vs LIME. In *Proceedings of the Korean Institute of Communications and Information Sciences Conference,* Seoul, Korea (pp. 1816–1817).

O'Neil, C. (2016). *Weapons of Math Destruction: How Big Data Increases Inequality and Threatens Democracy.* Crown Publishing Group, New York.

OECD.AI. (n.d.). *Algorithmic Impact Assessment Tool.* https://oecd.ai/en/catalogue/tools/algorithmic-impact-assessment-tool. *AI Principles Dashboard.* https://oecd.ai/en/dashboards/ai-principles/P7

Regulation (EU) 2016/679 of the European Parliament and of the Council of 27 April 2016 on the protection of natural persons about the processing of personal data and on the free movement of such data, and repealing Directive 95/46/EC (General Data Protection Regulation) (Text with EEA relevance). Official Journal of the European Union.

Regulation (EU) 2024/1689 of the European Parliament and of the Council of 13 June 2024 laying down harmonized rules on artificial intelligence and amending Regulations (EC) No. 300/2008, (EU) No. 167/2013, (EU) No. 168/2013, (EU) 2018/858, (EU) 2018/1139 and (EU) 2019/2144 and Directives 2014/90/EU, (EU) 2016/797 and (EU) 2020/1828 (Artificial Intelligence Act) [2024] OJ L 2024/1689.

Salih, A.M., Raisi-Estabragh, Z., Boscolo Galazzo, I., Radeva, P., Petersen, S. E., Lekadir, K., & Menegaz, G. (2024). A perspective on explainable artificial intelligence methods: SHAP and LIME. *Advanced Intelligent Systems,* 7, 2400304.

Sarker, I.H. (2021). Machine learning: Algorithms, real-world applications, and research directions. *SN Computer Science,* 2(3), 160.

Treaty of Lisbon. (2007). *Treaty of Lisbon Amending the Treaty on European Union and the Treaty Establishing the European Community.* https://eur-lex.europa.eu/legal-content/EN/TXT/?uri=CELEX:12007L/TXT

Urdhër i Kryeministrit të Republikës së Shqipërisë nr. 158 (25 nëntor 2019) *"Për marrjen e masave dhe rregullimin e dispozitave ligjore për aplikimin e shërbimeve vetëm online nga Data 1 Janar 2020"* [Order of the Prime Minister of the Republic of Albania No. 158 (25 November 2019) on the Adoption of Measures and Regulation of Legal Provisions for the Provision of Services Only Online from 1 January 2020].

Vendim i Këshillit të Ministrave Nr. 1147, datë 9.12.2020, *"Për krijimin e bazës së të dhënave shtetërore "Portali Unik Qeveritar e-Albania dhe për miratimin e rregullave për mënyrën e funksionimit të pikës së vetme të kontaktit"* [Decision of the Council of Ministers No. 1147, dated 9 December 2020, "On the creation of the state database E-Albania Unique Government Portal and approval of the rules on the functioning of the single contact point"].

Williams, R., Cloete, R., Cobbe, J., Cottrill, C., Edwards, P., Markovic, M., & Pang, W. (2022). From transparency to accountability of intelligent systems: Moving beyond aspirations. *Data & Policy,* 4, e7.

6 Fine-Tuning a Domain-Specific Large Language Model Using Low-Rank Adaptation Technique for Legal AI Applications
Case of India

V. S. Anoop and Mohammed Fawaz J.

6.1 INTRODUCTION

In the legal field, AI has become a tool that can facilitate the search for legal cases and documents (Ejjami, 2024). The traditional legal profession is extremely document-intensive and involves extensive research of precedents and case laws, as well as close reading of legal documents. However, with the rapidly growing amount of legal information and the increasing importance of legal problems, the role of AI is becoming more urgent to improve productivity, precision, and availability in legal practice. Legal professionals frequently spend numerous hours searching through large volumes of information. It is always a time-consuming task to examine relevant statutes, case laws, and legal precedents from unstructured legal text, which may also be influenced by human judgments. These routine activities, which require extensive human knowledge, can be automated using artificial intelligence techniques, significantly reducing the time that can be spent on other legal work (Said et al., 2023). Also, there are increasing demands from legal practitioners for faster, more effective, and cost-efficient solutions (Gandhi and Talwar, 2023) that can assist humans. Clients seeking legal aid may demand faster response times and better access to legal services, which may not be achievable through traditional, labor-intensive processes. AI provides solutions to overcome these challenges in activities such as legal research, document preparation, identification, assessment, regular review, and, in some instances, the ability to forecast the outcome of a case based on previous experience (Cohen et al., 2023). This not only reduces expenses but also enhances the

DOI: 10.1201/9781003541899-6

quality and standardization of legal services, thereby increasing client satisfaction (Marwala and Mpedi, 2024).

The recent advances in natural language processing (NLP), a subfield of artificial intelligence, have paved the way for the development of language understanding applications in various business domains and other areas. These same disruptive strides have been applied to the legal domain as well, to design NLP-powered applications that can understand legal language and contexts (Alexopoulos et al., 2024). The initial systems heavily relied on rule-based methods for language processing, where human subject matter experts handcrafted complex rules and stored them in rule bases (Dragoni et al., 2016). Later, rule-based systems were replaced with statistical approaches such as Conditional Random Fields (CRF) and Hidden Markov Models (HMM), which trained models using these rules. With advances in computational intelligence, machine learning became prominent, consuming large amounts of data during the training process and identifying patterns and relationships to make intelligent decisions (Khan et al., 2016). More recently, deep learning—a subfield of machine learning that uses complex neural networks for training models—has gained prominence due to its advanced capabilities, such as automated feature extraction and improved decision-making accuracy (Lauriola et al., 2022). These advances in machine learning have had a positive impact across different domains, leading to the development of more sophisticated context and text-understanding algorithms and techniques. These have been applied in area such as sentiment analysis (Anoop et al., 2024; Krishnan and Anoop, 2023), public discourse analysis (Anoop, 2024), entity recognition (Ardra et al., 2023; Devika et al., 2023), health-mention classification from user-generated text (Krishna and Anoop, 2023a), and relationship extraction to name a few.

The introduction of the "Attention" mechanism in the field of NLP revolutionized and entirely disrupted the landscape. Several algorithms and systems have since been introduced based on the Transformer architecture, which can capture the semantics of text in a way never seen before (Gillioz et al., 2020; Patwardhan et al., 2023). ChatGPT, the well-known AI chatbot that generates human-like responses, is based on Transformer architecture, and its release significantly increased interest in both the Transformer architecture and the attention mechanism. The core component in all AI chatbots and cognitive virtual agents that generate human-like responses is large language models (LLMs)—models trained on millions of documents that can generate new text (Ge et al., 2024). LLMs are now widely used to build generative and context-understanding applications across various domains such as healthcare (Sharaf and Anoop, 2023), banking (Xing, 2024), and education (Salminen et al., 2024). As outlined earlier, the legal domain is exceptionally complex, and applications of AI in this space remain limited. Very few studies have explored the use of artificial intelligence to solve complex legal tasks such as legal text summarization, judgment prediction, semantic segmentation, and statute identification. While some pre-trained LLMs have been introduced in the literature for the legal domain, fine-tuning them for country-specific laws and legal systems remains largely unexplored. In this context, this chapter attempts to use SaulLM (Colombo et al., 2024)—the largest pre-trained LLM for the legal domain, trained on Western legal documents—and fine-tune it for various legal tasks in the Indian legal system. The main contributions of this chapter can be outlined as follows:

a. Discusses the applications and relevance of LLMs in the legal domain.
b. Proposes an approach for fine-tuning SaulLM using the Low-Rank Adaptation (LoRA) Technique to develop Legal AI applications in the Indian context.
c. Elaborates on the fine-tuning process and highlights key applications developed for the Indian legal system using the fine-tuned LLM.

6.2 LARGE LANGUAGE MODELS IN LEGAL DOMAIN – THE NEED

LLMs trained for the Indian legal environment are unique AI systems developed to decode Indian legal text, which integrates a comprehensive range of statutes, case laws from High Courts and the Supreme Court, regulations framed by various governmental authorities, and legal opinions from legal scholars. These models are based on the wide range of NLP capabilities currently found in structures like GPT-4 and are trained on substantial material relevant to the Indian legal system, including texts in multiple languages recognized by the Indian judiciary. LLMs in the Indian legal context offer several major benefits. They help reduce the time consumed on document review tasks by rapidly assessing vast amounts of legal documents, identifying significant data, and highlighting main points. This capability is particularly useful for litigation support personnel, lawyers involved in due diligence, contracts analysis, and the discovery process in litigation. They also help in effective legal research by offering accurate citations of Indian cases, laws, or legal propositions to support lawyers' arguments and precedents. However, access to LLMs—especially those that are openly accessible and specialized for the Indian legal environment—remains scarce. This gap highlights the need for further development and greater localization of AI solutions to meet the legal peculiarities and linguistic diversity of India. Closing this gap would not only provide increased legal aid to the public but would also enhance the dissemination of legal information and improve the effectiveness of legal practice in the country.

6.3 RELATED STUDIES

The use of LLMs has been explored on a limited scale in the legal domain, with only a few studies published in the NLP and machine-learning domains. This section details some of the recent and prominent approaches to using NLP, specifically LLMs, in the understanding of legal text. An approach that explores the challenge of efficient fine-tuning for LLMs in NLP was introduced in 2021 (Hu et al., 2021). This study introduced a technique called LoRA to reduce the number of trainable parameters. This approach addressed two tasks that were prevalent in many LLM-based methods. The first was to reduce the requirement for GPU memory and the second was to maintain the performance of the model. Experimental results revealed that LoRA significantly decreased GPU memory requirements by reducing the number of trainable parameters.

LLMs face several challenges in domain-specific machine translation (MT), and techniques should be developed to address them. In this direction, Zheng et al. (2024) proposed a novel approach to tackling these challenges. It is an undeniable fact that LLMs have achieved significant advancements in general MT, but it is crucial to understand their applications in domain-specific scenarios. Many challenges remain that need to be addressed to make domain-specific MT systems robust, including sensitivity to input translation examples, increased inference costs, overgeneration requiring extra post-processing, and high training costs for domain adaptation. These methods also struggle with translating rare words in domain transfer contexts. The proposed approach introduced a prompt-oriented fine-tuning method named LlamaIT, which can effectively fine-tune a general-purpose LLM for domain-specific MT tasks. The approach involves constructing a task-specific mixed-domain dataset and fine-tuning the LLM using LoRA, eliminating the need for input translation examples and post-processing.

SaulLM-7B (Colombo et al., 2024), designed for the legal domain and developed using the Mistral 7B architecture, was introduced recently. As this LLM was trained on legal text, it was found to be better at capturing the context and semantics of legal language. However, there are several challenges in using this heavyweight model for text-understanding applications, and many researchers have suggested using quantization techniques (Gong et al., 2024). Quantization is a technique that makes minor changes to LLM weights and activations. This technique uses 4-bit and 8-bit quantization for both weights and activations, with only a small drop in performance. In general, quantization techniques help reduce the complexity of LLMs, which may lead to more manageable LLMs.

InternLM-Law (Fei et al., 2024), another language model, was introduced in 2024 and was specifically designed to handle complex legal questions about Chinese laws. The advantage of this model is that it can address both standard legal queries and more complicated, real-world legal scenarios. The authors used a dataset of over a million Chinese legal questions to train the model, employing a two-stage approach: fine-tuning on both legal and general content, then focusing solely on high-quality legal data to improve its structured responses. They evaluated the model's performance by comparing it with models like GPT-4 on 13 out of 20 tasks on the LawBench benchmark. Additionally, the authors published the model and the dataset to encourage further advancements in legal AI research (Fei et al., 2024).

6.4   MATERIALS AND METHODS

This section outlines the materials and methods used to fine-tune SaulLM for Indian legal applications.

6.4.1   SAULLM

SaulLM-7B can be seen as a significant step toward integrating AI into the legal domain. Trained on a large corpus of legal text, this model can understand unstructured legal text better than other models. It is estimated that SaulLM-7B was trained on over 30 billion tokens from English legal texts, giving it a deep understanding of legal language and the nuances that come with it. This means not only being able to identify legalistic language in the text but also understanding the contexts within which such terms are used (Colombo et al., 2024). SaulLM-7B has several advantages, including its ability to generate legal text that is highly fluent and accurate—at a human level (Colombo et al., 2024). It can write legal documents, including contracts, briefs, and pleadings, replicating the standard form and legal format used in the profession. Additionally, it can synthesize large documents, including legal opinions and cases, conduct legal analysis, and offer comprehensive and profound elaboration, given its extensive knowledge archive (Colombo et al., 2024).

6.4.2 PARAMETER-EFFICIENT FINE-TUNING (PEFT)

PEFT, which stands for Parameter-Efficient Fine-Tuning, is especially beneficial when there are limited resources and time as it is more efficient than complete model tuning in terms of computational and memory demands. The main concept related to PEFT is the selective update of some parameters. In contrast to the standard retraining method that adjusts the full set of parameters in a model, PEFT only fine-tunes a deliberately selected subset, which means that at any given time, only a small portion of the total number of parameters is adjusted. This selective adjustment can be realized using several approaches, including element-wise addition of small trainable modules called adapters or selectively retraining specific layers of the model. For instance, adapters are additional sub-components connected to the original model's structure and trained for the new task, leaving most of the initial model intact. Resource efficiency is one of the primary benefits of PEFT, which avails limited resources for efficient mastery. As will be discussed later, with fewer parameters to tune, PEFT decreases the overall computational resources and memory required for fine-tuning. This enhances the process to be faster and cheaper to undertake, making it possible to fine-tune larger models even on low-end devices with less computational power and memory.

6.4.3 LOW-RANK ADAPTATION (LoRA)

LoRA is one of several techniques falling under the family of PEFT, which aims at retraining large-scale models for another task efficiently. In this case, LoRA is achieved by incorporating low-rank matrix approximation. Therefore, LoRA appears to be an efficient solution to the problem of fine-tuning large models when computational resources are restricted by minimizing the number of trainable parameters. The primary advantage of this low-rank decomposition is that it drastically reduces the number of parameters that need to be fine-tuned, lowering the computational and memory requirements. Only the parameters in the low-rank matrices are updated during fine-tuning, while the original weights remain unchanged. This selective update mechanism ensures that the process is both efficient and effective.

6.4.4 MODEL SHARDING

To accommodate large-scale models on a machine-learning platform, sharding is a technique through which the model components are spread across many devices or nodes. This approach provides solutions to the problems of training and using models that are too large for any individual device to handle, a key factor in the scaling of most modern Machine Learning tasks. Model sharding is the process of splitting the model into segments of smaller sizes or "shards" that are assigned to different devices or nodes in a multi-tier system. The individual shards encompass portions of the model parameters and operations, facilitate parallel processing, and provide optimal resource utilization within the available computing system. It also enables the management of models that are too large to fit on a single device, which is typical in the distribution of exceptionally large models. Model sharding thus benefits from the utilization of memory space and computational capabilities of parallel devices. It allows for increased batch size and the ability to work with larger models simultaneously, thanks to data distribution across different nodes. This not only helps address the scale of training procedures but also improves model performance on large datasets.

6.5 FINE-TUNING SAULLM USING LOW-RANK ADAPTATION TECHNIQUE

This section discusses the approach for fine-tuning SaulLM, the largest legal LLM for the Indian legal context, using the LoRA technique (see Figure 6.1 for the overall workflow). This work uses two publicly available datasets for fine-tuning SaulLM.

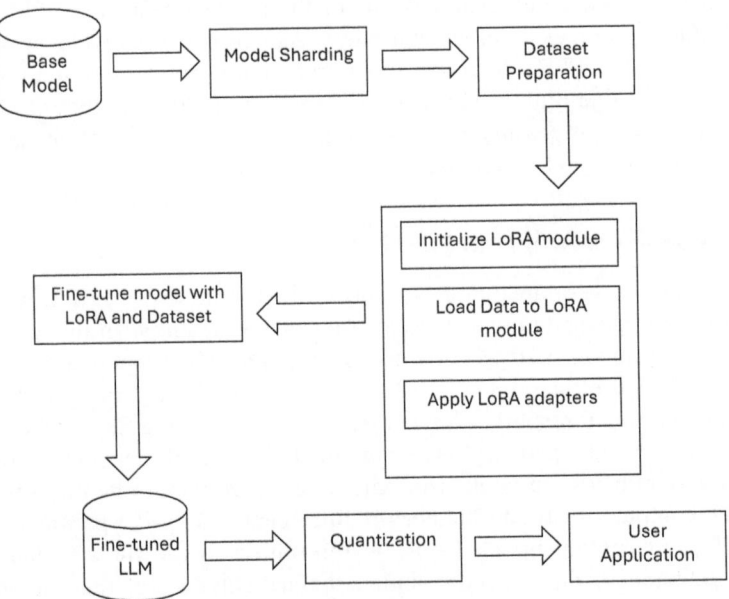

FIGURE 6.1   The overall workflow of the proposed approach.

6.5.1 DATASETS

The proposed work uses two datasets to fine-tune the SaulLM model. The first dataset is the Indian Legal Statute Identification (ILSI), and the second is the Indian Supreme Court Semantic Segmentation (ISS). The ILSI dataset comprises approximately 100,000 court case documents from various Indian courts. It focuses on identifying statutes cited within cases, specifically targeting the 100 most frequently cited sections of the Indian Penal Code (IPC). The ISS dataset, on the other hand, consists of 50 Supreme Court judgments from the top five legal domains and is designed for semantic segmentation, identifying and classifying seven key rhetorical roles within legal documents. These two datasets were used specifically to fine-tune the SaulLM model for different legal text-understanding tasks, such as semantic segmentation and statute identification.

The ISS dataset comprises legal judgments from the Supreme Court of India. It was retrieved from Thomson Reuters Westlaw India, containing 53,210 legal documents. From these, fifty documents were randomly selected from various legal domains, in proportion to their frequency: fifteen from the Criminal domain, ten from the Land and Property domain, nine from the Constitutional domain, eight from the Labour and Industrial domain, and seven from the Intellectual Property Rights domain. These documents were annotated to identify seven rhetorical roles: Background (simple facts, i.e., the timeline of events leading to the case), Lower Court Decision (judgment made by the lower court), Analysis (arguments made by the Court and applicable statutes), Precedent Case(s) (references to previous cases), Ratio of the Decision (applying the law and providing reasoning), and Supreme Court Decision (the final decision made by the Supreme Court). This dataset was used to retrain the SaulLM model for the semantic segmentation of legal documents, enabling the model to segment Supreme Court judgments into distinct roles and classify them accurately (Bhattacharya et al., 2019).

6.5.2 DATA PREPROCESSING

To prepare the ILSI and ISS datasets for fine-tuning the SaulLM model, we converted both datasets into the Alpaca format. This format, widely used for instruction-tuned LLMs, consists of inputs, outputs, and corresponding instructions. For the ILSI dataset, the Facts section of each court case document was used as the input, while the identified relevant IPC sections were used as the output. The instructions guided the model in identifying the appropriate statutes based on the provided facts. Similarly, for the ISS dataset, each Supreme Court judgment was segmented into seven rhetorical roles. Each segment served as an input, with the corresponding rhetorical role label as the output. Instructions were crafted to help the model accurately classify these segments.

6.5.3 MODEL SHARDING

Many open-source models have developed to the point where they are capable of producing human-like text similar to OpenAI, GPT J or PaLM. However, as these models become increasingly complex to enhance performance, they also face issues such as call size and resource utilization. A major difficulty is the application of such models, as it is impossible to load these giant models in platforms like Colab, Kaggle notebooks, or locally with comparatively limited RAM, let alone use them effectively. One potential solution to this problem is model sharding, which divides large models into smaller parts, allowing the loading of these massive models to take less time and occupy less space.

The original SaulLM-7B model, with a size of 30 GB, posed significant challenges in terms of loading and computational resource requirements. To address these issues, model sharding was implemented. Sharding divides the model into smaller, more manageable pieces, allowing it to be loaded and processed more efficiently. In this work, the SaulLM-7B model was effectively sharded, reducing its size to approximately 15 GB, a significant decrease. As a result, the model could be stored within the limited memory of the computing resources used for this project.

6.5.4 Fine-tuning of SaulLM

Once the data was structured in Alpaca format, the next phase was to optimize the SaulLM model using the PEFT approach with the application of LoRA. This technique is designed to improve LLMs with less computational power and relatively minor changes to the model structure. The fine-tuning process began with the LoRA initialization, which involved creating special LoRA layers within the SaulLM model. These layers were designed to integrate seamlessly into the rest of the model architecture, allowing the parameters to be updated smoothly during training. Once the LoRA setup was complete, the preprocessed ILSI and ISS datasets were loaded into the LoRA module. The Alpaca-formatted inputs, along with the outputs and instructions, were used for the next step. These adapters allowed the model to update its operations based on the new data with minimal additional computation. The final step was to adapt the SaulLM model by utilizing the LoRA-adapted layers and the loaded data. This process was iterative, adjusting the model weights according to the instructions and desired output to enhance its performance on legal statute identification and semantic segmentation tasks. The detailed fine-tuning process is shown in Figure 6.2.

The proposed approach conducted several experiments for fine-tuning the SaulLM model using the LoRA technique. The hyperparameters were tuned during these experiments to ensure the best performance of the fine-tuned model. One such parameter, the number of iterations, was varied to 100, 250, and 500 to find the optimal duration for fine-tuning. This variation was necessary to determine where the model exhibits balanced behavior between training time and performance. The model's scalability was evaluated using datasets of assorted sizes, and experiments were conducted with datasets containing 10,000 rows, 20,000 rows, and 45,000 rows. As one of our research objectives was to develop an application for legal assistance for the needy, we used "llama.cpp" in Python to successfully quantize the models to 8-bit precision.

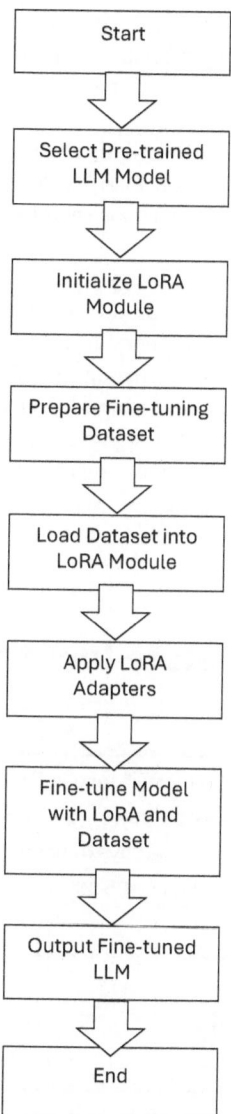

FIGURE 6.2   The detailed process flow for the fine-tuning process.

6.5.5   WEB APPLICATION INTERFACE

This work also created a web interface using Python Flask to interact with the model for common users. The model is hosted in the HuggingFace repository, and a Streamlit application that interacts with the fine-tuned model has been developed. This application features two distinct chat boxes dedicated to specific tasks: legal statute identification and semantic segmentation, allowing users to interact seamlessly with the models.

- **Legal Statute Identification Chatbot**: This chatbot allows users to enter queries related to identifying relevant legal statutes based on the provided facts. The model responds with the pertinent sections of the Indian Penal Code.
- **Semantic Segmentation Chatbot**: This chatbot is designed for input queries related to semantic segmentation in legal documents. The model provides segmented responses based on various rhetorical roles in legal judgments.

The web application is implemented using Flask, a web application framework in Python. The core functionality is centered around handling user inputs and model interactions. When a user submits a query in either chatbox, the input text is processed and passed locally to the respective quantized model. Utilizing the capabilities of llama.cpp, the model generates real-time responses. With llama.cpp, a powerful library for efficient model handling, the application can manage these models locally without requiring extensive computational resources. The response from the model for the legal statute identification task is shown in Figure 6.3, and the response from the model for the semantic segmentation task is shown in Figure 6.4.

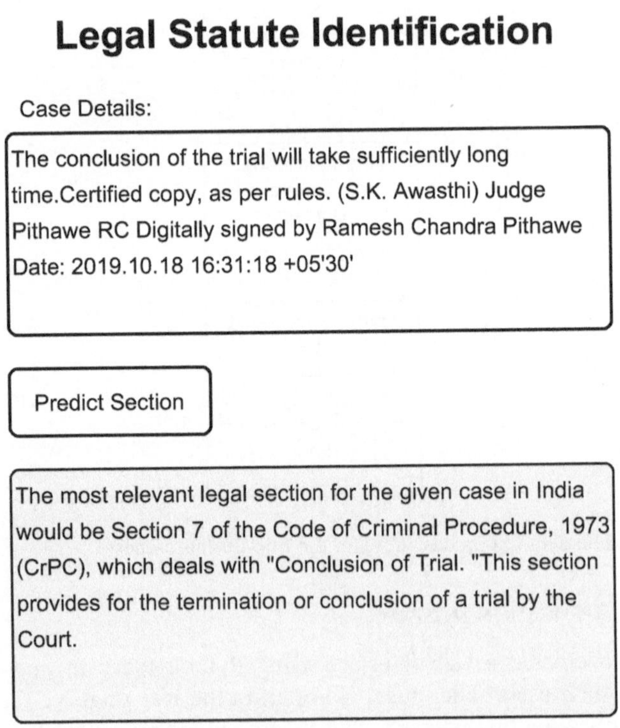

Legal Statute Identification

Case Details:

> The conclusion of the trial will take sufficiently long time.Certified copy, as per rules. (S.K. Awasthi) Judge Pithawe RC Digitally signed by Ramesh Chandra Pithawe Date: 2019.10.18 16:31:18 +05'30'

Predict Section

> The most relevant legal section for the given case in India would be Section 7 of the Code of Criminal Procedure, 1973 (CrPC), which deals with "Conclusion of Trial."This section provides for the termination or conclusion of a trial by the Court.

FIGURE 6.3   The response from the model for the legal statute identification task.

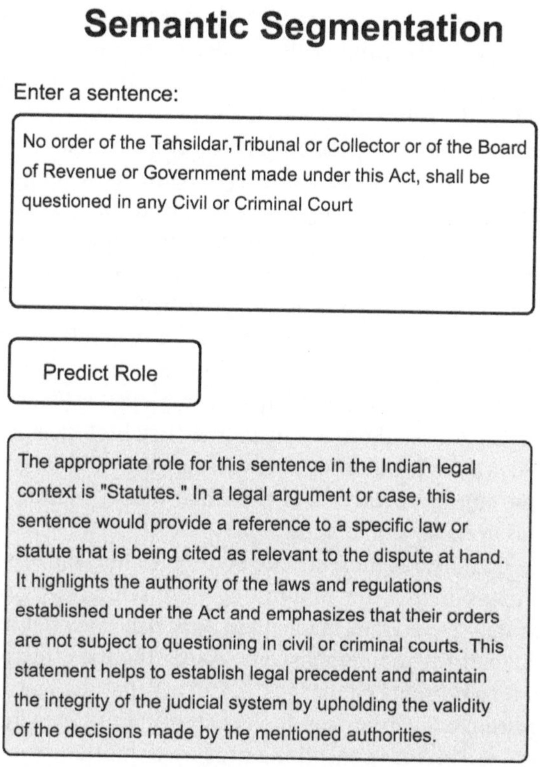

Semantic Segmentation

Enter a sentence:

> No order of the Tahsildar, Tribunal or Collector or of the Board of Revenue or Government made under this Act, shall be questioned in any Civil or Criminal Court

Predict Role

> The appropriate role for this sentence in the Indian legal context is "Statutes." In a legal argument or case, this sentence would provide a reference to a specific law or statute that is being cited as relevant to the dispute at hand. It highlights the authority of the laws and regulations established under the Act and emphasizes that their orders are not subject to questioning in civil or criminal courts. This statement helps to establish legal precedent and maintain the integrity of the judicial system by upholding the validity of the decisions made by the mentioned authorities.

FIGURE 6.4 The response from the model for the semantic segmentation task.

6.6 DISCUSSIONS

The SaulLM model was chosen for this study due to its well-thought-out structure and its success in previous language tasks. SaulLM's language comprehension and production proficiency make it suitable for specific application areas, such as legal text processing. With extensive pre-training on various datasets, it provides a solid starting point for fine-tuning to perform specific tasks, such as identifying legal statutes and semantic segmentation. This study specifically used SaulLM because it performed exceptionally well on natural language benchmarks. The work employed the LoRA technique for fine-tuning due to its effectiveness and adaptability, as highlighted in several machine-learning studies. Additionally, LoRA fine-tunes the model in a way that is different and more efficient than other methods, as it updates only a portion of the model parameters, requiring significantly less computational power. Given the limited computational resources for this experiment, LoRA proved to be a suitable mechanism for fine-tuning large models such as SaulLM-7B.

Like LoRA, low-rank updates do not prevent the original model from generalizing but improve its performance on task-specific data. This technique not only speeds up the fine-tuning process but also helps maintain the model's ability to solve various language tasks. One significant challenge of this work is the overfitting that may occur due to repeatedly training the model on a specific dataset. During this process, the model will try to capture the patterns from the training data but may perform poorly on unseen data. The ideal solution would be to use different data samples for fine-tuning and the validation process, such as cross-validation, to prevent overfitting. However, working with a large model like SaulLM is computationally expensive and time-consuming. Even though we have used the LoRA technique for the fine-tuning process, we found that the computational requirements are still remarkably high. This limitation draws attention to using different, representative data during fine-tuning and the necessity of applying methods such as cross-validation to observe overfitting. Fine-tuning large models, in general, can be very resource-hungry, as in the case of SaulLM, and it takes time. However, the computational costs are still high even when the LoRA technique is employed efficiently to fine-tune the model. Due to this limitation, there is a need to utilize high-performance computing resources, which could be limited for some researchers and organizations. As with most activities, fine-tuning requires less data than model training from scratch, but small data volumes are also challenging.

More extensive and diverse datasets can be used to fine-tune the model; however, in this study, the datasets used for fine-tuning were selectively compiled. This suggests that failures may stem from inadequate data that does not allow the model to learn task-specific features comprehensively. Assessing the effectiveness of a LoRA fine-tuned model also presents challenges. Ensuring that the learned features represent the task requirements while simultaneously retaining generalization ability is difficult. Moreover, it is a time-consuming process that often relies on human evaluation and requires substantial expertise.

Also, the automated measures might not always reveal the fine behavior of the model when it has been deployed in certain specific legal domains. The decision to fine-tune the current model of SaulLM using the LoRA technique arose from a desire to develop an efficient, scalable, and high-performing model for legal text analysis. Despite these enhanced potentialities, the approach faces challenges such as overfitting, high demand for computational resources, limitations in data volume, and difficulty in evaluation.

6.7 CONCLUSIONS AND FUTURE WORK

This work proposed an approach for fine-tuning a domain-specific LLM using the LoRA technique for Indian legal AI applications. The legal domain is one of the areas where the disruptive nature of artificial intelligence has not been explored to its full potential. The legal domain involves many complex documentation and processing techniques, mostly carried out using manual techniques that require a lot of time and effort and are prone to errors. Also, the enormous demand for legal assistance and the number of pending cases in the courts contribute to many issues faced by legal stakeholders. SaulLM, an LLM for law, was recently introduced in the machine-learning literature. The model was trained on a large legal corpus focused on Western law, which poses several challenges when applying it to other geographies, including the Indian judicial system. This work attempted to fine-tune SaulLM using a popular fine-tuning approach called the LoRA technique and to extend the fine-tuned model for developing web applications that can perform two crucial functions of legal document understanding: legal statute identification and semantic segmentation. The developed model was made publicly available for other researchers and developers to use and to build legal artificial intelligence applications for the Indian legal system, thereby making legal assistance more accessible to all citizens.

This is only an early attempt to use a heavyweight but feature-rich LLM for building semantic legal applications for Indian law. Thus, there are many avenues for future research and development. Some of the future work dimensions worth exploring include extended evaluation, additional fine-tuning, and model integration. Critically tuned models should be evaluated elaborately to establish their performance and credibility. We have used only a subset of the dataset for fine-tuning SaulLM, and a larger dataset may significantly enhance the model's performance. Also, integration and deployment of the fine-tuned model with legacy legal systems may be worth attempting.

REFERENCES

Alexopoulos, C., Saxena, S., & Saxena, S. (2024). Natural language processing (NLP)-powered legal A (t) Ms (LAMs) in India: Possibilities and challenges. *Journal of the Knowledge Economy*, 15(2), 8513–8533.

Anoop, V. S. (2024). Analyzing public concerns on Mpox using natural language processing and text mining approaches. In: Intersection of AI and Business Intelligence in Data-Driven Decision-Making, pp. 309–330. IGI Global, New York.

Anoop, V. S., Krishnan, T. A., Daud, A., Banjar, A., & Bukhari, A. (2024). *Climate Change Sentiment Analysis using Domain Specific Bidirectional Encoder Representations from Transformers*. IEEE Access, Piscataway, NJ.

Ardra, K. R., Anoop, V. S., & Panta, P. (2023). OralMedNER: A named entity recognition system for oral medicine and radiology. In: *2023 9th International Conference on Smart Computing and Communications (ICSCC)*, Kochi, Kerala, India, pp. 262–267.

Bhattacharya, P., Paul, S., Ghosh, K., Ghosh, S., & Wyner, A. (2019). Identification of rhetorical roles of sentences in Indian legal judgments. In: M. Araszkiewicz and V. Rodríguez-Doncel (Eds.) *Legal Knowledge and Information Systems*, pp. 3–12. IOS Press, Amsterdam, the Netherlands.

Cohen, M. C., Dahan, S., Khern-Am-Nuai, W., Shimao, H., & Touboul, J. (2023). The use of AI in legal systems: Determining independent contractor vs. employee status. *Artificial Intelligence and Law*, 30, 1–30.

Colombo, P., Pires, T. P., Boudiaf, M., Culver, D., Melo, R., Corro, C., & Desa, M. (2024). Saullm-7b: A pioneering large language model for law. arXiv preprint arXiv:2403.03883.

Devika, N., Anoop, V. S., & Thekkiniath, J. (2023). Biomedical named entity recognition from malaria literature using BioBERT. In: *2023 9th International Conference on Smart Computing and Communications (ICSCC)*, Kochi, Kerala, India, pp. 239–244.

Dragoni, M., Villata, S., Rizzi, W., & Governatori, G. (2016). Combining NLP approaches for rule extraction from legal documents. In: *1st Workshop on MIning and REasoning with Legal texts (MIREL 2016)*, Sophia Antipolis, France.

Ejjami, R. (2024). AI-driven justice: Evaluating the impact of artificial intelligence on legal systems. *International Journal for Multidisciplinary Research*, 6(3), 1–29.

Fei, Z., Zhang, S., Shen, X., Zhu, D., Wang, X., Cao, M., & Ge, J. (2024). InternLM-Law: An open source Chinese legal large language model. arXiv preprint arXiv:2406.14887.

Gandhi, P., & Talwar, V. (2023). Artificial intelligence and ChatGPT in the legal context. *International Journal of Medical Sciences*, 10, 1–2.

Ge, Y., Hua, W., Mei, K., Tan, J., Xu, S., Li, Z., & Zhang, Y. (2024). Openagi: When llm meets domain experts. *Advances in Neural Information Processing Systems*, 36, 5539–5568.

Gillioz, A., Casas, J., Mugellini, E., & Abou Khaled, O. (2020). Overview of the transformer-based models for NLP tasks. In: *2020 15th Conference on Computer Science and Information Systems (FedCSIS)*, Kochi, Kerala, India, pp. 179–183.

Gong, Z., Liu, J., Wang, J., Cai, X., Zhao, D., & Yan, R. (2024). What makes quantization for large language model hard? An empirical study from the lens of perturbation. In: *Proceedings of the AAAI Conference on Artificial Intelligence*, vol. 38, no. 16, pp. 18082–18089.

Hu, E. J., Shen, Y., Wallis, P., Allen-Zhu, Z., Li, Y., Wang, S., & Chen, W. (2021). Lora: Low-rank adaptation of large language models. arXiv preprint arXiv:2106.09685.

Khan, W., Daud, A., Nasir, J. A., & Amjad, T. (2016). A survey on the state-of-the-art machine learning models in the context of NLP. *Kuwait Journal of Science*, 43(4), 95–113.

Krishna, C. S., & Anoop, V. S. (2023a). Figurative health-mention classification from social media using graph convolutional networks. In: *2023 9th International Conference on Smart Computing and Communications (ICSCC)*, Kochi, Kerala, India, pp. 570–575.

Krishnan, A., & Anoop, V. S. (2023b). ClimateNLP: Analyzing public sentiment towards climate change using natural language processing. arXiv e-prints, arXiv-2310.

Lauriola, I., Lavelli, A., & Aiolli, F. (2022). An introduction to deep learning in natural language processing: models, techniques, and tools. *Neurocomputing*, 470, 443–456.

Marwala, T., & Mpedi, L. G. (2024). *Artificial Intelligence and the Law*, pp. 1–25. Springer Nature, Singapore.

Patwardhan, N., Marrone, S., & Sansone, C. (2023). Transformers in the real world: A survey on nlp applications. *Information*, 14(4), 242.

Said, G., Azamat, K., Ravshan, S., & Bokhadir, A. (2023). Adapting legal systems to the development of artificial intelligence: Solving the global problem of AI in judicial processes. *International Journal of Cyber Law*, 1(4), 49.

Salminen, J., Jung, S. G., Medina, J., Aldous, K., Azem, J., Akhtar, W., & Jansen, B. J. (2024). Using Cipherbot: An exploratory analysis of student interaction with an LLM-based educational chatbot. In: *Proceedings of the Eleventh ACM Conference on Learning@Scale*, Atlanta, GA, USA, pp. 279–283.

Sharaf, S., & Anoop, V. S. (2023). An analysis on large language models in healthcare: A case study of BioBERT. arXiv preprint arXiv:2310.07282.

Xing, F. (2024). Designing heterogeneous llm agents for financial sentiment analysis. *ACM Transactions on Management Information Systems*, 16, 1–24.

Zheng, J., Hong, H., Wang, X., Su, J., Liang, Y., & Wu, S. (2024). Fine-tuning large language models for domain-specific machine translation. arXiv preprint arXiv:2402.15061.

7 Application of Artificial Intelligence in the Indian Legal System
Pros and Cons

Madhavi Kilaru and Rajasekhara Mouly Potluri

7.1 INTRODUCTION

Artificial intelligence (AI) systems are not intended to fully replace human decision-makers. Instead, they contribute to increased human productivity and decision-making capacity. Fortunately, AI should support judges rather than replace them (Zerilli et al., 2019). AI advancements will have far-reaching social implications. Self-driving technology has the potential to replace millions of driving jobs in the coming decade. In addition to potential job losses, the transformation will present additional issues such as reconstructing infrastructure, preserving vehicle cybersecurity, and modifying laws and regulations. Law enforcement, military technology, and commercial applications will all present new hurdles for AI developers and policymakers (Morgan et al., 2020).

Proponents of AI in legal operations frequently tout its potential to transform the profession, promising better efficiency, accuracy, and cost-effectiveness. While AI has several advantages, it is critical to realize its limitations and acknowledge that technology alone cannot solve all the complicated difficulties inherent in legal operations. Companies cannot automate this process, and legal services are slightly more expensive than those of other firms in the industry (Pasquale, 2019). Although AI applications play a significant role in law firms, their practical use is limited. As a result, this book chapter focuses on how AI plays an essential part in the Indian judicial system and the limitations of AI's practical use.

7.2 INDIAN LEGAL SYSTEM

When we examine the Indian judicial system, we discover that there are legal delays. The judiciary is overburdened with more than 5.1 crores pending cases, causing undesirable delays in administering justice to the people, and as the proverb goes, "Justice delayed is justice denied." As a result, various efforts must be made to improve the current situation, such as shortening vacation periods. Advanced tools such as data science and AI will assist courts in improving judicial strength by using predictive technology to provide critical information about ongoing cases based on prior cases

DOI: 10.1201/9781003541899-7

of a similar nature (Moses, 2017). One of the most significant improvements that AI can bring is to law firms today. As a result, the Indian legal system is constantly evolving, and lawyers can gain distinct advantages in this field by utilizing AI. The Indian legal system is a complicated framework based on common law and heavily impacted by British colonial control. It consists of different branches, including civil, criminal, constitutional, and administrative law, and is governed by the Indian Constitution, which is the supreme law of the land. The judiciary is independent, with the Supreme Court at the top, followed by the high courts and lower courts. The legal process consists of several stages, including case filing, hearings, and judgments, which are frequently characterized by lengthy procedures and backlogs (Chalakkal & Prabhakaran, 2021). In recent years, there has been an increase in the use of AI in the legal system, with the goal of improving efficiency and accessibility.

AI technologies are being integrated into various legal practice areas, including legal research, document analysis, and case management. AI-powered technologies can assist lawyers and judges in quickly identifying important material for a specific case and streamlining workflows. Furthermore, AI-powered tools can assist in forecasting case outcomes, allowing legal experts to improve case strategies through tactical approaches. Advanced data can be extracted using advanced techniques such as big data and Natural Language Processing (NLP), allowing legal practitioners to forecast data trends, legal principles, and data complexity, all of which may influence the conclusion of a legal matter. This would help improve the accuracy of legal procedures and the system's general efficiency (Frankenreiter & Nyarko, 2022). Predictive analytics can help analyze patterns and connections in legal datasets. This will allow legal practitioners to make more informed decisions. It can also help to ensure consistency and justice in legal decisions, particularly in cases where subjective judgment is important.

While frequently regarded as a more traditional form of AI, Expert Systems have major legal applications. These AI systems encode domain-specific knowledge and rules to replicate expert decision-making. In the legal arena, expert systems may provide crucial procedural assistance, maintaining uniformity and efficiency in court processes. They could also provide preliminary assessments of basic legal concerns, potentially assisting in case triage and identifying those that require more in-depth human attention. While not immediately applicable to many legal activities, computer vision technology has the potential to play important roles in the judiciary (Chalakkal & Prabhakaran, 2021). Computer vision could aid in evidence analysis, such as processing surveillance footage in criminal cases or examining documents for signs of forgery.

As digital evidence becomes more widespread in court procedures, computer vision systems' capacity to interpret visual data quickly and accurately may be crucial. These key AI technologies can be applied to a variety of judicial processes, with each having the potential to speed up operations. The uses of AI in the judiciary are numerous and promising, ranging from streamlining case administration and scheduling to improving legal research capabilities, automating document review, and providing decision support to judges (Vivek & Nilakshi, 2024). However, it is critical to understand that various factors, including the quality and amount of available data, precise implementation details, and stakeholders' willingness to adopt and adapt to new technology, must be considered. To learn more about how these technologies are used in India, we must consider both their revolutionary potential and the limitations associated with their adoption (Chatterjee, 2020).

7.3 ADVANTAGES OF AI IN LEGAL SYSTEM

Sundar Pichai, CEO of Google, believes that India is well positioned as the shift to AI takes place. The use of AI in judicial systems could potentially reduce the time required to deliver judgments. Traditional legal processes often involve significant manual labor, such as document examination and case preparation, which consumes time and causes delays in case resolution. AI technology can automate and optimize many areas of the legal process, enabling more advanced and efficient decision-making. NLP algorithms, for instance, can evaluate and extract relevant information from vast amounts of legal data, such as statutes, rules, and legal opinions (Bommarito et al., 2021).

This will accelerate the legal research process and allow legal practitioners to swiftly access crucial materials, saving valuable time when drafting arguments and analyzing cases. Furthermore, AI can simplify the process of categorizing massive numbers of legal documents, such as contracts, pleadings, and evidence. By automating document inspection, AI may drastically reduce the time necessary for this task, ensuring that relevant information is readily available when needed. This increased efficiency allows legal practitioners to focus on higher-level duties, such as case planning and analysis, ultimately accelerating the decision-making process. AI technologies can potentially improve the study of legal features, leading to increased accuracy and thoroughness in legal evaluations. Additionally, AI has the potential to evaluate vast amounts of legal information effectively, enabling it to find data trends, extract accurate and relevant information, and provide valuable insights to legal professionals. AI-powered predictive analytics may analyze past cases to identify correlations and data trends. AI algorithms can forecast case outcomes or the success rate of similar cases for specific legal arguments by considering elements such as case characteristics, parties involved, and jurisdiction. This can assist legal professionals in understanding the strengths and weaknesses of their cases, allowing them to make better-informed decisions and develop effective legal strategies. To save time and money, in-house legal counsel frequently skips the inquiry process or hires a first- or second-year attorney to carry it out. AI can assist humans in asking straightforward legal questions and receiving responses based on research, case law, and other sources. Furthermore, AI can be used as a FAQ service for internal customers, answering basic legal, HR, and compliance issues while determining when to refer the case to a human lawyer. The key here is that not only can the use of AI save time and money, but it also provides in-house teams with the one indulgence that is often missing: the advantage of time to carefully consider the issue and provide the best possible solution (Bell et al., 2023).

Furthermore, AI systems can help with thorough legal research by rapidly collecting pertinent case law, statutes, and legal precedents. By analyzing and summarizing such a large amount of legal knowledge, AI technology can assist legal practitioners in understanding legal principles, arguments, and counterarguments. Not only does this save time, but it also improves the precision and comprehensiveness of legal analysis. Additionally, AI can assist with the structure and synthesis of legal materials. It automatically categorizes and tags legal documents based on their content, making them easier to retrieve and analyze (Kusabi et al., 2024). Effective legal management information helps legal practitioners find and use relevant materials, thereby boosting the quality of research and discussion. Using AI in legal decision-making, especially for individuals struggling to understand the current system, makes legal services more accessible to many people with low incomes or limited resources. AI-powered solutions can address these issues and provide effective, efficient legal help. Before seeking legal assistance, chatbots and virtual assistants can provide individuals with preliminary information, guidance, and self-help options. These tools are accessible at any time of day or night and offer basic information to individuals. Furthermore, AI algorithms can assist in translating legal documents, interpreting legal procedures, and facilitating communication between legal experts and individuals to overcome language barriers. This ensures that all parties involved in judicial proceedings comprehend and participate effectively.

We know that legal procedures are often lengthy, but AI algorithms can help simplify legal forms and procedures, making them more accessible and understandable to laypeople. Advanced tools, such as machine learning (ML) and NLP, help reduce errors, streamline procedures, and empower individuals to engage effectively in the legal system. A more significant transformation of AI in the legal field involves using AI to reduce judgment time, improve legal documentation, and enhance access to justice. Legal experts, policymakers, and stakeholders must accept and investigate the benefits of AI if technology is to be used responsibly and effectively in the legal domain (Coglianese & Dor, 2020). It is equally important for every legal professional to consciously analyze and address the ethical implications associated with AI technology implementation. AI-generated technologies can automate and optimize various aspects of legal document management, such as contract analysis and task execution based on priority and urgency. ML algorithms can assist in detecting risks, saving documents, and quickly processing information. Automation through AI offers countless benefits, including reduced labor, a faster review process, and greater accuracy in document analysis.

7.3.1 CHALLENGES AND LIMITATIONS OF AI IN LEGAL SYSTEM

In general, legal professionals employ AI in legal operations to investigate contracts, evaluate documents, establish legal research processes, and perform predictive analytics. These processes can assist legal authorities in streamlining specific operations, thereby saving time and resources. For example, AI algorithms can help examine many legal papers and find the essential information required to mitigate potential risks, whereas humans can take much longer, often many days, to review the relevant data. Legal experts can also use AI technology to identify patterns to predict case outcomes accurately. During the manual review process, data may be overlooked when it involves large documents; AI can assist in this direction to identify uncovered data, thereby enhancing legal operations in a more transformative manner (Sil et al., 2019). Even though AI has excellent innovations, it has certain limitations, particularly regarding the complex case-generative outcomes and context-dependent nature of legal work. AI may not perform adequately in these situations because human interactions are always challenging and may not agree or come to a fixed point, as the legal system is evolving with social norms and subjective matters, which leads to a significant challenge. One of the major challenges of AI in legal operations is its reliance on historical data and AI technology to learn from past outcomes while generating and predicting outcomes for current and future scenarios. This may be beneficial for specific cases; nevertheless, when uniqueness and special legal challenges exist, AI may not be able to deliver relevant insights or outcomes. In today's environment, unexpected events may arise that AI cannot fully solve (Benbya et al., 2020).

One of the most significant issues in legal decision-making is AI's lack of openness. Complex models of AI algorithms are often difficult for humans to understand, providing accurate forecasts without clear explanations of the factors associated with the supplied document and failing to explain why a specific reason was mentioned for the given situation. This makes it harder to establish trustworthiness and accountability in AI automation results. Without a clear explanation, people will be unsure if they are following the correct technique or making accurate predictions. The judicial system is very broad and sensitive. Thus, clear explanations are crucial to enable legal experts, litigants, and the public to comprehend and evaluate the reasoning behind AI-generated results (Awasthy et al., 2022).

Significant work is required to construct AI models that produce interpretable and explainable outcomes to address these difficulties. It is tough to achieve openness in policymaking, but transparency is very important for the success of any system. Proper analysis is required to identify and rectify errors with AI algorithms, as well as to properly test the implementation process before it collects enormous volumes of data. Particularly for algorithms with private or secret codes, this is necessary for the development of advanced instruments like AI (Ejjami, 2024). Automatically maintaining such data necessitates high security and must be protected from hackers. Legal professionals and AI engineers must collaborate, understand the system's data protection priorities, and build the necessary technologies to protect individuals' privacy rights and comply with applicable laws and regulations. The specifics of a case can be gathered and retained, raising privacy concerns. Data consent must be obtained freely and voluntarily to collect the details; feeding the details entails access control, system updates, and monitoring. The number of cyber-attacks is increasing, so we need to establish efficient cyber-control measures to safeguard against the misuse of AI technologies. Legal professionals and AI developers must create awareness among individuals and parties involved when sharing data with third parties. Transparent terms and conditions must be set to ensure data privacy, including the tenure of the case systems, which should be considered a vital tool to help legal professionals find the right path rather than completely replacing human judgment. Humans can understand, question, and dispute AI-generated solutions. Hence, legal professionals must have the knowledge and expertise to use AI technology effectively and critically examine and evaluate its outcomes. Furthermore, appropriate mechanisms for testing and appealing AI-generated solutions or outputs must be devised, especially when legal experts are required to uncover and examine alternatives and explanations for AI-generated solutions in a broader and ethical context that they believe to be unjust or inaccurate. This promotes transparency, accountability, and fairness (Dronadul & Bhaskar, 2023).

Strict norms and appropriate regulatory frameworks must be established and enforced to encourage the responsible and ethical use of AI in legal decision-making. For this collaboration among stakeholders, AI experts, and policymakers—as well as ethics experts—is critical for developing effective and accurate recommendations. Individuals involved in formulating and executing the rules include legal professionals, associations, and the government. These rules should cover a variety of topics, including providing explanations, mitigating bias, protecting data privacy and security, establishing accountability, and using AI responsibly. It is critical that detailed rules are established to assist in the development, deployment, and assessment of AI systems in the legal arena. Regular evaluations and modifications to these rules are required to keep up with technological advancements and evolving ethical considerations. Ethical considerations and adherence to rules on explainability, bias reduction, data privacy and security, accountability, and responsible AI use are essential for ensuring AI's responsible and efficient incorporation into legal decision-making processes. Legal practitioners must prioritize transparency, impartiality, and the protection of personal information.

7.3.2 SUCCESSFUL IMPLEMENTATION OF AI IN LEGAL SYSTEM

AI encompasses a wide range of computational approaches that allow machines to accomplish tasks that would normally require human intelligence. Several fields of AI are especially relevant for judicial applications, with each offering unique capabilities to address various aspects of legal proceedings. ML is at the forefront of AI technologies relevant to the court. ML algorithms can find patterns in vast datasets and improve their performance on tasks with experience. The most important approach in legal systems is supervised learning, which is used to anticipate future-oriented data classification and case outcomes using previous data. This domain can assist legal systems in correctly predicting datasets, making the role of legal experts easier. This could be extremely useful in revising case bargains and offering more knowledge to both lawyers and judges. On the other hand, unsupervised learning may reveal hidden patterns in case management, which can help the legal system by informing policy decisions and addressing systematic issues within the legal framework (Bardhan et al., 2024). Reinforcement learning is an important AI technique for training software to make informed decisions to achieve the best possible results. The ability of this technique, particularly in legal systems, aids in the optimization of protracted procedures over time, such as refined court scheduling systems, resulting in increased system efficiency and proper resource allocation. NLP, another crucial and advanced AI tool, is utilized in the court system to automate the processing of legal documents, allowing cases to be evaluated more efficiently. NLP has numerous uses in the legal profession; it may employ complex legal research methods to analyze large amounts of data quickly. NLP can also help computers understand, analyze, and interpret human language. Additionally, NLP has the capability of automating lengthy documents and identifying crucial elements in the legal system for rapid assessment. Furthermore, NLP systems could even assist in regularizing and routing document texts, allowing legal practitioners to save time and focus on more complex topics (Hassan et al., 2021).

While widespread implementation of AI in Indian courts remains in its initial stages, various initiatives have been launched to investigate its potential. These revolutionary initiatives span a wide range of applications, from language translation to case management, and reflect a growing realization of AI's disruptive potential in the legal system. The Supreme Court Vidhik Anuvaad Software (SUVAS), announced in 2019, is a major step toward improving language accessibility in the legal system. This AI-powered language translation technology is intended to translate Supreme Court decisions from English to vernacular languages, increasing access to justice by making legal material more available in regional languages. The implementation of SUVAS acknowledges India's linguistic diversity and seeks to bridge the language gap, which sometimes hinders understanding of legal proceedings and judgments.

Another significant innovation is the Supreme Court Portal for Assistance in Court Efficiency (SUPACE), launched in 2021. This AI application is specifically created to help courts by extracting key facts and legislation from case documents. SUPACE's goal is to reduce the time judges spend on preparatory work, allowing them to focus more on key decision-making processes by automating routine research tasks. The Supreme Court of India has developed an SCI Interact tool that is entirely AI-based and helps streamline procedures related to case status, judgments, and court circulars. While this AI application does not directly solve case backlogs, it does improve transparency and access to information, both of which are critical components in fostering public trust in the court system and reducing unnecessary litigation. The E-Courts Project, while not solely an AI endeavor, lays the framework for future AI applications by developing a comprehensive digital infrastructure for court procedures. This initiative includes e-filing of cases, digital case records, and virtual hearings, all of which produce significant data that AI systems will use in the future. The National Judicial Data Grid (NJDG) is an online portal that provides real-time data on case status across all levels of courts. Currently focused on data collection and visualization, the NJDG generates a significant dataset that could power future AI analytics tools, providing insights into case flow patterns and bottlenecks in the judicial process. Several high courts have deployed Automated Case Flow Management Systems, which use simple algorithms to automate case listing and allocation. While not employing advanced AI, these technologies provide the framework for more sophisticated AI-driven scheduling in the future, potentially optimizing court resources and reducing delays (Aithala et al., 2024). Finally, while not particular to the judiciary, the national AI plan outlined by NITI Aayog, the government think tank, mentions justice delivery as a priority. This high-level policy direction signals government support for AI adoption in the legal sector and provides a broader context for AI initiatives in the judiciary. These innovations, collectively, demonstrate a growing recognition of AI's potential to address longstanding challenges in the Indian judicial system.

7.4   CONCLUSION AND IMPLICATIONS

In India, AI has the potential to cause an immense paradigm shift in the legal profession by improving operational efficiency, precision, and cost-effectiveness. Also, in the Indian legal system, one of the most crucial algorithms AI provides in terms of benefits and uses is its ability to assist in the resolution of ongoing cases. As the number of pending cases grows, AI may help minimize court workload and speed up case resolution. For example, by assisting with document analysis, legal research, and evidence appraisal, AI systems can allow judges to focus on more important aspects of the case. This may result in faster case resolution and less buildup. Furthermore, AI can facilitate drafting legal documents and pleadings, especially in litigations that rely on vast datasets and information. AI integration in India's legal industry brings both potential and problems for legal practitioners, governments, and society. While AI technologies have the potential to increase efficiency, lower costs, and enhance access to justice, they also raise worries about job displacement, skill shortages, ethical challenges, and the loss of human expertise. As the legal profession navigates the complications of AI adoption, a balance must be struck between using technology to complement human talents and safeguarding the legal profession's core beliefs. Otherwise, it is difficult to maintain applications in the legal sphere overall since it creates a schism between the public and government. By embracing AI responsibly and investing in continuous learning and skill development, legal professionals can adapt to the evolving landscape of the legal industry and ensure their relevance in the AI-powered future. Moreover, policymakers need to enact appropriate regulations and safeguards to address ethical and regulatory challenges associated with AI adoption in the legal sector, fostering an environment of trust, accountability, and responsible innovation. This chapter describes the lawyer's duty of technology competence to advise their clients while discussing the ethical implications of using AI technologies in the lawyer's own legal practice.

It also describes a judge's duty of technological competence to understand the legal and ethical challenges associated with AI, as well as the advantages and disadvantages of using or allowing the use of AI technology tools in their own courtroom. Fundamental rights are protected by lawyers and judges through the courts, which means competence with AI technologies is of utmost importance for lawyers, judges, and other judicial officers. Lawyers and judges must understand what an AI tool can and cannot do while also understanding its effectiveness and biases when accomplishing its objectives. Lawyers and judges must, therefore, possess a higher level of competence when AI tools impact their practice. Education is at the center of this competency. Understanding AI in the legal field starts with educating stakeholders about the fundamental aspects of AI, its challenges, and how to create frameworks for addressing these challenges. Dataset Disclosure Forms and Model Disclosure Forms are necessary to ensure that lawyers and judges are sufficiently educated regarding the contents of data, models, and related algorithms. While Dataset Disclosure Forms and Model Disclosure Forms are only one transparency tool among many, they are necessary for lawyers and judges to uphold their ethical duties (Shope, 2021).

AI solutions can speed up legal research and automate repetitive procedures, which can lead to more efficient processes and better use of resources. Furthermore, the emergence of online platforms and AI-powered virtual assistants helps to overcome geographical limitations, promoting a more inclusive judicial system. Nevertheless, this progression in technology is not devoid of its obstacles. Significant ethical concerns arise, encompassing worries over algorithmic bias, transparency, and the necessity of human supervision. Ensuring the responsible implementation of AI in the judiciary requires a crucial balance between technical progress and protecting individual rights. An essential aspect of this shift is the requirement for a strong legal and regulatory framework that can adapt to the ever-changing nature of AI. Ensuring clear and precise regulations for using AI in the judicial system is crucial for minimizing potential dangers and building a solid basis of confidence among all involved parties. The success of AI integration is heavily influenced by technological literacy. Legal professionals and stakeholders must possess the necessary expertise to utilize AI systems to their maximum capabilities effectively. Thorough training programs and continuous education campaigns are crucial in this context. The foundation of a functional judiciary relies on public confidence, and it is crucial to communicate transparently about the role of AI in shaping good opinions. Ensuring comprehension and trust among the public is crucial as AI becomes an indispensable component of the legal decision-making procedure. To ensure the future of AI in the Indian courts, it is imperative to consistently engage in innovation and collaboration. The legal industry should adopt developing AI technology, utilizing knowledge from international benchmarks to guide strategic decision-making. Despite obstacles, employing a considerate and morally upright strategy and continuous improvement presents AI as a powerful agent in the continuous endeavor to create a judicial system in India that is more accessible, efficient, and fair for its varied and ever-changing population.

REFERENCES

Aithala, V., Sachan, A., Sen, S., Payal, H., & Bhattacharya, C. (2024). Decision time: Illuminating performance in India's district courts. *Data & Policy*, 6, e32.

Awasthy, S., Babu, P., & Singh, S. (2022). Application of artificial intelligence and machine learning in the Indian legal system: Use cases for judiciary, law firms, and lawyers. *Part 2 Indian Journal of Integrated Research in Law*, 2(4), 1.

Bardhan, T. K., Chintale, P., Gouravaram, R. R., Gardezi, S. H. I., Patnaik, J. R., & Khade, A. (2024). Utilizing AI for enhanced predictive analytics in financial projections: Significance in corporate planning and risk mitigation. *Journal of Electrical Systems*, 20(7s), 3983–3987.

Bell, F., Bennett Moses, L., Legg, M., Silove, J., & Zalnieriute, M. (2023). *AI Decision-Making and the Courts: A Guide for Judges, Tribunal Members and Court Administrators*. Australasian Institute of Judicial Administration, Sydney, NSW.

Benbya, H., Davenport, T. H., & Pachidi, S. (2020). Artificial intelligence in organizations: Current state and future opportunities. *MIS Quarterly Executive*, 19(4), 9–21.

Bommarito II, M. J., Katz, D. M., & Detterman, E. M. (2021). LexNLP: Natural language processing and information extraction for legal and regulatory texts. In *Research Handbook on Big Data Law* (pp. 216–227). Edward Elgar Publishing, Cheltenham.

Chalakkal, K., & Prabhakaran, A. (2021). The importance of structural reforms for an efficient Indian judiciary. *IUP Law Review*, 11(3), 36–50.

Chatterjee, S. (2020). AI strategy of India: Policy framework, adoption challenges and actions for government. *Transforming Government: People, Process and Policy*, 14(5), 757–775.

Coglianese, C., & Dor, L. M. B. (2020). AI in adjudication and administration. *Brooklyn Law Review*, 86, 791.

Dronadul, S. D., & Bhaskar, D. V. (2023). Impact of artificial intelligence (AI) on the legal profession and justice system. *International Journal of Law, Management, and Humanities*, 6(2), 1084.

Ejjami, R. (2024). AI-driven justice: Evaluating the impact of artificial intelligence on legal systems. *International Journal of Multidiscipline Research*, 6(3), 1–29.

Frankenreiter, J., & Nyarko, J. (2022). Natural language processing in legal tech. *Legal Tech and the Future of Civil Justice (David Engstrom ed.)* Forthcoming.

Hassan, F. U., Le, T., & Lv, X. (2021). Addressing legal and contractual matters in construction using natural language processing: A critical review. *Journal of Construction Engineering and Management*, 147(9), 03121004.

Kusabi, V., Jain, P., Palesha, R., Khandelwal, K., Potdar, G. P., & Kohok, P. T. (2024). Advancements in legal document processing and summarization. *Computer*, 24(6), 158–166.

Morgan, F. E., Boudreaux, B., Lohn, A. J., Ashby, M., Curriden, C., Klima, K., & Grossman, D. (2020). *Military Applications of Artificial Intelligence*. RAND Corporation, Santa Monica, CA.

Moses, L. B. (2017). Artificial intelligence in the courts, legal academia, and legal practice. *Australian Law Journal*, 91, 561.

Pasquale, F. (2019). A rule of persons, not machines: The limits of legal automation. *George Washington Law Review*, 87, 1.

Shope, M. L. (2021). Lawyer and judicial competency in the era of artificial intelligence: Ethical requirements for documenting datasets and machine learning models. *Georgetown Journal of Legal Ethics*, 34, 191.

Sil, R., Roy, A., Bhushan, B., & Mazumdar, A. K. (2019, October). Artificial intelligence and machine learning based legal application: The state-of-the-art and future research trends. In *2019 International Conference on Computing, Communication, and Intelligent Systems (ICCCIS)*, Kochi, Kerala, India, pp. 57–62.

Vivek, T., & Nilakshi, N. (2024). Artificial intelligence in the Indian judiciary: A systematic analysis of potential applications and challenges in addressing case backlogs. *Journal of Trends and Challenges in Artificial Intelligence*, 1(3), 91–96.

Zerilli, J., Knott, A., Maclaurin, J., & Gavaghan, C. (2019). Transparency in algorithmic and human decision-making: Is there a double standard? *Philosophy & Technology*, 32, 661–683.

8 An Analysis of the EU Artificial Intelligence Act

Reald Keta

8.1 INTRODUCTION

Apart from a vague public discussion about how information technology systems are becoming crucial for everyone's daily life or appear as futuristic creations in cinematography, artificial intelligence (AI), until recently, stood as a mirage of the future. Undoubtedly, in the general perception, it was a short-term future full of fears and hopes for progress, but it had not yet arrived in our everyday lives.

This was the general panorama of universal society until the advent of different models of AI systems in our daily lives. For example, on November 30, 2022, the "ChatGPT" chatbot debuted as open source. Since then, the use of open-source chatbots has massively increased in many aspects of society, with many alternatives emerging with their own features, such as "Copilot," "Gemini," and others.

Beyond basic uses, such as students preparing assignments, office workers preparing analytical materials, and those in media creating audio-visual content, the range of applications is expanding ever more widely. AI is increasingly being used in the fight against tax fraud (e.g., automated detection of swimming pools based on satellite images), security (e.g., advanced video surveillance systems analyzing human behavior), healthcare (e.g., diagnostic assistance), and education (e.g., through learning analytics aimed at personalizing learning paths) (Felicien, 2023).

With the rise of generative AI programs for consumers, such as Google's Bard and OpenAI's ChatGPT, the generative AI market is expected to gain even more economic weight. According to a new report from Bloomberg Intelligence (BI), this weight is projected to increase from a market size of just $40 billion (about $120 per person in the United States) in 2022 to $1.3 trillion (about $4,000 per person in the United States) over the next 10 years (Bloomberg Intelligence, 2023).

In the face of such developmental reality, and with the effort to keep up with socio-economic dynamics, in 2021, the European Commission undertook a significant regulatory step regarding AI systems. This initiative culminated on July 12, 2024, when the Official Journal of the European Union published "Regulation (EU) 2024/1689 of the European Parliament and of the Council of June 13, 2024, laying down harmonized rules on artificial intelligence and amending Regulations (EC) No 300/2008, (EU) No 167/2013, (EU) No 168/2013, (EU) 2018/858, (EU) 2018/1139, and (EU) 2019/2144, and Directives 2014/90/EU, (EU) 2016/797, and (EU) 2020/1828." For ease of communication, it will be referred to hereafter as the "EU AI Act," as it is widely known.

DOI: 10.1201/9781003541899-8

The drafting and adoption of such an act, as a flagship initiative from the European Commission, also represents the first approval of a horizontal regulatory framework for AI systems, not only for the European Union. The regulation took time to reach a consensus since its proposal and will require time to achieve full implementation. The act came into force in the 27 European Union countries on August 1, 2024, but implementation of the regulation is anticipated to be progressive according to a calendar timeline. To a major extent, the act is expected to be applied by August 2, 2026.

As an act of such magnitude, covering such a dynamic field and with such broad impact, it has elicited numerous responses from various stakeholders and considerations of different natures. In this context, the article aims to provide an overview of the fundamental issues of the act and a contextual analysis of the regulations it implements.

In this historical context, this chapter primarily aims to provide an introduction to the regulatory framework of the act in question from a jurisprudential perspective. This reading seeks to present the regulatory act in an understandable way to a non-legal audience. Alongside the presentation and in the conclusion of the analysis, this chapter intends to outline some of the short-term and, where possible, long-term implications of the act. In the analysis, the author also considers, for reference, the opinions of experts with specialized profiles in information technology.

8.2   LEGAL CONTEXT

While the "EU AI Act" rightly holds the merit of being the first regulatory framework for regulating AI systems, it does not mean there were no prior normative regulatory acts that partially governed the use of AI. Moreover, many non-governmental organizations and authors have prepared regulatory documents or guidelines for the use of AI systems. This normative and theoretical legacy undoubtedly helped and found its place in the mentioned regulation.

8.2.1   BROAD CONTEXT

A normative approach before the "EU AI Act," within the framework of a politically autocratic society, was pioneered by China. Under the authoritarian leadership of the Chinese Communist Party, a regulatory and governance framework for the use of AI was implemented in China in 2021 and 2022 (Sheehan, 2024).

Meanwhile, on the other side of the Atlantic, regulatory development had been underway before the approval of the "EU AI Act." For example, American tech giants Google and Microsoft had agreed to collaborate with OpenAI and the start-up Anthropic to launch the "Frontier Model Forum," a self-regulatory industry body that would promote safe and responsible AI.

However, even in the United States, unlike the normative approach in Europe, there have been regulatory efforts. It is worth mentioning that in the United States, there have been non-normative regulatory acts such as the "NIST AI Risk Management Framework." There have also been normative efforts, such as the Presidential Executive Order "On the Safe, Secure, and Trustworthy Development and Use of Artificial Intelligence," adopted in October 2023.

However, the United States has not yet managed to establish a more detailed normative framework. The long journey and the still ongoing inability to adopt the "Algorithmic Accountability Act" in the US Senate since 2019 demonstrate this. Among other factors, the regressive pressure from the industry, due to the costs a regulatory framework would bring, has led to the blocking of such legislation (MacCarthy, 2020).

8.2.2 EUROPEAN CONTEXT

Within its legal and political tradition to positively regulate matters in every field, the European Union institutions have long been striving to be at the forefront of developments in AI systems. This effort began with the European Commission's publication in 2018 of the strategy "Artificial Intelligence for Europe." This strategy, accompanied by a budget of 1.5 billion euros for the 2018–2023 period, is set as the EU's goal to place AI in the service of human development.

However, the preparation and theoretical framework on which the "EU AI Act" was based started with the white paper titled "On Artificial Intelligence – A European Approach to Excellence and Trust." Through this document, it was stated that "a common European approach to AI is necessary to achieve sufficient development scale and avoid the fragmentation of the single market." It also outlined two objectives the EU should maintain regarding AI and its regulatory activity. According to this document, the EU should aim for AI use to expand within an excellent and trustworthy ecosystem. A balanced approach with two perspectives, targeting the promotion of innovation as economic progress while also keeping in mind the guarantee of citizens' rights, especially as consumers.

In this regard, the first concrete step was taken on April 21, 2021, when the European Commission proposed the first draft of a regulatory framework for AI. Following discussions and legislative procedures, several key issues gained attention. Among these, some of which will be addressed in detail later in this chapter, are as follows:

i. The definition and purpose of an AI system.
ii. Risks associated with public and private sector AI use.
iii. The classification and listing of high-risk AI systems.
iv. The classification and listing of systems exempted for national security concerns.
v. Considering "Foundation Models" as high risk.
vi. The exemption of AI systems used for public purposes.

On December 6, 2022, the European Council approved the general approach, allowing negotiations with the European Parliament to begin. On December 9, 2023, after three days of "marathon" talks, the Council of the EU and the Parliament reached an agreement. The law was passed in the European Parliament with dedicated support from MEPs on March 13, 2024, with 523 votes in favor, 46 against, and 49 abstentions. Subsequently, the act was approved by the Council of the EU on May 21, 2024.

8.3   ANALYSIS OF THE ACT

Due to its nature and regulatory magnitude, the "EU AI Act" has been regarded as the "GDPR of AI," with the General Data Protection Regulation considered a benchmark for challenging regulatory acts in the EU. This comparative approach will be explored several times throughout this chapter while addressing various issues.

Many commentators argue that the "EU AI Act" is not just comparable to the General Data Protection Regulation (GDPR) but extends beyond it. This is partly because many issues will remain within the domain of secondary regulatory acts for specific regulations. These secondary acts, among others, include practical implementation guidelines for the regulation, which are expected to be developed by the European Commission.

In this context, the European Commission's initiative to assist entities in implementing the regulation is commendable. As part of a two-year transitional implementation period according to a calendar, the Commission has launched the "AI Pact." The Commission has promoted the AI Pact, seeking the voluntary commitment of the industry to begin implementing its requirements ahead of the legal deadlines. To gather participants, the first call for expressions of interest was published in November 2023, receiving responses from over 550 organizations of assorted sizes, sectors, and countries.

Below, we will focus on some of the key issues regulated by the act and provide a summary of the regulations. The following topics will be addressed:

  i. The scope of the act.
  ii. Definition of AI systems.
  iii. Categorization of AI systems.
  iv. Subjects of the regulation.

8.3.1   THE SCOPE OF THE ACT

Briefly, the "EU AI Act" aims to establish a set of rules for AI systems within the European Union. This regulation ensures that AI systems are safe, transparent, and respectful of fundamental human rights. More specifically, in Article 1, the "EU AI Act" outlines seven areas it regulates as follows:

- Harmonized rules for placing products on the market, putting them into service, and using AI systems in the Union.
- Prohibitions of certain AI practices.
- Specific requirements for high-risk AI systems and obligations for operators of such systems.
- Harmonized transparency rules for certain AI systems.
- Harmonized rules for placing general-purpose AI models on the market.
- Rules on market monitoring, market surveillance, governance, and enforcement.
- Measures to support innovation, focusing on Small Medium Enterprise (SMEs), including start-ups.

8.3.2 DEFINITION OF AI SYSTEMS

It is challenging to translate a technical process into a legal definition, especially in the case of information technology systems. This task becomes even more difficult when it comes to AI systems. The difficulty of this task, as universally experienced, has led many normative acts on AI systems to avoid this challenge by not defining the concept itself (Kluge Corrêa, 2023).

Point 1 of Article 3 of the act defines an AI system, specifically stating that: "(Artificial Intelligence System) means a machine-based system that is designed to operate with varying levels of autonomy and that may exhibit adaptiveness after deployment, and that, for explicit or implicit objectives, infers, from the input it receives, how to generate outputs such as predictions, content, recommendations, or decisions that can influence physical or virtual environments."

It is necessary to mention that defining what constitutes an AI system was a debated issue during the drafting process. The discussion included issues regarding the differentiation of AI systems from other software and the need for a more specific definition. This discussion and the criticisms presented led to the rejection of the initial proposal in the Commission's draft. In the final act, an agreement was reached, harmonizing with the OECD definition in the "Recommendation on Intelligent Systems." For context, this definition is similar to that mentioned above.

From reading the definition in the relevant provision, six characteristics of the nature of an AI system emerge. Of these characteristics, four are essential, and two others are also essential and serve as nuances that differentiate AI from software. More specifically:

  i. Machine-based system.
  ii. Designed to operate with a degree of autonomy.
  iii. Operates with clear or implied objectives.
  iv. Based on the provided information (input), it generates processed information (output) in the form of predictions, content, recommendations, or decisions.
  v. Can exhibit adaptability post-deployment.
  vi. The system's output may affect physical or virtual environments.

First, the criticism of this definition is that the definition borrowed from the OECD was not intended to serve as a legal provision but as a policymaking guide. This is emphasized to highlight that, in principle, the referred definition was created for a different functional purpose and will inevitably suffer from shortcomings when applied as a legal regulation.

Second, the key elements in the above definition are 'infers' and 'autonomy,' which attempt to distinguish an AI system from any other software where the outcome is predetermined (if x then y) by a strict algorithm. However, some authors argue that, even in this form, we are mostly still dealing with a definition of software, not AI (Hacker, 2024). They support this with the example of Excel's auto-sum function. It has a goal (constructing a sum), inputs (the entered values), and an output that can affect environments (depending on the importance of the sum for each decision).

Compared to the definition, the only difference with AI in this example is the ability to "conclude."

To address this criticism, recital 6 offers some clarification, specifying that: "The notion of AI [...] should not cover systems that are based on the rules defined solely by natural persons to automatically execute operations. A key characteristic of AI systems is their capability to infer. [...] The techniques that enable inference while building an AI system include machine learning approaches that learn from data how to achieve certain objectives; and logic- and knowledge-based approaches that infer from encoded knowledge or symbolic representation of the task to be solved. The capacity of an AI system to infer goes beyond basic data processing, enable[ing] learning, reasoning or modelling."

There are also two other legal gaps in the phrasing of the definition that, in practical reality, could create issues. The first is a reference to a machine-based system, which is outdated (machinery) and allows for different interpretations. Secondly, the phrasing of a system created to be autonomous raises questions regarding the relationship between creation and functioning as such. However, these remarks are based on a theoretical approach. As would be argued again, the definition itself or the entire act will show its merits during adaptation and court rulings.

8.3.3 CATEGORIZATION OF AI SYSTEMS

One of the fundamental issues addressed by the act is the provision of a categorization of AI systems and AI usage practices. The strategy used for this overall regulation and categorization is built according to the "pyramid of criticality," supported by the risk faced in practice or the targeted sector. In dividing these systems, the act uses an approach based on the levels of risk that the consumer may face. This is an attempt to manage risk in proportion to the measures enforced (Mahler, 2022).

Regarding the definition of risk, it is specified that "risk means the combination of the probability of the occurrence of harm and the severity of that harm." This two-component approach has been considered a definition made within the framework of ISO Standards. More specifically, the "EU AI Act" highlights four levels of risk and, consequently, three categories of systems, for each of which specific regulations are provided depending on the risk level.

8.3.3.1 Unacceptable Risk

This category exhaustively lists prohibited AI practices under any circumstances. For clarity, the act prohibits specific AI functionalities, not the systems themselves. The prohibited functionalities summarized are:

- **Subliminal Techniques**: Manipulative or deceptive methods that distort behavior and hinder informed decision-making, resulting in significant harm.
- **Exploitation of Vulnerabilities**: Targeting individuals based on age, disability, or socio-economic status to manipulate behavior, causing considerable harm.
- **Biometric Categorization**: Systems that infer sensitive attributes like race, political beliefs, or sexual orientation, with exceptions for legally obtained data use or law enforcement.

- **Social Scoring**: Evaluating individuals based on social behavior or characteristics, potentially leading to harmful treatment.
- **Risk Assessment via Profiling**: Assessing criminal risk based solely on profiling or personality traits, except when supplementing objective, factual assessments.
- **Facial Recognition Databases**: The uncontrolled collection of facial images from online sources or CCTV for creating recognition databases.
- **Emotion Detection**: Monitoring emotions in workplaces or educational settings, prohibited unless for medical or security purposes.
- **Remote Biometric Identification**: Real-time biometric identification in public spaces for law enforcement, raising privacy concerns.

The ban on real-time biometric identification for law enforcement was the subject of much debate in European institutions. The prohibition does not apply when these systems are used for any of the listed specific purposes, such as searching for victims of human trafficking or sexual exploitation, or for the prevention of terrorist attacks. In principle, relying on such an exception will require thorough assessments, technical and organizational measures, notifications, and a warrant (Fernhout, 2024).

8.3.3.2 High Risk

This category includes systems used in critical areas such as biometrics, infrastructure, education, and finance, which are allowed but must comply with requirements and undergo a conformity assessment. The act provides a dual definition, categorizing cases into an exhaustive list and defining the second as a category. The second category includes AI systems deemed high risk, which are either standalone products or security components of a product.

In summary, the following obligations must be fulfilled for these systems:

- **Risk Management**: Developers and providers of high-risk AI systems must implement a risk management system throughout the product lifecycle, including identifying, analyzing, and minimizing potential risks that the AI system may pose to safety, health, or fundamental rights.
- **Data Governance**: Systems must utilize high-quality data for training, testing, and validation. The data should be appropriate, accurate, and representative to ensure proper functioning and minimize errors and exclusions.
- **Technical Documentation**: Providers must maintain detailed technical documentation describing design, algorithms, data, risk assessments, and compliance measures. This should enable users to understand how the system operates and to be aware when interacting with an AI system. Products must indicate that they are AI-based, especially if they are used for critical safety purposes.
- **Human Oversight**: Systems must be designed in such a way that allows human intervention and oversight. Users should be able to interrupt or correct AI system decisions when they are dangerous or inaccurate. High-risk applications should not operate fully autonomously where human intervention is critical.
- **Transparency and Information Provision**: Providers must maintain detailed technical documentation as described above. Systems should be

designed so that users understand how they function and know when they are interacting with an AI system. Products should display that they are AI-based, particularly for critical safety purposes.

- **Conformity Assessment**: Before being placed on the market, high-risk AI systems must undergo a conformity assessment by an independent third party to ensure compliance with all EU legal and technical requirements.
- **Accuracy Oversight**: Providers of high-risk AI systems must have mechanisms for reporting incidents related to system failures or anomalies. They must monitor and improve AI systems throughout their lifecycle to minimize risks that may arise during use.
- **Record Keeping**: Developers and providers must retain technical documentation and risk assessment results for an extended period, even after the product is on the market, to provide evidence of compliance during inspections or investigations.

Foundation Models (FMAI) and General-Purpose Models (GPMAI) fall under this category, depending on their use and receive comprehensive treatment under the "EU AI Act." However, they are not the only models addressed. General-Purpose Models (GPMAI) refer to AI systems not developed for a specific task but capable of being adapted for a wide range of applications. In comparison, Foundation Models (FMAI) can also process substantial amounts of data and can be used for a wide range of tasks. Unlike GPMAI, which is more flexible and broadly applicable, FMAI is more advanced and serves as a foundational base for developing other AI models tailored to more complex tasks.

8.3.3.3   Limited Risk

In the second group of this category, systems permit information and transparency. These models can create additional content, such as text, images, videos, or sounds. It is essential to mention that "Generative Models" are referred to and regulated in the approved version but were not part of the first draft of the Act by the Commission.

Limited risk refers to the outcome associated with a lack of transparency in using these systems. In the case of Generative Models, these systems may fall under high-risk regulation if used in ways that affect privacy, ethics, or copyright.

The "EU AI Act" establishes specific transparency obligations to ensure that individuals are informed when necessary, promoting trust. For example, when using AI systems like chatbots, people should be aware that they are interacting with a machine in order to make an informed decision about continuing or withdrawing.

Providers must also ensure that AI-generated content is identifiable. Additionally, AI-generated text published to inform the public about matters of public interest must be labeled as artificially generated. This requirement also applies to audio and video content that constitutes "deep fakes." "Deep fakes" are considered "content generated or manipulated by AI in the form of images, audio, or video that resembles existing persons, objects, places, entities, or events and would appear authentic or true to a person."

According to the "EU AI Act," using AI systems to create deep fakes must disclose that the content has been artificially created or manipulated by labeling it as such and revealing its artificial origin (except when the use is authorized by law to disclose, prevent, investigate, or prosecute a criminal offense). When the content is part of an artistic work, the transparency obligations are limited to disclosing the existence of such generated or manipulated content in a manner that does not impede the presentation or enjoyment of the work (Hickman, 2024).

8.3.3.4 Low or No Risk

In this case, we are referring to AI systems that are permitted for use and do not carry any obligations, apart from the standards for the use of products.

8.3.4 SUBJECTS OF THE REGULATION

In summary, the regulation identifies four subjects to which it applies obligations regarding "artificial intelligence systems" placed on the EU market or affecting those located in the EU. Similar to the GDPR, the act aims for broad jurisdictional reach, often referred to as the "Brussels effect." These subjects are:

- **Providers**: Entities that develop or place AI systems on the EU market.
- **Importers**: Those importing AI systems from outside the EU.
- **Distributors**: Entities involved in the supply chain within the EU.
- **Deployers**: Public and private users of AI systems.

Like the rules on product liability, whereby an entity other than the provider may be considered the provider, in this Act any importer, distributor, deployer, or any third party will be considered a provider of the high-risk AI system and will therefore be subject to the extensive list of obligations under the AI Act if one of three conditions is met:

- they have put their name or trademark on the system after it has already been placed on the market or put into service;
- they have made substantial modifications after that placing on the market or putting into service, provided that the system remains high risk; or
- they have modified the intended purpose of the AI system, which renders the system high risk.

On the other hand, the Act provides exclusions regarding the obligations of providers. Firstly, the Act does not apply to providers of free and open-source models, with some exceptions. For example, general-purpose artificial intelligence (GPAI) models—even if open source—will be subject to regulation.

Additionally, the obligations do not apply to AI systems used for national security, military, or defense purposes, or to research, development, and prototyping activities prior to their entry into the EU market. "EU AI Act" also excludes certain categories from its scope, such as:

- Research and development of AI prior to commercial deployment.
- Free and open-source software, unless it is high risk or has significant impact.

- AI systems used for military or defense purposes.
- AI systems used solely for scientific research.
- AI systems placed on the market before the Act, unless they have been significantly modified.
- AI systems used solely for personal, non-professional purposes.

The Act provides for the establishment of several regulatory, supervisory, and advisory structures at the EU level. The following bodies are foreseen:

- An Artificial Intelligence Office within the European Commission.
- An Artificial Intelligence Board as a collegial body with representation from member states.
- An advisory forum to provide technical expertise, advise the Board and the Commission, and contribute to their tasks under this Regulation.
- Scientific panels composed of independent experts. The Commission shall establish a scientific panel of independent experts to support enforcement activities under the Regulation. These experts will be selected by the Commission based on their up-to-date scientific or technical expertise in the field of AI.

It is also anticipated that responsible authorities will be established in each member state, with at least one designated as a notifying authority and at least one other as a market surveillance authority.

8.4   IMPLEMENTATION CHALLENGES

The law, following its publication in the Official Journal of the European Union, entered into force 20 days (about three weeks) later. After August 1, 2024, a phased implementation began that allows provisions to come into force over three years, depending on the type of AI system. The law will be fully effective on August 2, 2026, and will be fully in effect by this time, including the implementation of full enforcement mechanisms by mid-2027.

However, some regulations will be applicable earlier than the deadlines mentioned. The prohibitions of AI systems that pose unacceptable risks will apply six months after entry into force. Codes of practice will apply nine months after entry into force. The rules for general-purpose AI systems that must meet transparency requirements will apply 12 months after entry into force. High-risk systems will have more time to comply, as obligations for them will become applicable 36 months (about three years) after entry into force. Like the GDPR, local enforcement authorities are tasked with conducting random checks.

Timeline / Progressive Grace Period

- **February 2025**: Six months after entry into force: Prohibitions on banned AI practices will apply.
- **August 2025**: Twelve months after entry into force: Obligations for general-purpose AI systems, including governance requirements, will apply. Penalties will also come into force.

- **August 2026**: Twenty-four months after entry into force: The Act becomes generally applicable, including obligations for many high-risk AI systems.
- **August 2027**: Thirty-six months after entry into force: Obligations for all remaining high-risk AI systems will apply.

Failure to comply with the provisions of the "EU AI Act" may result in a maximum penalty of €35 million or 7% of global annual turnover, whichever is higher. The AI Act grants any natural or legal person the right to file a complaint with a market surveillance authority if they have grounds to believe that the Act has been infringed. This represents an unusually broad personal scope for exercising this right, as there is no requirement for standing. This differs notably from other instruments, such as the GDPR, where data subjects may submit a complaint only if the processing of personal data relates to them.

Like any normative act in the field of information technology that seeks to guarantee human rights, the "EU AI Act" also faces two challenges that could lead to side effects or counterproductive outcomes.

First, considering the dynamics of the market—and information technology in particular—the Act risks becoming outdated very quickly and may prove inefficient. This inefficiency, besides failing to achieve the goals of the Act, could also result in regulatory costs.

Second, in contrast to the first argument but based on the same premise, the Act risks being restrictive. Although, as argued at the beginning of the document, the EU aims to promote innovation and support small businesses through this Act, the EU AI Act could have the opposite effect. This is because the administrative burden it imposes could weigh heavily on small businesses and stifle innovation in the sector.

8.5 CONCLUSIONS

As mentioned, the "EU AI Act" is a regulatory act within the framework of a broader regulatory context in the EU. This Act and the entire legal framework listed below interact in many aspects. It includes references to product safety, product liability, copyright, and others. More specifically, "the EU AI Act" interconnects with:

- General Data Protection Regulation (GDPR)
- Product Liability Directive (PLD)
- European Cyber Resilience Act (CRA)
- Data Governance Act (DGA)
- General Product Safety Regulation (GPSR)
- Digital Services Act (DSA)
- Digital Markets Act (DMA)
- Copyright

The European Union's framework for regulating the digital ecosystem—aside from the Single Market—is built on three legislative pillars: the DSA, the Digital Markets Act (DMA), and the Artificial Intelligence Act (AI Act). The DSA focuses on user safety and rights, creating a safer online environment. The DMA ensures that markets remain competitive and free from monopolistic practices. The AI Act promotes the safe and ethical use of AI, ensuring it benefits society. These acts are complementary and, in certain circumstances, may overlap.

Like any legislation of this magnitude—one that affects numerous economic interests and social actors—criticisms and reservations have accompanied its drafting, approval, and implementation. However, this inevitability should not be used to dismiss legitimate critiques or to overlook the Act's positive elements. The author supports the view (Hacker, 2024) that, although this regulation requires strong political consensus and is far from perfect, it is a more positive alternative than having no regulatory framework at all.

Firstly, it establishes minimum rules for the functioning of AI systems, considering the risks to public safety. In line with this, it also sets minimum standards for the protection of privacy and personal data. An example of the benefits of these standards is the month-long ban on OpenAI's chatbot in Italy by the data protection authority in 2023.

Most importantly, the "EU AI Act" guarantees human oversight of AI systems. Systems must be designed and developed in such a way that they can be "effectively overseen by natural persons during the period in which the AI system is in use." This goes beyond mere transparency or explanation of how the AI system "works"; it involves enabling the "human overseer" to spot anomalies, recognize "automation bias," correctly interpret the system's outputs, and override or disregard the system when necessary. Explicitly, one aim is to prevent or minimize risks to fundamental rights (Edwards, 2022).

It also addresses political data in the context of remote biometric identification (RBI). In both areas—foundation models and RBI—more protective measures would be possible and desirable, but the current regulation is still better than having none.

Thirdly, it will allow companies to create codes of conduct that could gain broad validity through Commission-approved self-regulation. This offers flexibility, provides room for concrete implementations across various sectors, and leverages industry expertise.

As argued at the beginning, two factors will determine the regulatory success of the Act: the framework of secondary legislation and the case-by-case progression in the courts.

REFERENCES

BBC. (2023). ChatGPT accessible again in Italy. BBC News. Retrieved from https://www.bbc.com/news/technology-65431914

Edwards, L. (2022). The EU AI Act: A summary of its significance and scope. Ada Lovelace Institute. Retrieved from https://www.adalovelaceinstitute.org/wp-content/uploads/2022/04/Expert-explainer-The-EU-AI-Act-11-April-2022.pdf

Felicien, V. (2023). Is it possible to regulate AI? Commission Nationale de l'Informatique et des Libertés (CNIL). Retrieved from https://www.polytechnique-insights.com/en/columns/society/is-it-possible-to-regulate-ai

Fernhout, F. (2024). The EU Artificial Intelligence Act: Our 16 key takeaways. Stibbe. Retrieved from https://www.stibbe.com/publications-and-insights/the-eu-artificial-intelligence-act-our-16-key-takeaways

Hacker, P. (2024). Comments on the Final Trilogue Version of the AI Act. European New School. Retrieved from https://www.europeannewschool.eu/images/chairs/hacker/Comments%20on%20the%20AI%20Act.pdf

Hickman, T. (2024). Long-awaited EU AI Act becomes law after publication in the EU's Official Journal. White & Case. Retrieved from https://www.whitecase.com/insight-alert/long-aw aited-eu-ai-act-becomes-law-after-publication-eus-official-journal#:~:text=Under%20 the%20EU%20AI%20Act,detect%2C%20prevent%2C%20investigate%2C%20and

Kluge Corrêa, N., & Others. (2023). Worldwide AI ethics: A review of 200 guidelines and recommendations for AI governance. Science Direct. Retrieved from https://www.scien-cedirect.com/science/article/pii/S2666389923002416

MacCarthy, M. (2020). An Examination of the Algorithmic Accountability Act of 2019. Georgetown University. Retrieved from https://papers.ssrn.com/sol3/papers.cfm?abstract_id=3615731

Mahler, T. (2022). Between risk management and proportionality: The risk-based approach in the EU's Artificial Intelligence Act Proposal. SSRN. Retrieved from https://papers.ssrn.com/sol3/papers.cfm?abstract_id=4001444

Sheehan, M. (2024). Tracing the Roots of China's AI Regulations. Carnegie Endowment for International Peace. Retrieved from https://carnegieendowment.org/research/2024/02/tracing-the-roots-of-chinas-ai-regulations?lang=en

9 Merging Artificial Intelligence with the Existing Legal Frameworks

A Comparative Analysis of the EU's AI Act

Sourav Mandal, Sonika Bhardwaj, Rita Ghiyal, and Sandra Jini Saju

9.1 INTRODUCTION

In the last few years, financial services and technology have come together to create substantial changes in India's banking and Non-Banking Financial Companies (NBFCs) sectors. Operations have improved in major areas like customer service and risk management with the help of Artificial Intelligence (AI) (Moharrak & Mogaji, 2024; Singh et al., 2024). Financial institutions are using AI more often because it offers benefits like better efficiency and analytical capabilities, allowing them to simplify services, automate tasks, and evaluate credit risk in competitive markets. Still, adding AI is not easy; it requires manoeuvring through a confusing regulatory environment that lacks clear rules for addressing the unique risks and ethical issues that come with AI (Md. Molla, 2024). The main research problem this chapter will investigate is the legal and regulatory challenges that banks and NBFCs in India face as they begin using AI technologies in a rapidly changing financial market. This study will aim to identify gaps in current regulations and how these gaps impact compliance and risk management. The goals of this research are diverse: to clarify the regulatory atmosphere affecting AI use in finance, examine case studies of institutions that faced compliance issues, and suggest practical steps to improve existing legal frameworks.

By achieving these goals, the research aims to shed light on how regulatory and legal issues can slow down technological progress in finance, which can hinder digital transformation efforts. This section is especially important because it builds the basic understanding needed to tackle the larger implications of using AI in financial services. From an academic standpoint, the findings will add to the ongoing discussions about fintech innovations and provide important insights into the relationship

DOI: 10.1201/9781003541899-9

between technology and regulation, an area that has not been deeply studied or much worked upon. From a practical viewpoint, this research is vital for policymakers, financial institutions, and stakeholders who aim to deal with the challenges of integrating AI while ensuring they follow the rules and manage risks tied to technological advancements in banking (Allen et al., 2021, pp. 259–339; Suryono et al., 2020, pp. 590–590). Therefore, this chapter aims to clarify how to use AI in India's banking sector in a way that is regulated and ethically responsible, working to strike a balance between innovation and governance.

9.2 EVOLUTION OF TECHNOLOGY IN THE FINANCIAL SECTOR

The rise in AI has changed many industries globally, offering new ways to improve efficiency and decision-making. In India's financial services, banks, and NBFCs are starting to use AI technologies to handle operations, evaluate credit risks, personalize customer service, and fight fraud. Yet, using AI in finance comes with regulatory and legal issues. These problems include concerns over data privacy, the clarity of algorithms, and keeping up with changing laws. Such challenges affect not just the institutions but also consumers and the financial system overall. This research is important due to the increasing role of AI in India's financial sector, which is quickly expanding thanks to technology and digitalization. As banks and NBFCs make more use of AI, understanding the regulations surrounding these technologies is vital. Recent literature stresses the need for a regulatory framework that can adapt to the quickly changing AI landscape, which remains unregulated. Experts highlight that while AI offers great possibilities for improving financial services, it might also create systemic risks without proper regulation. Key topics from existing research include data protection and consumer rights, responsibility in AI decision-making, and the need for current regulatory frameworks that keep pace with technological changes. Many studies underline the difficulty regulators have in keeping up with the fast pace of AI development. For example, existing laws often do not address the specific challenges unique to algorithms and machine learning. Authors point out the urgent need for regulators to craft guidelines ensuring transparency and fairness in AI-related decisions, especially in areas like credit scoring and lending. While much academic work has been done on the effects of AI in financial services, there are still significant gaps, particularly concerning practical regulation implementation.

Few studies have focused on how to put AI governance frameworks into action, and there is a strong need to look at specific examples of banks and NBFCs that have successfully handled these issues. Additionally, how local regulations interact with global best practices is usually not examined, leaving a key area of research for how Indian institutions can meet international standards while respecting local differences. This literature review aims to explore the regulatory and legal hurdles that AI poses in Indian banking and finance by summarizing existing research and identifying key areas for future study. By outlining the challenges financial institutions face in adopting AI technologies and the related regulatory issues, this examination hopes to provide a clearer picture of how different stakeholders can work together in this challenging environment. Insights from this review are intended to guide recommendations for policymakers, regulators, and financial institutions as they strive for a balanced approach that encourages innovation while protecting consumer rights and financial stability. The use of AI in India's banking and NBFC sectors has created several regulatory and legal challenges. AI technologies began making headlines in 2017 for improving operational efficiency and customer service. However, this swift adoption revealed deficiencies in existing regulations, as highlighted by Dalsaniya et al. (2025), who point to inadequate policies for the special needs of AI in finance. In response to rising concerns about data privacy and the transparency of algorithms, regulatory bodies like the Reserve Bank of India (RBI) started to develop guidelines specifically for AI use. For example, the RBI published the "Technology Vision for the Financial Sector" in 2019, which advocated for a strong regulatory base while supporting fintech solutions, as noted by Panwar (2024). Due to the lack of necessary resources for quick adoption of new regulatory demands, NBFCs face significant challenges regarding compliance. Recently, during the COVID-19 pandemic, there was a spike in the demand for AI-driven solutions. This prompted India to draft the Data Protection and Digital Privacy Bill, primarily intended to regulate the data used by AI to provide personalized solutions (Moharrak & Mogaji, 2024; Singh et al., 2024). Critics have argued that the bill might hinder innovation through strict compliance measures. In an ever-evolving industry, the pertinent discussion among stakeholders remains the need to balance innovation and creativity with proper regulatory measures while preserving consumer trust. The inclusion of AI in India's banking and NBFC sectors holds great promise for efficiency and innovation but simultaneously creates regulatory and legal challenges. Current regulations were designed with the traditional financial operations in mind, not how these rules would apply to AI-driven methods in the banking sector. For example, the authors Dalsaniya et al. (2025) and Panwar (2024) have observed that the use of AI in determining loan approvals raises concerns about accountability and transparency, particularly when algorithms make automated decisions that impact individual creditworthiness. Moreover, concerns regarding data privacy and security are crucial. AI technology deployment requires substantial amounts of data, complicating adherence to laws such as the Information Technology Act and the Personal Data Protection Bill, which aim to protect consumer information (Moharrak & Mogaji, 2024; Singh et al., 2024). Banks and NBFCs must navigate these challenges to avoid data breaches that could lead to considerable liabilities. While AI applications can improve operations, they must undergo thorough testing and validation to rigorously comply with legal obligations. Therefore, this becomes the very reason of concern for the financial institutions. Lastly, continuous updates in AI systems might make the present laws and guidelines outdated eventually requiring regulations to be proactive rather than reactive. Quantitative studies have frequently focused on empirical data analysis to evaluate how AI impacts regulatory compliance in financial operations. For instance, some studies analysing banking performance data show a direct link between AI use and improved operational efficiency, indicating the need for updated regulations that account for these changes (Dalsaniya et al., 2025).

On the other hand, qualitative methods have stressed the need for a regulatory approach to protect consumer interests, keeping in mind the stakeholders' perspectives while promoting technological progress (Panwar, 2024). This viewpoint is supported by interviews with bank leaders, highlighting concerns over data privacy and the compliance challenges posed by AI (Moharrak & Mogaji, 2024). Also, mixed-method research has effectively combined these viewpoints, using both qualitative and quantitative data to explore how AI affects compliance practices amid regulatory complexities (Singh et al., 2024). These approaches reveal the complex relationship between innovation and regulation. At a surface level, AI may seem to streamline compliance processes, but on a deeper level, it brings new risks that current regulations may not sufficiently address. Additionally, regulatory impact assessments have become the primary tools for examining how AI integration interacts with legal frameworks that can adopt technical changes with flexible regulations without hindering innovation. AI's incorporation in Indian financial institutions highlights a major gap that needs further research and policy adjustments to ensure good governance and effective regulation. Thus, an overall range of research methods has been applied to study the advent of AI in the banking and NBFC sectors in India, raising complex regulatory and legal challenges, and calling for a broad theoretical analysis of organizational behaviour. The present legal and regulatory frameworks in India create significant obstacles for AI adoption, as banks and NBFCs must deal with complicated compliance requirements that often fail to keep up with rapid technological change (Dalsaniya et al., 2025). These frameworks can unintentionally inhibit innovation, as institutions may focus more on following rules instead of integrating AI capabilities. From a technology acceptance standpoint, the perceived risks of AI—like data privacy, security, and potential bias—affect acceptance by both customers and regulators. The apprehension about non-compliance with laws further complicates the AI integration process (Moharrak & Mogaji, 2024; Singh et al., 2024). Accountability for AI-driven decisions is also important, as it presents a dilemma within the existing laws, which are not equipped to handle modern technologies. Hence, critical theory reflects the gaps in regulation and the socio-economic effects of implementing AI, thereby reducing the ability to partake in business with larger companies that can better manage compliance expenses. To collate the understanding so far, these theoretical perspectives together highlight the urgent need for cohesive policies that will bring a balance between innovation and regulation to support the safe and just use of AI in finance. Such alignment will promote a favourable environment for technological growth while safeguarding the interests of all. Integrating AI into the banking and NBFC sectors in India brings a host of complex regulatory and legal challenges thoroughly examined in academic literature. Key findings show that current regulatory frameworks are insufficient for the fast-evolving AI technology. Many studies stress that existing laws were primarily designed for traditional banking functions, revealing considerable gaps in algorithmic transparency, data protection, and compliance. The literature consistently suggests that AI's capability to both transform and disrupt financial services overlaps significantly, and the thin line between the two needs stringent regulations to enhance efficiency and customer experience. The absence of a unified regulatory strategy poses risks that could weaken consumer trust and financial stability. This chapter sheds light on the regulatory and legal challenges faced by banks and NBFCs in India regarding AI integration. The scope of the research includes several issues, such as stakeholder views on compliance challenges, regulatory delays, and the consequences of insufficient consumer protection due to the evolving technology. The findings highlight an immediate need for regulatory bodies to adapt and create more specific guidelines and rules to keep up with AI innovations while ensuring systemic security and consumer rights.

The broader implications of this study extend beyond theoretical discourse. As banks and NBFCs endeavour to adopt AI, the highlighted challenges indicate a strong need for collaboration between financial institutions and regulatory bodies. This collaboration is crucial for developing frameworks that encourage innovation while managing risks. The findings suggest that a proactive regulatory stance, including technological knowledge, can create a more supportive environment for financial institutions to take advantage of AI, leading to better services for consumers. Such alignment can aid in managing AI-related risks and enhancing India's competitiveness in the global financial services arena. However, notable limitations exist within the current literature. A significant gap is the lack of empirical studies examining specific cases of successful regulatory adjustments within India. Furthermore, most research focuses primarily on theoretical and advocacy perspectives, frequently neglecting the quantifiable effects of AI integration on compliance and institutional performance. Future research should aim to conduct empirical studies offering data-driven insights into the practical impacts of AI governance in banks and NBFCs. Analysing specific examples of where regulatory frameworks have effectively aligned with technological advancements would also enrich this discussion. In conclusion, tackling regulatory and legal challenges regarding AI implementation in India's banking and NBFC sectors is crucial for fully realizing the benefits of AI while preserving financial integrity. This literature review lays the groundwork for ongoing exploration and dialogue among academics, practitioners, and regulators as they work collaboratively in this fast-changing environment. The call for adaptable and well-informed regulatory frameworks is vital not only for the sustainability of financial institutions but also for fostering a safe and innovative financial system in India (Table 9.1).

TABLE 9.1
Regulatory Challenges for Banks and NBFCs in India with AI Implementation

Year	Challenge	Description	Impact
2020	Lack of Clear Guidelines	Absence of comprehensive AI regulatory frameworks leads to operational uncertainties.	Increased compliance costs and risk of penalties.
2021	Data Privacy Regulations	Concerns around data collection and processing as per the Personal Data Protection Bill.	Potential fines and reputational damage.
2022	Insufficient AI Competence	Inadequate knowledge and skills within regulatory bodies to oversee AI technologies.	Delayed approvals and implementation of AI solutions.
2023	Ethical and Bias Issues	Challenges in ensuring transparency and fairness in AI algorithms used for credit scoring.	Risk of discrimination and loss of consumer trust.

9.3   AI IMPACTS THE FINANCIAL SECTORS

The implementation of AI in India's banking and NBFC sectors highlights that regulations and related legal issues require more understanding. As financial institutions increasingly use AI, data privacy issues, accountability of algorithms, and unclear regulations lead to tough compliance problems that are not yet addressed by present research (Dalsaniya et al., 2025). This study aims to explore these issues using a mixed-methods approach that incorporates both qualitative and quantitative research methods. The primary research question focuses on identifying the specific regulatory challenges that banks and NBFCs face in using AI technologies, especially regarding compliance while still allowing for innovation (Panwar, 2024). The main objectives are to investigate the current legal frameworks, conduct interviews with key individuals in the financial industry, and assess the impact of regulatory guidelines on AI adoption (Moharrak & Mogaji, 2024). By comparing the details obtained from interviews and survey data, the research will help understand the challenges and opportunities in the space where AI meets regulation in banking (Singh et al., 2024). This solid framework is important for capturing a broad view of the legal landscape, which is needed for both theory development and practical use. This approach has its value not only in guiding policymakers and regulators on the changing role of AI in finance but also in shaping industry practices that support responsible AI use while reducing risks. By positioning the study within recognized methods such as case studies and empirical research, this approach follows established practices in regulatory research (Kumar, 2024). Furthermore, using both qualitative and quantitative methods allows for data triangulation, which helps confirm the findings and fill in gaps found in previous studies (Md. Molla, 2024). Finally, results from this study will contribute to the discussion on changes in regulations by promoting flexible legislation that responds to change, hence ensuring consumer safety and financial stability at the same time (Goto et al., 2019) (Table 9.2).

TABLE 9.2

Regulatory Challenges Faced by Banks and NBFCs in India Regarding AI Implementation

Year	Regulatory Challenge	Impact on Banks	Impact on NBFCs
2020	Lack of clear guidelines on AI usage	Operational inefficiencies and high compliance costs	Limited adoption of AI technologies
2021	Data privacy and protection regulations	Increased scrutiny on customer data usage	Challenges in accessing customer data for AI models
2022	Complying with evolving AI regulations	Need for constant monitoring of regulations	Difficulty in adapting AI strategies to regulatory changes
2023	Ethical concerns about AI decision-making	Increased demand for transparency in AI algorithms	Challenges in addressing biases in AI models

The changing scene of financial services in India shows a complicated situation where banks and NBFCs are extensively using AI to improve operations and engage customers. However, this mix brings up many regulatory and legal challenges that must be addressed to ensure the safe and proper use of AI. Important results of this study reveal that banks and NBFCs face significant issues in handling fuzzy regulations, wherein AI-related technologies are not clearly defined. Three important challenges of unclear rules, dealing with data privacy, accountability of algorithms, and protection of consumers, affect the widespread adaptation of AI in these organizations (Dalsaniya et al., 2025). Many firms are finding it challenging to make their AI practices comply with existing financial regulations, increasing uncertainty and risks (Panwar, 2024). In prior studies, many of these same issues were discussed, where fast-paced tech change often exceeds regulatory systems developed to control such inventions (Moharrak & Mogaji, 2024; Singh et al., 2024). For instance, the IMF pointed out that weak risk assessment and management might put banks and NBFCs at risk of financial instability. The RBI's AI regulations have been mentioned as positive steps in these findings; however, their application varies between financial institutions. The combination of the above results highlights the academic and practical need for developing flexible regulatory approaches, which foster innovation while maintaining consumer trust and financial stability (Kumar, 2024; Md. Molla, 2024). It is important, as it emphasizes that policymakers need to create detailed regulations that allow the integration of AI while protecting against risks. This could help the financial sector in India effectively harness the evolving power of AI (Goto et al., 2019; Singla, 2025). Additionally, these findings add to the current literature by showing how financial institutions can manage the blend of technology and regulation, thus setting the stage for future research in this lively area (Hegde, 2024, pp. 1380–1388; Banerjee, 2024). It is important to work together across fields, with legal experts, tech professionals, and financial regulators, to craft a stronger framework that fits the changing digital environment (Giuliano et al., 2023, pp. 178–210).

As financial institutions start using AI technologies more, it is evident that the rules and laws governing these technologies often do not fit well with the specific problems they create. Research has indicated that AI has made operations more efficient and improved customer interactions. However, compliance with existing rules is still complicated and inconsistent, causing significant difficulties for banks and NBFCs (Dalsaniya et al., 2025). It was observed that concerns over data privacy, algorithm transparency, and consumer protection might hinder the adoption of AI developments by institutions (Panwar, 2024). Previous research also highlighted how the existence of clear regulations is crucial in allowing the use of technology in finance, indicating that without appropriate guidelines, institutions are at risk of operational issues (Moharrak & Mogaji, 2024). Unlike other markets, where rules have changed faster to keep pace with digital advancements, India's regulatory system has been criticized for being slow to change, thus creating a situation that stifles innovation (Singh et al., 2024). This difference has huge theoretical implications, thus compelling a rethinking of traditional regulatory methods and a call for rules that are flexible and forward-looking. In practical terms, this study reiterates how urgently policymakers and industry leaders, combined with tech developers, should work as a team to build a solid regulatory framework that not only reduces low risks

TABLE 9.3

Regulatory Challenges Faced by Banks and NBFCs in India Related to AI

Year	Challenge	Description	Regulatory Body	Impact
2021	Data Privacy and Security	Concerns over data protection laws and the secure handling of customer data.	Reserve Bank of India (RBI)	Prevention of data breaches and fines for non-compliance.
2022	Bias in AI Algorithms	Risks of discrimination and bias in AI decision-making affecting lending.	Ministry of Finance	Legal repercussions and loss of customer trust.
2023	Lack of Clear Guidelines	Uncertainty surrounding AI usage in financial services due to insufficient regulatory frameworks.	Securities and Exchange Board of India (SEBI)	Hindering innovation and implementation of AI solutions in financial services.
2023	Compliance with Existing Regulations	Struggling to comply with traditional regulatory frameworks while adopting AI.	RBI, SEBI	Increased compliance costs and operational challenges.

but is also friendly to innovations. Building on other countries' models of regulatory sandboxes may be a sensible approach to creating a test phase for AI with solutions or fixes for such regulatory issues (Kumar, 2024). In addition, stakeholder engagement that cuts across different sectors will play a significant role in ensuring fair and effective regulation (Md. Molla, 2024). After all, the challenges and insights drawn from this research highlight the need to change regulatory frameworks in favour of a model of flexibility and adaptability in response to the rapidly evolving world of financial technology (Goto et al., 2019). This transformation is critical not only for safely deploying AI but also for protecting the consumer and ensuring that the benefits of AI technologies are available to all (Table 9.3).

9.4 COMPARATIVE ANALYSES OF THE AI REGULATORY FRAMEWORKS

The General Data Protection Regulation, California Consumer Privacy Act, California Data Protection Act, Personal Information Protection and Electronic Documents Act, Financial Industry Regulatory Authority Act, AI Act of the EU, and Digital Personal Data Protection (DPDP) Act of India would primarily serve as sources for the comparison of these nations. This chapter shall further bring forth the differences existing in these laws that may very well be pertinent to bringing about a structured change in the Indian regulatory framework. The General Data Protection Regulation (GDPR) is among the most vivid data protection laws globally. One of the intriguing features of the GDPR is its extraterritorial application, in the sense that it applies not only within the EU but also to any entity processing the personal data of EU citizens, irrespective of the location of such an entity. The DPDP Act, on the other hand, is much narrower legislation that solely concentrates on the processing of data within India but also considers cross-border data transfers in recognition of the growing global data flows. Another area of comparison is personal data categorization. The GDPR provides various categories of personal data; among them is sensitive personal data, which is subject to strict processing conditions. The DPDP Act classifies personal data but provides fundamental concepts that may not be as comprehensive as those under the GDPR. Such differences illustrate the varying levels of detail between the two frameworks. Discussions are also made on legal grounds of data processing. The GDPR categorically provides certain conditions under which data processing shall be carried out; these include consent, legal obligations, and legitimate interests. The DPDP Act provides for some legitimate reasons for the processing of data.

However, the conditions here might be even lighter for businesses that recognize the practical strain these pose in obtaining compliance. Additional grounds for data processing are data-processing legal grounds. The GDPR establishes specific legal conditions for the possibility of processing data: consent, obligations or rights of the controller, and interests. Legal grounds for data processing exist in the DPDP Act, although the conditions may be even more lenient for businesses that acknowledge the practical strain these pose in obtaining compliance. One of the significant findings of the analysis is that while the GDPR provides detailed instructions and comprehensive guidelines, the DPDP Act lays down fundamental concepts that aim to balance the interests of data subjects with the practical challenges faced by businesses. From this observation, it can easily be noted that the GDPR and California's Consumer Privacy Act (CCPA) are substantial statutes aimed at protecting personal data and improving rights to privacy. Even though they were implemented with the same purpose of protecting individual privacy, there are differences in the scope of application, consent requirements, individual rights, enforcement mechanisms, business obligations, and international data transfer regulations between the two.

One of the major differences in the scope of application between GDPR and CCPA is that the CCPA has a much narrower scope than the GDPR, as it only applies to for-profit organizations collecting consumers' personal information, which falls under the purview of the CCPA if they possess, access, or maintain California state residents' personal information. On the other hand, the GDPR applies to all organizations processing personal data concerning a resident of a Member State of the EU. Where an organization is established does not matter. This means that non-EU companies must comply with the GDPR if they handle the personal data of EU residents. In contrast, the CCPA specifically targets California businesses with revenues above certain thresholds or that process a particular amount of personal data. Geopolitically, the geographically limited nature of the CCPA makes it less pervasive, as opposed to the GDPR, which affects larger populations. Another difference lies in the stipulations for obtaining consent embedded in each regulation. This contrasts sharply with the CCPA, which grants consumers the right to know what personal data is being collected about them, the right to delete their data, and the right to non-discrimination for exercising privacy rights. However, the level of rights offered under the CCPA is fewer than those under the GDPR, which downsizes consumer control over data in California.

Enforcement and penalties for non-compliance also vary widely between the two regulations. The GDPR is enforced by independent supervisory authorities in each EU member state, with considerable powers to levy enormous penalties for breaches. Non-compliance with respect to the GDPR can result in fines of up to as much as 4% of an organization's global annual turnover, or €20 million, whichever is higher. Such a strong enforcement mechanism reflects the seriousness with which the EU approaches data protection. In direct contrast, the CCPA is primarily enforced by the California Attorney General. While penalties under the CCPA for non-compliance exist, they are less severe than those in GDPR, and fines are typically not more than $7,500 per violation. This reflects the difference in the intensity of enforcement between these two laws and reveals a difference in the regulatory environments in which they operate. The burden of responsibilities on businesses differs between the GDPR and the CCPA. Under the GDPR, organizations are mandated to conduct data protection impact assessments, appoint data protection officers, and maintain precise records of processing activities in strict observance of the rules on accountability and transparency in data handling practices. While the CCPA imposes some obligations on businesses regarding data practices and rights granted to consumers, it is less comprehensive than the GDPR. This may result in differences in compliance and data protection accountability for organizations complying with these two regulations.

Finally, the requirements differ in how international transfers of data are treated. Since data is exported from the EU, the GDPR states that third countries have obligations to ensure an adequate level of protection for such data. This condition ensures that the data remains safe, irrespective of the countries to which it is being transferred. The CCPA does not have regulations for international data transfers, as this law focuses on consumer rights in California. However, this presents a problem: the CCPA has not placed any precise requirements on cross-border data transfers, which could cause obstacles for global operations of business corporations. A comparative analysis of the Indian DPDP Act, CCPA, and the European GDPR reveals several key differences in their data protection and privacy approaches.

9.5 DRAWBACKS OF EXISTING LAWS

The advancement of technology has indeed revolutionized the face of the financial industry. The numerous opportunities brought along have posed serious challenges to the sector. Among the highest impacts of technology on financial services are efficiency and access. Now, with advancements in online banking, mobile applications, and automated services, managing finances can be done by a customer anywhere.

This shift improves customer service and the operations of the financial institutions by speeding up transactions and lowering the cost of doing business. In this regard, access to financial services is therefore made possible for a much wider audience, and the finance industry has been democratized. Fintech companies have also accelerated innovation in financial products and services. They have brought disruptive technologies such as peer-to-peer lending platforms, robot-advisors, and blockchain technology into the industry, which have disrupted traditional banking models. Innovation has given consumers more choices, and traditional banks are being compelled to change and improve their services to stay ahead of the competition.

The ability to employ technology in the development of products has led to a more liquid financial environment where consumers can leverage tailored financial solutions that address their specific needs. Moreover, where efficiency and innovation have been advanced, so too have developments in managing data as well as analytical techniques that allow financial institutions greater insight into consumer behaviour and preferences. Financial institutions use advanced data analytics tools to offer customized services and effectively tailor their marketing strategies, enhancing customer satisfaction and loyalty (Santhosh, 2023). Based on the data approach, banks can predict what their customers will need and act proactively in advance, which is a critical feature for the current fast-paced financial environment. However, with technology implemented across the financial sector, the chances of data breaches have increased as well. The collection and maintenance of comprehensive, sensitive customer information by financial organizations make them an attractive target for cybercriminals. This can result in monetary loss, reputational damage, and legal consequences for banking organizations. The impact of such data breaches is not limited to short-term fiscal consequences; the aftermath may lead to a long-term erosion of trust with customers. People will not want to interact with financial organizations if they feel their private information is at risk. Advancement in technology is happening too fast, leaving old regulatory structures behind. This is yet another challenge financial corporations face. Financial companies have had to endure numerous challenges to ensure cybersecurity. The operating cost is generally higher compared to other expenses and requires constant updates to their security measures.

This added regulatory burden may be particularly difficult for smaller financial institutions, which do not have the capability and resources to build robust cybersecurity infrastructures. Trust among consumers is another critical issue born out of the challenges created by technological progress. The potential risk of data breaches can damage consumer confidence in financial institutions. These entities, therefore, have more reasons to take additional measures to strengthen their cybersecurity. Banks and other financial establishments must rebuild and maintain customer confidence because the ability to attract and retain customers depends on how well their confidence is handled in the digital environment. This is one of the significant negative impacts of technological advancement: it has exposed financial institutions to cyberattacks.

Through this integration, online banking and mobile applications have greatly elevated the possibility for customers to access their accounts from anywhere in the world to execute a transaction. However, there are significant disadvantages to the same. Cyberbullies, thieves, and stalkers are continuously innovating in their lines of attack to leverage these weaknesses in the given systems. Since financial institutions collect and retain enormous amounts of sensitive data, including personal identity details, account numbers, and transaction histories, they constitute high-value targets for breaches in the cyber world. The effects of a breach may be nothing short of disastrous: monetary loss, legal exposure, and even irreparable damage to the good name of a bank. Technical progress, in addition, tends to be much faster than the pace at which a financial institution can implement adequate security measures. This is open warfare in a new way with technologies like AI and machine learning because the same tools, while exploited by cybercriminals to develop novel and quirky attacks, can also be applied by financial institutions to upgrade their security simultaneously. This continuous battle creates an unyielding environment for financial institutions to continually invest in security strategies to protect their systems and customer information.

The regulatory environment for data security is also changing, but often at a pace much slower than the rapid technological upgradation. Financial institutions must comply with a wide range of regulations meant to protect consumer data, including the GDPR in Europe and the CCPA in the United States. However, rapid technological progress makes it difficult for regulators to keep up, hindering their ability to inspect and enforce. This regulatory response lag may leave financial institutions vulnerable to data breaches since they are not entirely aligned with the latest security standards. In addition to the direct financial costs associated with a data breach, there are also significant indirect costs. Customers could become wary of all financial organizations, leading to an overall decline in the sector's trust level. Therefore, such a lack of trust may block innovation, as customers may fear using innovative technology and services that require exposing personal information. The Information Technology Act, Banking Regulation Act, and Payment and Settlement Act demonstrate various weaknesses in addressing data piracy and breaches within the banking sector even though these acts contain provisions that safeguard consumer data. Liability in cases of data breaches is given to the corporation under Section 43A of the IT Act, but the penalties imposed are abysmally low. Section 72A offers protection for personal data; however, it is limited in applicability and lacks clear guidelines. Consequently, measures to protect data and privacy are insufficient. The Act also lacks clarity on data localization and international data transfer. The Banking Regulation Act, Section 26A, mandates banks to maintain confidentiality but does not require data breach notification or customer compensation. Under Section 35A, the RBI has the right to issue guidelines on banking operations but does not address contemporary cyber threats and data safeguards.

Such data breaches have not only short-term fiscal consequences but also lead to an erosion of customer trust in the long term after the incident has occurred. There is no other reason people might not want to interact with financial organizations in case they get the feeling that their private information is not safe and secured. Developments in technology move too fast compared to the remaining old regulatory structures. Financial corporations face this problem again. Financial companies have endured many regulations meant to protect consumer data or ensure cybersecurity, often operating with the highest expenses compared to other expenses and requiring constant changes in their security measures.

This added regulatory burden might particularly be challenging for smaller financial institutions, which lack the capability and resources to build robust cybersecurity infrastructures. Trust among consumers is another significant issue born out of the challenges created by technological progress. The potential risk of data breaches can damage consumer confidence in financial institutions.

The lacunas common to all these acts are a lack of emphasis on data protection and privacy, penalties that are insufficient for data breaches and non-compliance, and unclear guidelines for data localization, cross-border data transfer, and data breach notification. Their archaic provisions do not tackle the newest forms of cyber threats and technologies, exposing the banking sector to data piracy and breaches. Therefore, there is a requirement for comprehensive amendments to the existing legislation to address these gaps and ensure robust data protection and security in the banking sector.

9.6   FINDINGS FROM THE SURVEY

A structured questionnaire was employed to conduct a study to understand awareness of the use of AI in the finance sector. The questionnaire was answered by 200 respondents out, of whom 84 were students from diverse backgrounds, 52 were research scholars in the field of law and finance, 40 were working professionals in the field of law and banking, and 24 were legal academicians, as outlined in Figure 9.1.

Upon analysing the data from the 200 respondents, it was observed that 136 respondents had faced payment-related issues and had immediately approached

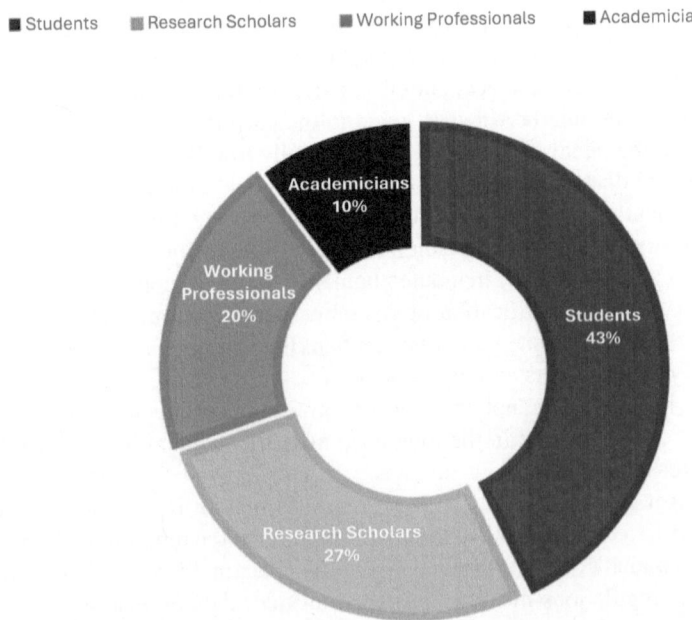

FIGURE 9.1   List of respondents who responded to the questionnaire.

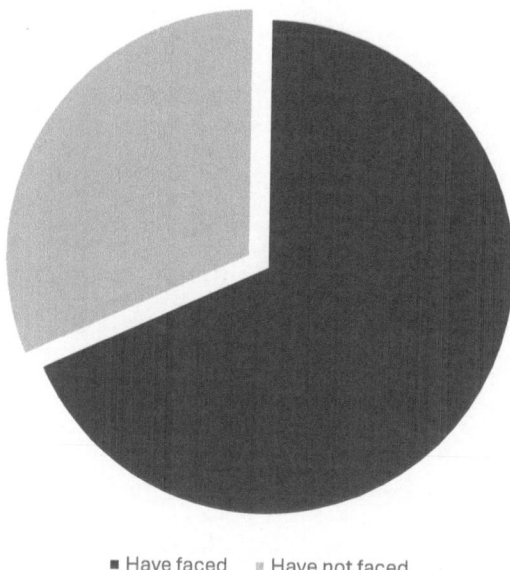

■ Have faced   ■ Have not faced

FIGURE 9.2   Respondents who have faced payment issues while using the financial applications and sought help from the integrated chatbots, and whether resolutions provided by the chatbots were of any help.

chatbots to seek resolution for the transaction issue, while 64 respondents had not faced such issues while using digital payments. From this data, the authors understand that transactional issues do occur, but most of them do not receive immediate resolution, as banks do not have a robust regulatory framework to mitigate these issues (Figure 9.2).

The sample was asked whether they were at least aware of the laws that could protect them in case there was a data leak. All the respondents replied that they were aware, and in fact, 75% of them specifically mentioned Section 43A of the Information Technology Act (Figure 9.3).

Around 50 of the respondents believe that the new DPDP Act would be able to better safeguard consumers from data leakage in banks. However, it was pretty surprising to find that around six respondents, when a follow-up question was asked to understand whether they were aware of how banks store their personal data to provide lucrative offers, were in fact surprised to learn that not only do banks store their data, but they also sell it (Figures 9.4–9.6).

It can be observed from the responses that a selected few respondents want other financial institutions to have their data so that they can receive more lucrative offers. Thereafter, the respondents were asked if they knew how to seek redressal in case of data leaks. To sum up, it can be observed that people are aware of how to seek redressal and are also aware that their data is being stored, but at the same time, the common issue they opined was that no matter where they approach the amount of moncy as well as time, they have to spend to receive a resolution is much more than

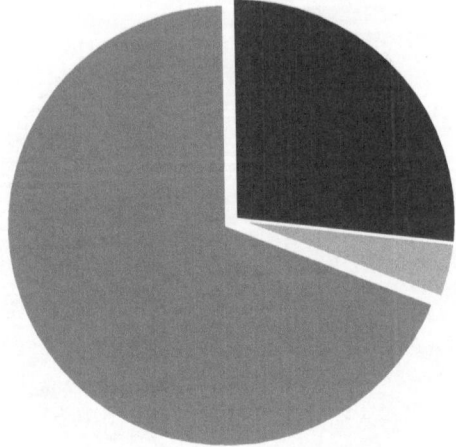

■ Information Technology is sufficient   ■ Amendment to IT Act+ DPDP Act   ■ Not aware of applicable laws

FIGURE 9.3 The awareness of the law that regulates privacy concerns arising from the use of AI in finance and banking.

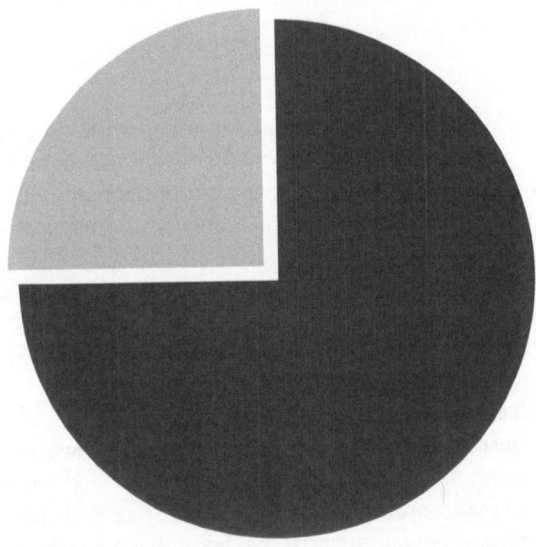

■ Knowlegde of DPDP Act   ■ Only IT Act can provide remedy

FIGURE 9.4 Pie chart showing whether the respondents were aware that banks, fintechs, and e-commerce websites have integrated AI into their respective platforms to provide a seamless experience for consumers, which in turn requires a large amount of user data to be stored which could lead to data theft or data leaks and whether they were aware of the laws under which they could seek remedy.

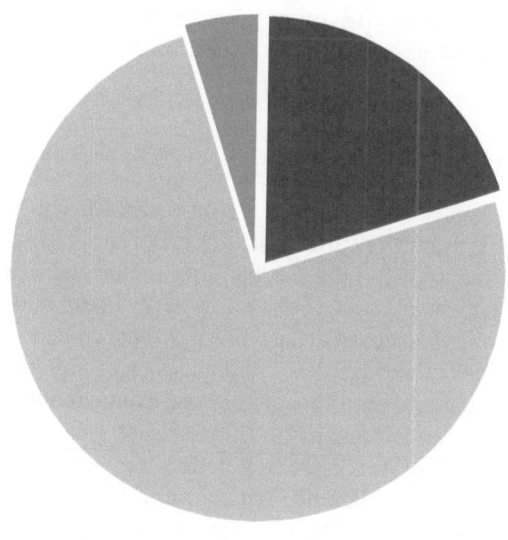

■ Aware of Data Storage   ■ Not aware of data storage   ■ Want more offers from bank

FIGURE 9.5   Pie chart that shows whether the respondents wanted their data to be stored by banks/financial institutions for further offers.

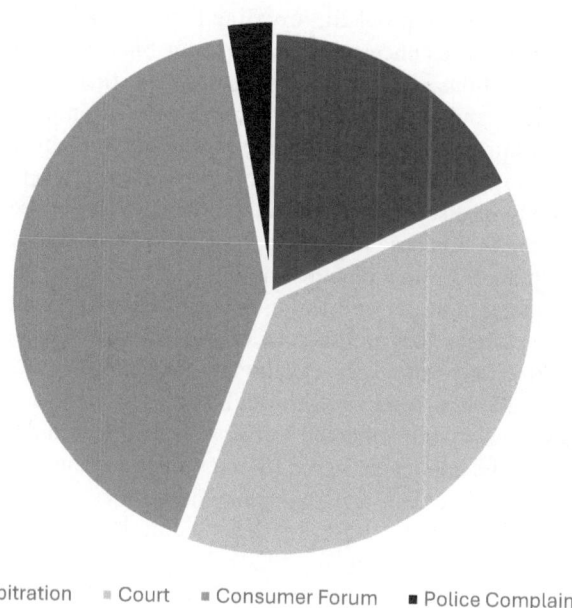

■ Arbitration   ■ Court   ■ Consumer Forum   ■ Police Complaint

FIGURE 9.6   Pie chart showing which platform would be the feasible redressal mechanism for identity theft or data breach.

the amount in dispute. Hence, the study proposes that a stricter regulatory framework must be introduced to curtail these issues; otherwise, such cases will remain undocumented.

9.7 CONCLUSION

In conclusion, this chapter aims to foster a secure and efficient financial ecosystem with strict regulatory framework like that of the European Union. The integration of AI technologies has transformed the banking sector and enhanced operational efficiency, risk management, and customer service while introducing significant challenges related to cybersecurity, data privacy, and ethical considerations. The DPDP Act of India seeks to bridge these challenges by establishing a comprehensive structure for data protection, even though it is still compared with more established regulations that exist in the EU and in the United States—namely, the GDPR and the Algorithmic Accountability Act. These regulations provide a significant framework to uphold transparency, accountability, and consumer rights in AI applications. The AI-based assessment of creditworthiness is at once a representation of the best that such technology can do and an exemplar of the worst it can do. Improving credit appraisals, and access thereto, with AI-based assessment means there is plenty of cause for concern. This includes the complex regulatory and legal issues involved in using AI technologies with banks and NBFCs in India. An exhaustive analysis has found that problems in data privacy, algorithmic bias, and fitting regulatory frameworks have hindered the effective use of AI in the financial sector. This study carefully addresses the research problem, revealing how the lack of flexible regulations and clear guidelines causes uncertainty and risk for financial entities when they try to implement AI solutions. Therefore, it becomes clear that regulatory changes are needed to encourage and stimulate innovation in an environment that, at the same time, protects consumers and ensures financial stability, thereby guiding the future. Two outcomes emerge from this research: on the academic level, they complement the increasing body of discourse regarding the connection between technology and regulation, pointing in this case to significant gaps in the literature that concern the effects of AI in finance. From a practical point of view, results can assist policymakers, financial organizations, as well as regulatory bodies to review and reform their ways and design policies that embrace technological advancements while remaining well within the norms of ethics and the law (Dalsaniya et al., 2025). Moreover, the suggestions made hint towards empirical studies so that one could understand the implications of newly implemented frameworks and search for international best practices that could be applicable in the Indian scenario (Panwar, 2024). Interaction between industry stakeholders and regulatory authorities on the long-term results of AI adoption in the banking sector, becomes increasingly significant as the financial landscape changes (Singh et al., 2024). In conclusion, the need for ongoing research, especially regarding the long-term results of AI adoption in the banking sector, becomes increasingly significant as the financial landscape changes (Singh et al., 2024). In conclusion, this chapter puts forward the urgent need for adaptive and future-looking regulations that will help banks and NBFCs address the challenges associated with AI adoption while protecting the interests of consumers and ensuring financial integrity in the evolving financial system of India.

REFERENCES

Allen F, Gu X, Jagtiani J. (2021). A survey of fintech research and policy discussion. *Review of Corporate Finance*, 1, 259–339. https://doi.org/10.1561/114.00000007

Banerjee S. (2024). The advent of virtual digital assets: Analysing its status in the fintech sector. *International Journal for Multidisciplinary Research*, 6, 1. https://doi.org/10.36948/ijfmr.2024.v06i02.14881

Dalsaniya A, Patel K, Swaminarayan PR. (2025). Challenges and opportunities: Implementing RPA and AI in fraud detection in the banking sector. *World Journal of Advanced Research and Reviews*, 25, 296–308. https://www.semanticscholar.org/paper/32a79685f ec4fb14c1c474ad99418e7c397c3551

Giuliano GC, Ēriks KS, Arner DW. (2023). *The Emergence of Financial Data Governance and the Challenge of Financial Data Sovereignty*. Oxford University Press, Oxford, pp. 178–210. https://doi.org/10.1093/oso/9780197582794.003.0009

Goto SP, et al. (2019). Management and 1-year outcomes of patients with newly diagnosed atrial fibrillation and chronic kidney disease: Results from the prospective GARFIELD-AF registry. *Journal of the American Heart Association: Cardiovascular and Cerebrovascular Disease*, 8, e010510. https://www.semanticscholar.org/paper/d13e4a8bbada3267a4f5278f3859f0d14e2e3952

Hegde SR. (2024). A study on the fintech penetration in rural Karnataka. *International Journal for Research in Applied Science and Engineering Technology*, 12, 1380–1388. https://doi.org/10.22214/ijraset.2024.60020

History of the Basel Committee. (2014). https://www.bis.org/bcbs/history.htm

Kumar PM. (2024). A study on accelerating digital financial inclusion for positioning India through AI-enabled banking services. *International Journal for Multidisciplinary Research*, 6, 4. https://www.semanticscholar.org/paper/a486f5df583c9486939fda2419888d1e1c88b76d

Md. Molla M. (2024). Barriers to AI integration in banks in Bangladesh. *International Journal of Science and Business*, 40, 1–18. https://www.semanticscholar.org/paper/5bcfeb8564d 53275b4df00d5ed265d3615854d8f

Moharrak M, Mogaji E. (2024). Generative AI in banking: Empirical insights on integration, challenges, and opportunities in a regulated industry. *International Journal of Bank Marketing*, 43, 871–896. https://www.semanticscholar.org/paper/d2ffdc789498d3a9716d82d907cd40de7d98b721

Panwar P. (2024). Challenges and opportunities of AI in banking sector. *International Journal of Scientific Research in Engineering and Management*, 8, 1–5. https://www.semanticscholar.org/paper/8744fc592afb67ba53a86dbbb8a31b934c554cbf

Santhosh, A. (2023). Current situation and challenges in Indian banking sector. *International Journal for Research in Applied Science and Engineering Technology*, 11(5), 3360–3363. https://doi.org/10.22214/ijraset.2023.52326.

Singh SK, Parida JK, Shekhar S. (2024). The landscape of AI in Indian banking sector: A theoretical perspective. *Journal of Informatics Education and Research*, 4, 1. https://www.semanticscholar.org/paper/c0e54194183f41aaeeadbeafb7c08e811425b041

Singla S. (2025). A study on scale base approach of RBI on NBFCs Banking in India. *Journal of Informatics Education and Research*, 5, 1960. https://doi.org/10.52783/jier.v5i1.1960

10 Public Procurement and Artificial Intelligence: The Case of Albania

Jonaid Myzyri and Valbona Ndrepepaj

10.1 INTRODUCTION

Albania has chosen to revolutionize public procurement law by introducing a new artificial intelligence (AI) system to manage and monitor public procurement procedures. This pioneering move, which sets Albania apart from many other European countries, presents a fascinating case for research into the use of AI technologies in public procurement.

This chapter deals with these legal changes by aiming to explore the system in both technical and legal terms. On the technical side, the type and level of AI technology used have been identified. On the legal side, several issues known from the relevant literature have been analyzed, such as the legal status of AI as a subject or object of the law, and the legal guarantees needed to avoid risks arising from the use of AI in this field—particularly regarding the protection of human rights, public safety, and accountability.

To carry out this exploration of Albania's new public procurement system, which relies on AI technologies, we used legal research methods involving the collection, processing, and analysis of documentation/data, as well as interpretation. Initially, we analyzed the new public procurement system, including legal, economic, and integrity risks. Secondly, we addressed some concerns, such as guaranteeing the legal protection of economic operators against decisions on the announcement of the winner made by AI.

Additionally, to identify this new system's legal and administrative features, we considered four indicators: the implementation context, the process phase in which the AI application is deployed, the impact of AI on the final decision, and the role of humans in reviewing that decision-making (Diaz, 2023).

10.2 LITERATURE REVIEW

Today, we are in a new wave of AI, as every country, big or small, invests considerable resources in its development to modernize public administration. AI refers to an intelligent technological machine that simulates human thinking and behavior. In essence, AI involves training an artificial brain to imitate the functions of the human brain. It entails collecting, processing, interacting with, and reading data from a machine to extract information. AI, as the simulation of human intelligence

DOI: 10.1201/9781003541899-10

through technology, was initially used to replicate cognitive abilities associated with the human mind and its actions, namely problem-solving and learning.

However, we must understand that AI technologies can produce excellent results in complex tasks. These technologies use computational mechanisms that do not resemble the human mind but imitate it. They cannot match higher-level human abilities such as reasoning, conceptual understanding, flexible comprehension, or other functions closely related to human intelligence (Krupansky, 2017). Currently, we have two types of AI: machine learning (ML) and logical rules with knowledge representation.

There are different discussions in the literature regarding AI. For example, Weizenhaum argues that computers should not make legal decisions, much less judicial ones, since such decisions cannot be supported by any model learned from rules extracted from continuous data (Weizenhaum, 1976). Berman and Hafner believe there is strong potential for use if such an "expert" system functions as an algorithmic tool to organize and present the facts of a relevant issue in support of human decision-makers. At the same time, the issue of the status and role of AI is directly related to the lack of AI regulation at the international level. In this regard, we agree with the opinion of many researchers on the need to improve the legal regulation of AI.

So, using AI in public procurement is a promising and relatively new phenomenon (Broadhurst, Brown, Maxim, Trivedi, & Wang, 2019). In this field, AI uses technologies that apply algorithms to extensive data sets (Khuan & Swee, 2018) or other types of software to enhance the daily work of public procurement agencies and review bodies. The potential benefits are significant, from improved decision-making processes to more efficient contract management (Yu, Liu, Yang, & Lan, 2020). Through the analysis of procurement data, a decision can be made on the definition of technical specifications (Broadhurst, Brown, Maxim, Trivedi, & Wang, 2019), supplier sourcing, request for quotation, purchase order issues, payment, and contract management, revealing the time and place of committing a future criminal act in procurement, especially at the stage of publication of the notice, such as corruption or fraud (red flags) (Modrušan & Rabuzin, 2019). Through the use of this data—which should be numerous in quantity and quality—collected by public procurement bodies such as the Public Procurement Commission of Albania, various AI technologies can be used to build models that predict the behavior of procurement actors or to create expert system in this field, such as e-procurement, e-advertising, e-invoicing, e-payment, e-complaints, etc. This leads to what Bartolini calls cognitive procurement, which is the application of cognitive computer systems by combining several technologies, such as neural networks and ML, to collect, process, and analyze large amounts of data to make quick, transparent, and efficient decisions in public procurement. It is easy to understand that AI, as the simulation of human intelligence in machines programmed to think and act like humans (Agarwal, Sharma, Sharma, Uniyal, & Yadav, 2013), can also play a vital role in this area of law.

But the literature also shows the risks of using AI in public procurement, such as violations of privacy, security, the environment, social justice, and human rights. Some authors, such as Jobin, Ienca, and Vayena, also discuss other risks, such as unemployment (Awuorc & Nagittaa, 2022), misuse, loss of human responsibility, and lack of impartiality. For this, Scheltema emphasizes that AI developers must eliminate these unnecessary risks and avoid violating human rights. Therefore, for the successful use of AI in procurement, two conditions are required:

1. Deep knowledge of the operation and principles of human-centered AI (HCAI).
2. Better interaction between AI developers and the public procurer.

Indeed, a study conducted with some public procurers revealed that they recognize the importance of using AI in principle. Still, they are concerned about the lack of legal regulation of AI, the lack of skills and knowledge in AI, and communication within AI-based public procurement teams, including procurement leaders, AI professionals, and economic operators.

The literature also suggests that the state must first take care of the well-being of its citizens—meeting their needs, security, privacy, and rights—so the use of AI in the proper functioning of a state system or public procurement system should first consider that. Secondly, the effectiveness depends on the context: the stage of public procurement in which AI is used, the role of AI in making the final decision, and the role of humans in that decision (Diaz, 2023).

On the other hand, the literature emphasizes that the impact of the use of AI will be the creation of a new profile of public procurer, and this will result in abundant information, increased productivity, cost reduction and savings, a more efficient system of risk management, changes in the behavior of the parties, improved quality, and enhanced safety (Simionescu, 2016). However, for this impact to materialize, public procurement must be seen as a social system rather than a technical one. Likewise, the challenges of this type of system should also be recognized, such as the lack of enabling data ecosystems, inadequate availability of AI expertise, workforce, and skilling opportunities, high resource costs, limited awareness for adopting AI in business processes, and unclear privacy, security, and ethical regulations (Jain, 2023).

Today, AI, in many countries around the world, is part of daily public procurement operations. For this reason, the European Parliament, after several efforts, has approved a regulatory framework for AI (Articles 33, 40, 41, and 42). The relevant EU structures should evaluate and promote the use of best practices in public procurement procedures, including AI technologies (Article 62).

E-procurement and AI are among the most important recent technological advances. If properly implemented—with a sound reform agenda, recognition of the country's context, and a legislative and regulatory framework—they can create a transparent, efficient system, etc. (Gadour, 2024). This emphasis on the importance of a sound reform agenda should make the audience feel optimistic about the future of public procurement.

In conclusion, we can say that by respecting ethics and human rights, and by increasing the sensitivity of AI developers to privacy, accountability, security, transparency, justice and non-discrimination, human control of technology, professional responsibility, and the promotion of human values, there are great possibilities for the use of AI in public procurement (Shneiderman, 2020) and its sustainable development (Dimitri & Naudé, 2021).

10.3 SIMILAR INTERNATIONAL PROJECTS IMPLEMENTING AI IN THE FIELD OF PUBLIC PROCUREMENT

Before starting the reform in the field of public procurement in Albania, the government of Albania studied similar international cases in this field to understand how this reform would impact the future of public procurement in Albania. There were 104 cases studied from all over the world, but 21 of them involved elements of AI, ML, blockchain, 3D printing, drones, and Robotic Process Automation (RPA) in procurement.

The project *Buy Smarter* in the USA was an attempt to use AI and ML in the field of procurement.

Department of Purchases and Strategic Support of the City Council of El Pasos (PSS) in the USA has undertaken a project focusing on AI and ML to improve communication and service to potential sellers. The project was realized through the integration of a chatbot solution called "Ask Laura" on their website.

ProZorro in Ukraine has implemented reforms in the procurement system, introducing electronic procurement through a platform called ProZorro. Beyond the digitization of the procurement process and the introduction of the electronic auction as the default tender type for all major procurements in all government entities, ProZorro and the legislative reform based on it introduced much greater transparency by adopting the Open Contract Data Standard (OCDS) as a publication standard and ensuring that information was available for small procurements (below the threshold), which had previously been unrecorded.

Procurement of New South Wales (NSW) in Australia has faced a major challenge: manually categorizing 2 million procurement transactions each quarter according to the NSW Government Procurement Taxonomy. This task required a lot of time and human resources. To address this challenge, the organization developed an AI tool called "CAITY," which automates the categorization of this data. The solution was developed using Python-based AI tools, provided on Microsoft Azure.

YPO (Your Procurement Organization) is an organization that provides framework contracts to its clients, who are public sector purchasers in the United Kingdom. Although it offers framework contracts, YPO clients have had trouble navigating the organization's website and identifying framework contracts that match their needs. To address this issue, YPO has integrated a chatbot solution on their website called the Procurement Information Provider (PIP). This chatbot can interpret users' written questions and direct them to the relevant parts of the YPO website, making it easier for customers to find and identify the framework contracts that interest them.

Hansel Oy, an organization in Finland, has aimed to improve the transparency of state spending by uploading e-invoicing data from the state's e-invoicing system to an open data portal called Explore State Expenditure. However, one challenge was that e-invoicing data was not categorized according to any procurement taxonomy, making it difficult to search and analyze. To address this problem, Hansel Oy piloted a ML solution that would categorize billing data according to the United Nations Standard Product and Service Code (UNSPSC). This solution was developed using tools from Azure ML. It integrated with the organization's Business Intelligence software, allowing users to manually classify data to train the algorithm.

Korean Public Procurement Service (PPS) provides an annual forecast of demand for goods by government bodies in South Korea. To do this, they use data from the Product Management System to analyze previous purchases in the public administration. However, this forecast has been inaccurate in recent years, causing unnecessary expense to the government. To improve this situation, Public Procurement Service (PPS) has implemented a pilot project. In this project, they used a deep learning (AI) solution to predict the government's annual demand for products. This AI solution was developed with the help of an external IT consultancy and uses data from the Product Management System. Data analysis was based on product purchases, changes in product use, and purchase plans by government agencies.

The Federal Ministry of Economy in Brazil has implemented a project to improve the price research process before the start of procurement procedures. Brazilian law requires price research to be carried out as a preparatory task before starting a procurement procedure. The traditional method, which involved getting cost estimates from three different suppliers, was time-consuming and inflated the estimated prices. To improve this process, the Ministry of Economy developed a price panel that provided visibility on historical prices paid. Users of this dashboard could search and filter data by many criteria, including material name, commodity code, and services and material description. The price panel is based on a Business Intelligence application, which was developed using Qlik Sense. This application allows data to be cross-referenced and standardized from several different sources, including the Integrated Management System of General Services (SIASG) and the public procurement market.

The Department of Mobility and Public Works in Belgium needed a tool that would provide visibility and the ability to analyze historical prices of goods and services. To address this shortcoming, they developed the MEDIAAN platform, which provides a searchable database of historical prices, along with a variety of applications for engineering and cost analysis. The primary source of data for MEDIAAN is the department's eDelta contract management system, with data on contracts dating back to 2001. This database is supplemented with data from other sources. The data is stored in an Oracle database, while the interface and other applications are built in Oracle Application Express. The platform includes a price review application, semi-automatic price estimation, and calculation of unit and hourly rates. The MEDIAAN development project started in 2009 and was formalized in 2013.

The Ministry of Public Administration in Slovenia has developed a data storage and business intelligence system, which will be offered as a horizontal service in the Government Cloud by 2022. This platform aims to promote data-driven decision-making in public administration and improve transparency in public procurement.

Open Contract Data Standard (OCDS) in Belarus, to address problems with the analysis and use of public procurement data, a solution was developed that includes the standardization of data from existing public procurement platforms and the creation of a single database. This platform is called the "Open Contract Data Standard (OCDS)" and was supported by the EBRD.

The city of Bilbao in Spain has launched a tender to find a company that would develop a digital platform based on blockchain technology for use in public services. The goal of this project is to facilitate the exchange of data between public institutions using blockchain technology and smart contracts.

Yeongdeungpo-gu, Council Office in South Korea, has developed a digital tendering platform coupled with a blockchain system. This project was created to improve the transparency and reliability of the tendering process for public contracts.

The Ministry of Internal Affairs and Communications in Japan has developed a project aimed at evaluating the use of blockchain technology to improve the security and auditability of public procurement processes, as well as to increase the availability and reuse of data.

IT agency Digipolis in Antwerp, Belgium, has developed an application based on blockchain technology in collaboration with their partner, BallistiX, to allow the publication and presentation of quotation requests in public procurement processes. The use of blockchain technology aims to ensure reliability at every stage of the procurement process, as its data will be recorded in a transparent manner.

The Department of Health and Human Services (HHS) in the USA has developed a project called "HHS Accelerate" to improve procurement processes and contract management through the use of blockchain technology.

The US General Services Administration (GSA), through the Federal Acquisition Service (FAS), provides procurement services to public organizations in the USA. They conclude central contracts, which allow public organizations to purchase a wide range of products and services. Vendors apply for hourly contracts, and the information they submit is extensive and must be processed manually.

The project *Consip* in Italy aims to better understand what is happening on the Consip platform and catalog. It observes user behavior and uses these observations to make recommendations for training, improvements to the catalog, proposals for new ways to interact, and to identify collusion, etc.

With *KONEPS* in South Korea, there has been a significant improvement in the transparency of public procurement administration since the early 2000s through the implementation of a national e-procurement system.

Deutsche project Bahn for 3D printing in Germany started as an effort to tackle challenges related to waiting times, spare part replacement, and price negotiations. This innovation was initiated in October 2015. Starting without a complete infrastructure and sufficient knowledge, they created the Mobility goes Additive network in September 2016, which aimed to bring together all aspects of the value of 3D printing and accelerate collaboration in this field.

E-procurement systems, excluding the ProZorro system built in Ukraine, were mainly developed during the years 2002–2004, as well as in 2017 and the years following. This study examined more than 104 cases of projects implementing AI, ML, robotic processes, drone technology, and 3D printing.

However, the Albanian project is more ambitious than all other projects implemented so far, as it includes several elements with advanced technology. Additionally, there is the possibility for the system to interact with the Air Albania 1 and 2 satellites in relation to projects in the field of infrastructure.

10.4   PUBLIC PROCUREMENT AND ARTIFICIAL INTELLIGENCE: THE CASE OF ALBANIA

Albania, a pioneer in the field, implemented the electronic procurement system in 2009. While not a fully electronic procurement system, this system allows economic operators to electronically submit documents and offers in procurement procedures and receive appropriate evaluations from contracting authorities. The approval of three laws on public procurement—from the fall of the communist regime until today—and over 15 amendments to these laws culminated in the approval of Law No. 16/2024. This law amended 54 articles of the current public procurement law, Law No. 162/2020 "On public procurement," as amended.

The amendments to the law provide for the creation of a standardized electronic system of public procurement, which will be used to carry out public procurement procedures, concessions, public-private partnerships, procurements in the field of defense and security, and public auctions, according to the provisions in this law and in other special laws, which interacts with other systems (Law No. 162/2020 "On public procurement," as amended, Article 4). This fact makes the Albanian case even more interesting, as it aims to establish a complex system that digitizes all public procedures for obtaining goods, works, and services. With a closed cycle on an electronic platform, this system aims to assist economic operators and contracting authorities at all stages of the public procurement procedure.

The development of the new system will highlight the need for interaction with many other systems. According to public information available as of September 2024, published on the official website of the National Agency for Society Information (hereinafter NAIS), there are 1,245 electronic services offered on the E-Albania portal and 63 state electronic systems that interact with the Government Interaction Platform. In other words, this gives Albania a technological advantage in quickly implementing the new public procurement system. Additionally, this results in AI operating within a closed circuit (closed AI). Ultimately, the ML process will be carried out within a closed data circuit, ensuring the quality and security of the data.

The public procurement system in Albania can be built based on AI technology in three phases:

1. The preparatory phase of public procurement procedures
   a. Drafting of technical specifications
   b. Calculation of procurement value (limit fund)
   c. Preparation of tender documents
2. The phase of development of public procurement procedures
   a. Submission of offers
   b. Evaluation of offers
   c. Submission and review of complaints
3. Monitoring and management of public contracts
   a. The risks of the AI system

The development of such a complex system certainly presents several risks, three of which are essential:

1. The risk of data integrity and security
2. The risk of interference by third-party systems with the electronic procurement system
3. The risk during the system's learning process.

As for the security risk and data integrity, this is the first risk when digital systems are implemented. Albania has over 63 systems that interact within a governmental platform of interaction, and these systems have been subjected to a strict process of registering their databases as national databases. A special law regulates the basis of state data in Albania. Therefore, the security and integrity of these systems are guaranteed. The connection of these systems with the new electronic procurement system may present risks that, if not appropriately managed, could compromise the integrity and security of the data. One way to mitigate this risk is by implementing blockchain technology, which increases the system's security level to the highest standards applied today. Although this technology is expensive, it is crucial for the success of this complex system.

Another risk in the process of operating the system and applying AI is the use of third-party systems with the public procurement system. As explained above, the primary data source that the system will process comes from third-party systems, so we have an AI based on closed data. Thus, the success or failure of these systems will also depend on the quality of the data received from the third-party systems, the level at which they are ready to communicate with the new public procurement system and their interaction.

As sensitive as the security of the data is, so is the process of ML and system training by the appropriate experts—the individuals whose life decisions are supported by the public procurement law. This is also a critical moment. Of course, the system must be built with more advanced technology, and the machine will be included in the self-learning and error correction process. Still, the foundation is the proper learning of the machine, and here is the only human element that can be set. The essence of these phases is the involvement of procurement experts at both the national and international levels, as well as researchers and developers of AI programs. Their involvement will mitigate risks and ensure the system's efficiency and effectiveness, leading to a successful implementation of the electronic procurement system.

10.4.1 Legal Protection of Economic Operators against AI Decision-Making

The debate on protecting subjects' rights subject to judgment by AI is not a debate that has only arisen in Albania. As we analyzed above, it is worth underlining the nature of AI decision-making concerning public procurement law, which can be grouped into two main categories. In the first group, the suggestive decision-making of AI takes part. This decision-making has a broad scope in public procurement law, such as in the case of drafting technical specifications, estimating the limit fund, drafting tender documents, and during contract monitoring and management. In these models, we have joint decision-making.

In the second group, the final decision-making of AI is included, especially in the process of evaluating offers. In one of these phases, AI plays a vital role in decision-making for an economic operator's final qualification or disqualification. In this way, AI is given the full role of the evaluation committee, in the case of automatic evaluation in the dynamic purchasing system, and in the procurement official's involvement in other procedures based on Article 82, point 9 of the Law on Public Procurement, where, for local economic operators, the electronic procurement system automatically verifies, through interaction with other systems, the fulfillment of mandatory disqualification conditions and specific qualification criteria, to the extent applicable.

Even though the legislator has provided for a significant role of AI in the administrative review system, the public procurement law remains unchanged in its approach to final administrative control of decision-making in public procurement procedures, as the right to appeal continues to be enshrined in law.

Article 109 of the law provides that: "any economic operator who has or had a legal interest in a procurement procedure according to the PP law and when he is damaged or is at risk of being damaged by the actions or inactions of the contracting authority or entity, for which he claims that they violate the law, has the right to complain to the contracting authority or entity and the PPC."

So, the active legitimacy of putting the procurement review body under review is based on the damage or the risk of damage to the legal interests of economic operators from the decision of the contracting authority. But how will the damage to the legal interests of economic operators from the decision of AI be handled?

Of course, legal doctrine has not yet provided an answer, nor has the European Court of Justice. However, according to Article 21 of the law, the contracting authority is responsible for procurement according to the law. A proactive approach is also the designation of the decision-making of AI as the decision-making of the contracting authority itself, where, in this case, the procurement officials are not humans but machines—preparing us for the future of AI in public procurement.

The fact remains consistent in supporting Article 24, point 1 of the law. The PPC remains the highest administrative body in the field of procurement, which examines complaints about procurement procedures and performs any other duties assigned to it by this law and other legal acts within the field of its powers. This reiteration of the Commission's role should instill confidence in the audience about the oversight of procurement procedures, providing a sense of assurance.

10.5 CONCLUSIONS

AI is an irreversible reality that will affect the facilitation of many processes in our lives. Public procurement cannot be an exception. Although a small country, Albania has shown for several years that it can be the first in the region and, more broadly, in developing innovative initiatives. In 2009, Albania became the first country in the world to mandate the development of procurement procedures in electronic systems, but 15 years later, the ambition is even greater: the creation of a fully electronic procurement system based on AI, where many procurers will be replaced from the preparation phase to the evaluation and monitoring of public contracts. If this level is reached, can we say that AI will also pass the Turing test? It will be a complete revolution in developing procurement procedures and the nature of doing business.

The three main risks posed by the development of the procurement system based on AI will be (a) data integrity and security, (b) the risk of interference from third-party systems with the electronic procurement system, and (c) the risk during the learning process of the system.

The development of a procurement system based on AI will also directly influence the evolution of legal terms, establishing as a subject of law the official authority of AI, whose decision-making remains under final human control.

Although AI will replace procurement officials, the public procurement law remains unchanged in its approach to the final administrative control of decision-making for public procurement procedures, as the right to appeal continues to be enshrined in law.

The application of such a level of AI can have a tremendous social and economic impact, starting with the increase in competition in public procurements, the reduction of risks to the integrity of procurement procedures—including those of corruption or conflict of interest—the increase of efficiency, effectiveness, and proper use of public funds, the acceleration of the delivery of works, goods, and services, and the enhancement of public confidence in public procurement procedures.

Reforming the public procurement system supported by AI is not simply a matter of technological development. The biggest challenge is not technology, but changing mindsets and the status quo. No one should be afraid of the development of procurement systems based on AI. The latter is neither more nor less than a tool to help people.

REFERENCES

Agarwal, P., Sharma, N., Sharma, S., Uniyal, R., Yadav, P., (2013), Research Paper on Artificial Intelligence, Case Studies Journal.

Awuorc, M., Nagittaa, O., (2022), Human-centered artificial intelligence for the public sector: The gatekeeping role of the public procurement professional. *Procedia Computer Science*, 200, 1084–1092.

Broadhurst, R., Brown, P., Maxim, D., Trivedi, H., Wang, J., (2019), *Artificial Intelligence and Crime*. Research Paper. Social Science Research Network.

Diaz, M.J., (2023), Artificial intelligence and its application to public procurement. *European Review of Digital Administration & Law*, 4, 2.

Dimitri, N., Naudé, W., (2021), Public procurement and innovation for human-centered artificial intelligence, https://ssrn.com/abstract=3762891.

Gadour, G., (2024), Corruption in public procurement: Can e-procurement and artificial intelligence make a difference in Africa? https://doi.org/10.5339/connect.2024.spt.2. https://www.europarl.europa.eu/RegData/etudes/STUD/2021/662908/IPOL_STU(2021)662908_EN.pdf.

Jain, N., (2023), A study on the impact of artificial intelligence techniques in enhancing electronic public procurement system. *International Journal of Innovative Science and Research Technology*, 8, 6.

Khuan, S., Swee, H., (2018), *Technologies for Procurement: Current Trends and Emerging Trends*, WOU Press, Athens, OH.

Krupansky, J., (2017), *Untangling the Definitions of Artificial Intelligence, Machine Intelligence, and Machine Learning, Medium.* Springer Nature, Singapore https://jackkrupansky.medium.com/untangling-the-definitions-of-artificial-intelligence-machine-intelligence-and-machine-learning-7244882f04c7

Law No. 162/2020, dated 23.12.2020, Article 109, "On Public Procurement", as amended.

Law No. 162/2020, dated 23.12.2020, Article 21, "On Public Procurement", as amended.

Modrušan, N., Rabuzin, K., (2019), Prediction of public procurement corruption indices using machine learning methods. In *Proceedings of the 11th International Joint Conference on Knowledge Discovery, Knowledge Engineering and Knowledge Management (IC3K 2019)*, Vienna, Austria, pp. 333–340.

Shneiderman, B., (2020), *Bridging the Gap between Ethics and Practice: Guidelines for Reliable, Safe, and Trustworthy Human-Centered AI Systems*, pp. 1–31, ACM Transactions on Interactive Intelligent Systems, New York.

Simionescu, V., (2016), The impact of artificial and cognitive intelligence on Romanian public procurement. *Revista Economică*, 68, 142–155.

Weizenhaum, J., (1976), *Computer Power and Human Reason*. W. H. Freeman and Company, New York.

Yu, H., Liu, L., Yang, B., Lan, M., (2020), Crime prediction with historical crime and movement data of potential offenders using a spatio-temporal cokriging method. *ISPRS International Journal of Geo-Information*, 9, 732.

11 Decentralizing the Law
Exploring the Potential of Blockchain Technology in Legal Processes

Saranya A, Rajiv Iyer, Vedprakash Maralapalle, and Shivali Wagle

11.1 INTRODUCTION TO BLOCKCHAIN TECHNOLOGY

The use of Artificial Intelligence (AI) in legal systems can be regarded as a new paradigm in legal processes, especially in terms of blockchain. This chapter focuses on how AI and blockchain intersect, particularly on how both technologies can alter and improve legal provisions and services to promote access to justice and rectify existing flaws within the legal system. Zekos (2021) presented AI as an essential part of business that has also made its way into the legal profession. It can perform tasks such as legal research and analysis, contract review, and predictive analytics to boost efficiency. Machine learning applications can process a vast amounts of legal information in a short period, providing attorneys with knowledge that was previously unavailable to them. For instance, using big data, it is possible to predict case outcomes based on previous similar cases, which helps lawyers determine the right strategies to use in the courtroom. Furthermore, with AI, online dispute resolution mechanisms are being adopted to help avoid litigation, which can be time-consuming and expensive. With the help of AI, routine tasks are handled, allowing legal professionals to spend more time on complex matters and thereby improve the productivity of legal services. While this shift is advantageous for legal practitioners, it also assists those seeking justice, as AI can act as a mediator for individuals who cannot afford legal assistance.

Blockchain technology is increasingly being considered a relevant phenomenon in the legal profession today because of its power to address some of the most recurrent and critical problems in the field, especially in terms of process transparency. The decentralized nature of blockchain leads to secure, tamper-proof records, which can enhance the management of legal papers and agreements. For example, smart contracts are self-executing contracts that embed commands directly into the blockchain, so they do not require the involvement of third-party service providers and eliminate human error. Such advantages are underlined by recent case studies. For instance, judicial enforcement officers have had to deal with the use of cryptocurrency assets during the debt recovery process because digital wallets are shielded

DOI: 10.1201/9781003541899-11

by cryptographic technologies. This scenario highlights the fact that existing law, if it fails to take note of emerging technologies, requires additional legal structures capable of offering enforceable mechanisms. Also, Estonia illustrates how blockchain technology can alter the execution of business processes and identification by offering government services via e-residency. Currently, legal environments globally face new challenges in regulating content and digital assets; blockchain provides solutions to address these challenges in legal practices and contributes to the overall effectiveness, security, and transparency of legal operations. Ongoing adoption may be viewed as heralding a new era and work environment for legal professionals and their clients.

11.1.1 BLOCKCHAIN TECHNOLOGY: A NEW PARADIGM

Blockchain, being relatively decentralized and allowing hardly any alterations, may positively impact legal processes. Using an unhackable distributed ledger, blockchain maintains transparency and greater accountability in legal transactions. According to Tan (2022), blockchain-based smart contracts—automated contractual relationships in which the terms of the agreement are coded into the program—represent this potential. They direct enforcement and execution, essentially eliminating the middleman as well as reducing the possibility of contract-related disputes due to misinterpretations. The integration of AI and blockchain can thus complement each other in improving the legal platform. For instance, AI can easily decode the data behind transactions made via blockchain channels to help develop patterns and trends for refining legal research and enhancing the consistency of monitoring.

11.1.2 ETHICAL CHALLENGES

However, there are several ethical and pragmatic issues in combining AI and blockchain in legal frameworks. A core issue is that AI has a potentially prejudiced nature; by discriminating, it may reinforce existing disparities in the legal field. According to Dimitropoulos (2020), these systems can become biased if they are developed with historical data that is itself biased. Therefore, there is a need to enforce strict monitoring of AI systems and constantly check their fairness. Furthermore, the reasoning behind AI decision-making is largely unclear, which poses essential questions regarding accountability and transparency. This will require extensive cooperation between the legal community and technologists to design solutions that allow the outputs of AI systems to be scrutinized and reviewed.

11.1.3 BLOCKCHAIN TECHNOLOGY ENHANCE THE SECURITY OF AI-DRIVEN LEGAL SYSTEMS

In the same way, the integration of blockchain technology into AI-driven legal systems can greatly improve security by taking advantage of its decentralized, immutable, and transparent features. In addition to reinforcing data quality, this integration of Technology and Enhance systems with legal processes also helps build trust and accountability.

a. **Enhanced Data Integrity and Security**: Another benefit often associated with the use of blockchain technology is the transparency of various transactions through the recording of those transactions in blocks that cannot be easily altered. In the legal AI context, this implies that any information input into the system—cases, evidence, or documents—cannot be modified once entered. This characteristic is extremely important, as it ensures that the data collected remains the same as when it was initially recorded. With blockchain, legal professionals will be able to work with data that has already passed through a validation process and cannot be altered, thereby minimizing the chances of fraud and mistakes in the legal process.

b. **Decentralization and Reduced Intermediaries**: The regular blockchain functions in a decentralized environment, which implies that no single entity can monopolize the blockchain. This decentralization can be seen as a strength in the sense that there will be no place where all the security measures are concentrated. Some legal middlemen play the role of checking the evidential value of documents in legal systems, such as notary public or registrars. Blockchain removes these intermediaries because entities have the opportunity to transact directly with an authoritative system. Smart contracts, which are digital contracts whose conditions are coded directly into the source code, do not require interaction with third parties to enforce and check compliance, making processes more efficient and minimizing fraud.

c. **Improved Transparency and Auditability**: One of the effective features of blockchain systems is the actual availability of data on the progress of a legal process to all participants. Florescu (2024) reported advantages in the application of AI in legal environments because the decisions made by AI can be stored on the blockchain. Due to independent documentation practices, the decision-making processes in AI systems can be audited by stakeholders in line with the legal framework and ethical norms. It also enables the elimination of bias in AI algorithms since all the data used in the formulation of the algorithms, as well as the decision-making processes involved, are transparent.

d. **Enhanced Anomaly Detection and Predictive Analytics**: The integration of AI with blockchain also has the potential to enhance security via more sophisticated means of anomaly detection and predictive modeling. Ramos and Ellul (2024) show that some blockchain data features can be analyzed by AI algorithms to uncover anomalous activities suggesting malicious attacks or fraud. For example, if a smart contract starts performing transactions that are not conventional, AI can report such conduct for further scrutiny. This means that there are fewer risks as legal systems can address potential threats promptly.

e. **Data Privacy and Control**: It is revealed that blockchain technology can advance proficiency in data privacy within AI-driven legal frameworks by enabling individuals to retain authority over their data. According to blockchain technology, the data owner has control over how and to whom the data is released. This capability is very important in legal areas, which involve a lot of significant data. In addition, the implementation of encryption types in blocks helps protect data against leakage or losses since no one can access the data without prior permission.

11.1.4 GLOBAL PERSPECTIVES ON BLOCKCHAIN AND AI REGULATION

Blockchain and AI are new technologies the use of which is actively regulated by states, and every country implements quite different measures to steer these opportunities and manage potential threats.

- **United States**: In the USA, the regulatory framework is decentralized, with agencies overseeing and regulating blockchain and AI in their respective ways. While the Securities and Exchange Commission (SEC) concentrates on securities-associated blockchain models, the Federal Trade Commission (FTC) covers consumer matters related to AI. A hot-point issue in the industry is the differentiation between cryptocurrencies and tokens, discussions of which shape existing regulations and business conformities. The focus is placed on stimulating creativity, with concerns about appropriateness concerns regarding the consumers and the rest of the market.
- **European Union**: The EU has been rather active with its ongoing proposal of the Artificial Intelligence Act, which will address the high-risk use of AI through heavy obligations for compliance. Also, the EU's Digital Services Act and Digital Markets Act would help make the online environment more secure by increasing responsibility for digital businesses. Speaking of blockchain, the EU is developing legislation that would govern assets and help the market embrace new technologies, creating more transparency and security in financial services.
- **India**: Responsible regulation remains a critically important theme in India, especially in banking, financial services, and insurance (BFSI). The Reserve Bank of India (RBI) has recently issued guidelines encouraging its adoption to increase transparency in operations related to asset management and compliance checking. As seen in the Payments Vision 2025, there is a strong focus on implementing AI and blockchain as part of stronger digital payment systems and improved cybersecurity. However, issues such as data localization remain, making compliance relatively challenging for these firms, especially when operating in India.
- **China**: China has assumed a more centralized model for the advancement of both AI and blockchain technologies. The country has adopted the New Infrastructure Policy to implement blockchain and integrate it into finance, supply chains, and public services. On the other hand, AI regulation aims to ensure that AI systems in use serve the country's best interests and are safe and ethical to use. China has a detailed set of rules governing technological advancement that seeks to keep such processes under state control;

notwithstanding, that innovative development is encouraged and guided to meet governmental aspirations.

11.2   APPLICATIONS OF BLOCKCHAIN IN LEGAL SYSTEMS

Blockchain technology presents innovative opportunities within legal frameworks, upending conventional approaches to speed, protection, and openness. Figure 11.1 shows applications of blockchain in legal systems.

a. **Smart Contracts**: These smart contracts execute the legal terms of the contracts when pre-established conditions are met. Smart contracts remove intermediaries; thus, they are faster and cheaper than traditional contracts and help ensure compliance and minimize disputes.
b. **Blockchain**: An immutable online database that contains numerous transactions in sections known as blocks linked sequentially for greater efficiency and safety. Each block hosts a list of transactions and is termed a block because it can only be related to the subsequent block using cryptography to change records.
c. **Block**: A block on a blockchain containing information about individual transactions. Each block is added successively in a chronological fashion.

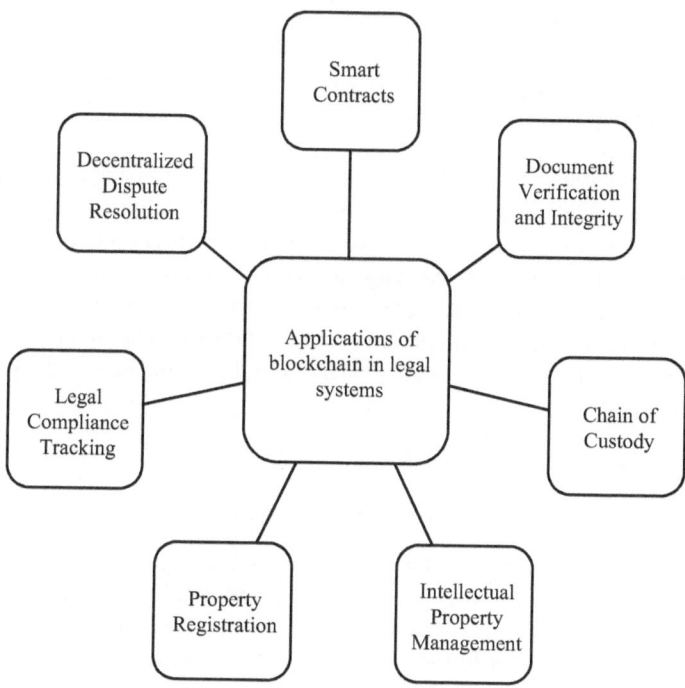

FIGURE 11.1   Applications of blockchain in legal systems.

d. **Node**: Any electronic platform that is involved in a blockchain network and has a copy of all the transactions that take place in the network.

e. **Consensus Mechanism**: This refers to how nodes in a blockchain network come to a consensus about the authenticity of transactions. These are Proof of Work (POW) and Proof of Stake (POS).

f. **Immutability**: The feature of the blockchain that guarantees once information is stored in the system, it cannot be tampered with. As with the previous feature, this increases confidence in the optimality of the data.

g. **Distributed Ledger**: A database on a distributed system where updates in one node are immediately copied or relayed electronically to other nodes, where they are also received by the other participants.

h. **Cryptographic Hash**: An example of a string transformation function that takes as input as many characterizing features as necessary to transform the input data into a string of characters with a fixed length, which is different for different inputs. Since retrieving the actual data from a hash is almost impossible, this ensures data integrity is upheld.

i. **Permissioned vs. Permissionless Blockchain**: A permissioned blockchain only allows some parties to be involved, while a permissionless blockchain is available to anybody who wishes to be involved.

j. **Land Registry**: By creating a record that cannot be easily altered, blockchain can help make land registration more efficient. This is especially helpful in areas that have no or poorly defined property rights, as it aids in increasing transparency and decreasing fraud.

k. **Intellectual Property Rights**: Blockchain also helps in the registration and protection of intellectual property (IP) assets. It provides creators with evidence to tag their creation at the point of creation and first use, thus assisting in the protection of IP rights and the enforcement of legal measures.

l. **Chain of Custody**: For evidence, specifically, it is important to retain continuity especially when dealing with issues of law. With blockchain, the process of examining evidence can be recorded and its complete history can be stored securely, making the data correct and valid in a legal trial.

m. **Litigation and Settlements**: Blockchain can improve litigation processes since the parties can file complaints and respond to allegations securely and transparently. This can eliminate delays and build confidence in the judicial system.

11.2.1 · CONTRACT MANAGEMENT AND SMART CONTRACTS

The roles of contract management and smart contracts are undeniable in driving the modernization of entire legal frameworks and improving the speed and effectiveness of operations. Course (2022) reported that smart contracts refer to forms of contracts coded to function autonomously and are designed to perform specific tasks whenever certain conditions are activated. This automation assumes that it reduces the need for middlemen, decreases the possibility of errors, and advances reputation time. Figure 11.2 shows key features of smart contracts.

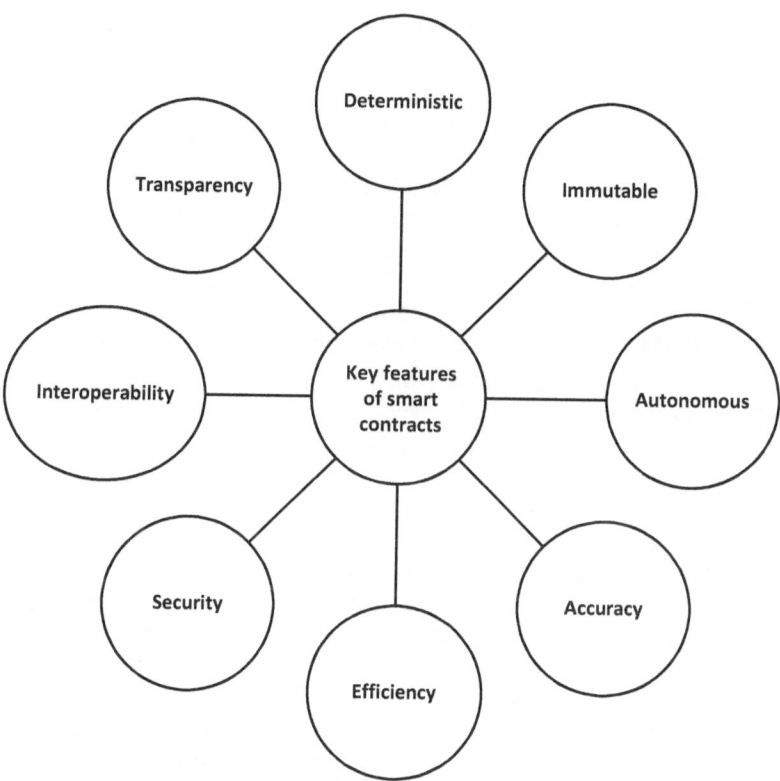

FIGURE 11.2 Key features of smart contracts.

11.2.1.1 Key Features of Smart Contracts

a. **Automation**: Smart contracts are predefined and perform contractual terms like payment, and delivery of goods and services when the conditions are met. They eliminate red tape and simplify many business processes.

b. **Transparency and Security**: Smart contracts are automated legal agreements enhanced with AI to operate on the blockchain, which makes all transactions reliable and unchangeable. This has a twofold effect of building trust among parties because every action is documented and can be traced for accreditation.

c. **Cost Efficiency**: Smart contracts reduce transaction costs because they eliminate human interference and intermediaries in contract fulfillment. It allows organizations to manage their resources better by outsourcing ongoing contract management tasks and concentrating on more important objectives.

11.2.1.2 Smart Contract Management Solutions

To efficiently leverage smart contracts in their operations, businesses are turning to smart contract management platforms. These platforms assist in creating, launching, and managing smart contracts to reduce risk and ensure the contracts remain accurate throughout their duration.

a. **Real-time Monitoring**: Smart contract managers can inform users about changes in the contract status or possible problematic situations, thus making management more effective.

b. **Version Control**: These solutions enable organizations to work with numerous versions of contracts while keeping the terms clear and consistent.

c. **Integration with AI**: The integration of smart contracts with AI tools complements each other in managing contract creation and negotiations by improving the efficiency of approvals and minimizing risks resulting from deviations in the contracts.

11.2.1.3 Quantitative Data Contract Management Using Blockchain

The use of statistics to evaluate blockchain's influence in legal processes, especially in contract management, is an added weapon in the arm. Here are some relevant statistics and case studies that illustrate the efficiency improvements realized through blockchain technology:

a. **Efficiency Gains**: Contract management through blockchain-powered contract lifecycle management (CLM) solutions can cut nonprofit overhead costs by as much as 30%. This is made possible by the integration of operational activities where major decisions can be directly made without the influence of other middle stakeholders, to make clear and precise contract vectors.

b. **Reduction in Contract Disputes**: Out of all the lawsuits filed in state courts in the United States, about 64% of them are part of a contract disputes. This highlights how through augmented contract visibility and precision by using blockchain, organizations can avert such disputes, in the end, lowering legal expenses and general legal effectiveness.

c. **Time Savings**: Smart internet can cut the time taken to draft a contract by up to 80% if the process is digitized using blockchain. This saves legal team's time on administrative tasks, allowing them to focus on more essential, valuable work, enhancing productivity several-fold.

d. **Cost Reduction**: Industries that incorporate smart contracts may reduce their costs by about 2% of their yearly spending due to the reduction in time and approvals from routine contract management methods. Further, weak contract management leads to revenue losses, particularly inefficiency, highlighting that over 92% of it can be resolved through blockchain.

e. **Improved Transparency**: Blockchain has a unique recording system that offers great assurance and accountability to the various parties involved. This transparency not only makes collaboration possible but also enhances the decision-making speed, resulting in enhanced contract cycles.

f. **Automation Impact**: A study predicts that the use of CLM systems integrated with AI alone will reduce manual work by 50% by 2024. Furthermore, the combined use of AI and blockchain will make many legal processes more efficient.

11.2.2 LEGAL RECORD MANAGEMENT

Blockchain technology is expected to bring change to legal record management through improved security, accountability, and effectiveness. Flat-file-based storage and search systems have limitations and problems inherent to them, such as fake documents, slowness, and vulnerability to tampering. Blockchain solves these challenges because it is decentralized and non-alterable; once a record is entered into the blockchain, it cannot be manipulated or edited. Through the application of blockchain in the management of legal records, the legal sector enjoys increased effectiveness, reliability, and security in the delivery of its services to the market.

11.2.2.1 Applications in Legal Record Management

a. **Immutable Record-Keeping**: Examples include contracts, property deeds, and court records, which can be safely stored on a blockchain. This helps avoid conflicts arising from one person having a different copy of the document than the other. Figure 11.3 shows the applications in legal record management.

b. **Smart Contracts**: These contracts can fulfill and enforcing terms when certain conditions have been met. Artzt and Richter (2020) presented this capability as one that simplifies processes and reduces the probability of

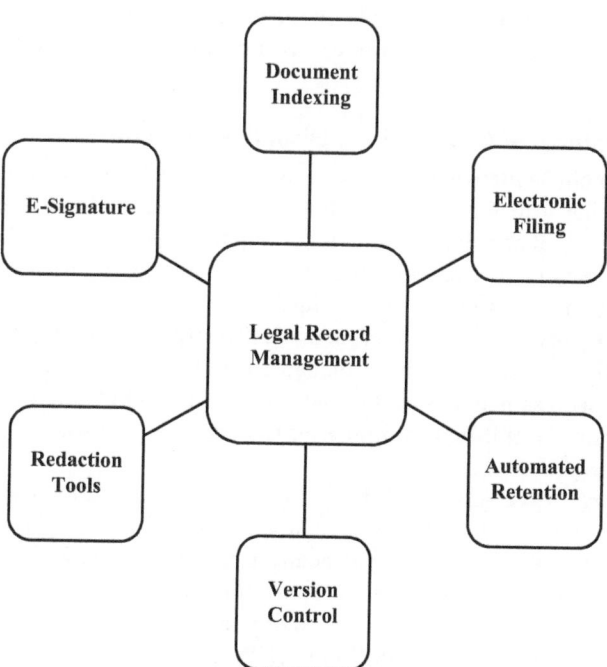

FIGURE 11.3 Applications in legal record management.

errant compliance and untimely fulfillment of the undertakings made in the agreements.

c. **Chain of Custody**: Blockchain can also ensure that there is a secure and verifiable record of ownership and transfer of evidence in a legal process. All transactions or changes that take place are timestamped, creating an easily understandable timeline that can be useful during a trial.

d. **Efficient Document Retrieval**: It also enables legal professionals to save time spent searching for documents and verifying information by automating the data retrieval process using blockchain.

e. **Enhanced Security**: Compared to centralized databases, blockchain offers the following advantage: it eliminates the possibility of unauthorized access to the information contained in legal documents.

11.2.3 DISPUTE RESOLUTION AND ARBITRATION

This chapter argues that the processes of dispute resolution and arbitration are rapidly changing as they adopt ideas from blockchain technology, which provides solutions to problems experienced in these processes. Due to the immutable, transparent, and decentralized consensus nature of blockchain solutions, these ideas are well-suited to developing effective and fair dispute resolution systems. According to Darwish (2023), with the continued development and deployment of blockchain technology, it is likely that even in the areas of disputing resolution and arbitration, a broader and more enhanced scope will be realized—especially in sectors involving a higher number of participants and complex contractual relations.

11.2.3.1 Features of Blockchain in Dispute Resolution

a. **Immutable Evidence**: Blockchain ensures that all messages and statements concerning a dispute are recorded, eliminating any doubt regarding the authenticity of communication. According to Haque et al. (2022), the generated records cannot be modified, thereby upholding the trust of all parties involved in the resolution proceedings.

b. **Smart Contracts**: Smart contracts are self-executing, meaning they automatically enforce the terms of an agreement between parties. For instance, actions such as penalties or payments can be triggered automatically when a condition is fulfilled, minimizing the chances of disputes arising from misunderstandings.

c. **Decentralized Decision-Making**: In contrast to the common use of arbitration where a single arbitrator is usually designated, blockchain incorporates juror networks to support a decentralized decision-making process. For example, platforms like Kleros offer a pool of randomly selected jurors who review cases, making the decision more impartial.

d. **Alternative Dispute Resolution (ADR)**: Blockchain enhances ADR processes by allowing the disputing parties to develop custom-made solutions based on their requirements. This flexibility can yield better results than traditional litigation processes, which is an important advantage.

11.2.4 Regulatory Compliance and Reporting

The use of blockchain in regulation and reporting systems is one of the beneficial opportunities and can strengthen legal frameworks by making processes more transparent, reliable, and efficient. In recent years, there have been numerous issues related to compliance with the steadily growing and changing legislation of countries. According to Centobelli et al. (2021), the incorporation of blockchain technology can play a crucial role in augmenting the capabilities of legal systems focused on regulatory compliance and reporting. Overall, organizations can leverage its distinctive characteristics to address the challenges of regulation and compliance while simultaneously promoting organizational integrity. It responds to these challenges in the following ways: Blockchain maintains a secure ledger of transactions and interactions that cannot be altered.

11.2.4.1 Benefits of Blockchain in Regulatory Compliance

a. **Immutability and Transparency**: Blockchain guarantees that all records are unalterable and open to the public since they are not stored on a centralized server. This is particularly important for compliance with relevant regulations, as it allows for the verification of transactions and data as they are entered. Companies can also ensure clear documentation of their audit trail, which is crucial in proving legal compliance.

b. **Automated Reporting**: Blockchain is capable of reporting compliance conditions through automation, as it is programmed to prepare reports once certain conditions are met. For instance, when a transaction occurs, information related to the transaction can be collected and automatically reported to regulatory bodies without much human input, thereby minimizing errors to a great extent.

c. **Real-Time Monitoring**: With blockchain, it is easier to monitor compliance-related activities in real time. Gürkaynak et al. (2018) suggest that combining AI with blockchain allows organizations to process large amounts of data in real time and quickly detect any abnormalities or compliance violations. This enables management to undertake timely corrective actions to eliminate risks before they worsen.

d. **Data Privacy and Security**: Blockchain improves the protection of data, which is essential in legal industries where compliance with Data Protection Acts is mandatory. Encryption and decentralized storage help organizations protect their data while also ensuring compliance with guidelines such as general data protection regulation (GDPR).

e. **Streamlined Processes**: AI integration with blockchain can greatly enhance the efficiency of compliance processes, as activities such as data checking for consistency and validity, risk analysis, and policy conformity checks can be performed by the system. Not only does this make workflows more efficient, but it also prevents compliance teams from being bogged down by administrative tasks, giving them more time to focus on work that will have a major impact on their organizations.

11.3 CHALLENGES AND LIMITATIONS OF BLOCKCHAIN IN LEGAL SYSTEMS

The adoption of blockchain technology in legal frameworks has some limitations and constraints that need to be overcome for its successful incorporation. Despite the potential advantages that blockchain offers, it has limitations, including legal and regulatory frameworks and technological barriers that may slow down its implementation. According to Sabharwal et al. (2024), despite the myriad opportunities that blockchain provides to legal systems, these issues need to be resolved for proper implementation of the technology. The ongoing discourse among legal experts, technologists, and authorities will be critical in providing a balanced examination of the legal and technical implications and ensuring that blockchain can be leveraged to enhance the favorable aspects of legal procedures without the threat of violating authoritative laws.

a. **Legal and Regulatory Challenges**: The first major issue facing legal innovation is the integration of existing laws into the concept of blockchain. For example, legal systems that implement the right to data protection or the right to erase information can face challenges ensuring compliance with blockchain technology due to its characteristics of immutability. Data on blockchains is irreversible, which is a problem for organizations operating in jurisdictions governed by such laws. Additionally, the legal nature of smart contracts is still ambiguous in most parts of the world. While these contracts bring efficiency to the automation and enforcement of agreements, their enforceability is still considered questionable by courts in relation to standard contract law. Pagallo et al. (2015) suggest that such a scenario may make some businesses hesitant to adopt blockchain solutions in their operations.

b. **Technical Limitations**: From a technical point of view, concerns include blockchain scalability and connectivity. For many distributed ledger technology systems currently in use, their effectiveness in handling transactions is a key issue, especially when traffic volume increases. Corea (2019) reported that this limitation can decrease the potential for applying the technology, particularly in scenarios where frequent transactions are expected, such as high-frequency trading. Additionally, there are no standardized interfaces for cross-chain communication and data exchange, which affects opportunities for international business and cooperation by limiting the potential of blockchain technology.

c. **Governance and Control Issues**: Other potential issues are related to governance structures in decentralized blockchain networks. According to Magnusson (2019), the decentralization of consensus also leads to

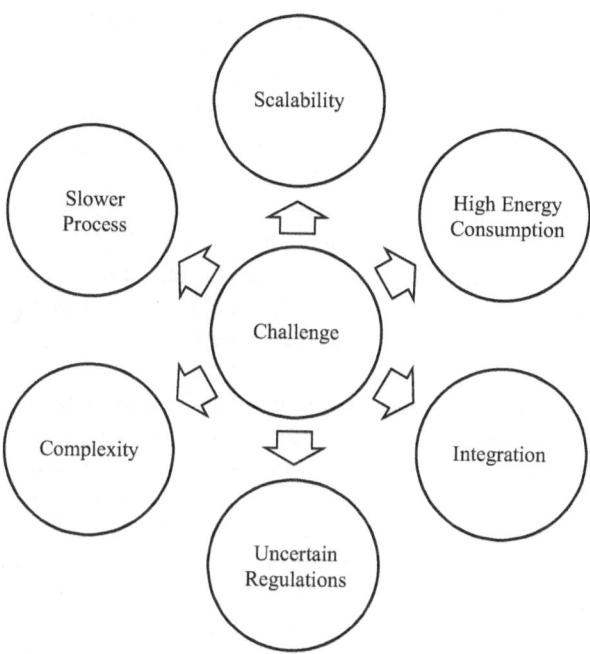

FIGURE 11.4 Disadvantages of blockchain.

disagreements among participants about changes or upgrades to the proto-col, which can create new chains that may confuse users and compromise the network's integrity. Additionally, it may cause discomfort for the management of enterprises working in a decentralized environment, as organizations can lose control over their data and actions. Figure 11.4 shows the challenges of blockchain in legal systems.

11.3.1 Regulatory Frameworks and Legal Considerations

There are various regulatory frameworks and legal aspects of blockchain technology in legal systems that are still emerging. As the use of blockchain solutions increases—including smart contracts and the storage of legal documents—legal advisors face significant challenges in maintaining compliance with existing legislation while also addressing the unique characteristics of blockchain technology.

a. **Legal Uncertainty and Compliance**: They argue that one of the major problems is that there is no recognized body of law governing blockchain as a technology. Most jurisdictions are progressive in implementing new laws due to the decentralized nature of blockchain-based systems, causing confusion about which ordinances to enforce, especially when operating across borders. Rhim and Park (2023) indicate that it remains somewhat unclear, which in turn poses challenges in compliance since organizations may face different legal framework requirements in different regions. For example, the legal regulation of smart contracts is still the subject of debate, since current laws on contracts may not be fully applicable to automated contracts.

b. **Data Privacy Concerns**: Another important issue is data privacy. Blockchain technology has an unalterable record which becomes an issue when supporting compliance with the most stringent data protection laws, such as the GDPR in Europe. The right to be forgotten, which means that a person has the right to request the erasure of personal data, contradicts the immutability and perpetual preservation of records kept on the blockchain. There is a set of demands which, by their nature, seem mutually exclusive, and legal professionals need to figure out how these challenges can be met to establish compliance and take advantage of blockchain at the same time.

c. **Jurisdictional Issues**: Other issues include jurisdictional complications because blockchain technology cuts across borders. The transactions recorded on a blockchain may involve people from more than one country, and thus it may not be clear which law will apply to resolve a conflict. This requires proper drafting of jurisdictional provisions in contracts to ensure legal certainty regarding the laws governing the contract and the mechanisms for resolving disputes. The steady evolution of blockchain technology suggests that further cooperation between legal scholars, IT professionals, and policymakers can be beneficial. This dialogue will assist in framing appropriate rules for using this technology, which creates new opportunities but must also meet the requirements of current legislation. Solving these problems is necessary for the further adaptation of blockchain technology in legal frameworks, which will lead to a more effective legal environment.

11.3.1.1 Barriers of Blockchain in Legal Systems

a. **Technological Barriers**: One of the most significant technological challenges is scalability. First-generation public blockchain systems, like those of Bitcoin and Ethereum, suffer from low transaction throughput (TPS) because of highly involved consensus algorithms. For example, the proof-of-work protocol used by Ethereum allows for the processing of approximately 30 transactions per second, which causes traffic jams and high fees at certain times. This inefficiency poses a challenge for blockchain in applications that require a fast rate of transaction processing, such as real-time contract signatories. Another challenge is integration, meaning that products and equipment need to be compatible with other systems within a network. Most organizations build their own unique blockchain systems that are separate from each other and thus are isolated. When there is no interoperability standard, the implementation of multiple blockchain solutions becomes complex. For example, the lack of interoperability has been a problem that has prevented supply chain projects seeking to link many players across different platforms.

b. **Social Barriers**: There is, however, a public relations problem that plagues potential users: a lack of trust. Some companies remain skeptical about integrating blockchain into their operations and processes because of existing doubts regarding the capacity of blockchain security and the stability of other participants in this kind of network. That lack of trust can then halt collaborative projects. For example, in the healthcare sector, where patient records are transferred from one organization to another, it can remain questionable whether the information will be protected, which can lead to the rejection of blockchain solutions.

c. **Legal Barriers**: From a legal perspective, the greatest difficulty stems from a lack of well-defined rules and regulations. There are few legal structures governing the use of blockchain technology in many jurisdictions; hence, there is a lot of confusion regarding compliance and legal responsibilities. For instance, smart contracts are still not legal permission contracts in some jurisdictions, making it inflexible to apply them in formal relationships. Officials' lack of definite guidelines in the regulation of blockchain hinders investments and slows down the deployment of such systems.

11.3.2 Integration with Existing Systems

Blockchain as part of the legal framework means understanding how it would work within existing infrastructure. Integration into current workflows is important, as it should not disrupt normal operations and be easy to adapt to the new technology.

a. **Compatibility with Legacy Systems**: Another critical concern when implementing blockchain is how well it will fit into existing architectures already adopted by organizations. Some legal organizations have already implemented conventional information technology systems and databases, and it may not be practical or efficient to replace them with blockchain-based systems. This means that legal professionals need to coordinate well with technology providers to develop solutions that can be implemented within existing systems, enabling a progressive transition to blockchain technology without compromising essential elements.

b. **Data Migration and Interoperability**: Equally important is the question of how to transfer data between blockchain networks and classical databases. Paper or electronic documents and contracts that are currently part of the legal system must be moved to the blockchain while keeping their chain of custody and their indexable properties intact. Sansone and Sperlí (2022) presented guidelines and procedures for exchanging data, which is crucial for data to be easily integrated between various systems and structures. Another requirement is compatibility with other blockchain platforms since legal procedures tend to involve users utilizing different systems.

c. **Process Reengineering**: Blockchain integration could also involve redesigning existing legal workflows so that they can leverage blockchain benefits. For instance, smart contracts enable some regular operations of business, for example, contract signing and dispute settlement. However, implementing these entails setting aside time to vet the existing processes to determine which steps can be automated successfully. For those in the legal profession, it is more likely that they will have to collaborate with process specialists and technologists in coming up with new and innovative processes that adapt to the heralded features of blockchain while at the same time continuing to meet the necessary legal standards.

11.3.3 LEGAL DISPUTES AND SMART CONTRACTS

It aims to analyze the potential challenges and opportunities associated with legal cases on smart contracts from an architectural framework perspective, focusing on the development of smart contracts in the matrix architecture of blockchain solutions. Smart contracts are digital contracts with specific rules residing in the smart contract that are implemented and self-executed once conditions are met. As handy tools for cutting out middlemen and dependencies, their legal status and the dispute settlement regarding the use of such contracts continue to be subjects of controversy.

   a. **Legal Status of Smart Contracts**: The first legal issue concerning smart contracts can be found in the question of whether they are enforceable as contracts. For the smart contract to be enforceable, it must fulfill the traditional legal elements of offer, acceptance, and consideration. However, this task becomes challenging due to the automated execution of smart contracts. The legal systems of different jurisdictions diverge when it comes to the treatment of smart contracts, with some considering them as legally binding contracts, while others may regard them as just code without any lawful recognition. This can result in issues regarding the legally binding force of such contracts, especially if there is a disagreement as to the meaning and execution of the code implemented in the smart contract.
   b. **Dispute Resolution Mechanisms**: Legal issues usually arise whenever disputes occur and given that smart contracts differ in many ways from conventional contracts, traditional legal models may not be capable of addressing them adequately. When disputes are considered to take place on the chain, often within the blockchain, they may need to be resolved by special means. For example, the Digital Dispute Resolution Rules introduced by the UK Jurisdictional Taskforce focus on providing certain recommendations on whether and how legal disputes related to smart contracts can be resolved digitally. These rules highlight the best-practice governance approaches as well as outlines for the handling of disputes related to blockchain decentralization.

11.4 ETHICAL CONSIDERATIONS IN THE USE OF BLOCKCHAIN IN LEGAL SYSTEMS

It is also important to consider the ethical issues underlying the implementation of blockchain technology in legal frameworks, which are quite complex. Despite its great importance, it cannot be considered without taking into account its ethical aspects. As blockchain is further applied in the legal processes, it is necessary to take into consideration the ethical concerns raised by the features of blockchain, including the immutability, transparency, and the exclusion of intermediaries.

a. **Privacy and Data Protection**: The first ethical issue revolves around privacy and data protection. Once records have been placed on the blockchain, they can neither be erased nor rewritten. This presents difficulties in areas where data protection regulations are strict, including the GDPR, where individuals are entitled to data erasure. This raises the issue of a discrepancy between legal systems that are required to retain records for accountability and the rights of individuals to privacy.

b. **Asymmetry of Power**: Another key ethical consideration related to blockchain is the risk that it could entrench existing inequalities. Given the possibility of contracting under conditions of asymmetric information and bargaining power, blockchain solutions can support highly opportunistic and authoritarian transactions. While reducing the possibility of intermediaries' intervention may be advantageous in various ways, it also removes safety nets that can prevent dubious actors from exploiting the potentially weaker party. This raises questions about the obligations that developers and legal practitioners have to ensure that the blockchain does not facilitate unlawful behavior.

11.4.1 Bias and Fairness

The infusion of AI in legal frameworks is widely believed to be beneficial in terms of improving speed, impartiality, and precision. Nevertheless, the ever-present threat of bias that can be built into AI algorithms is a major issue that must be addressed to ensure fairness and justice. Further, without proper design and integration of AI systems into the legal system, biased outcomes will be furthered and compounded because of the algorithms used to filter through legal databases.

11.4.1.1 Understanding AI Bias

a. **Prejudices in Training Data**: When the historical data used in developing AI models contain human bias and discrimination, the AI system will also incorporate them and act on them.

b. **Algorithmic Design Choices**: The choices of algorithms and modeling techniques made by developers are a source of bias, some of which are based on personal discretion. Some models may introduce too much or too little emphasis on patterns in the data and therefore, make imprecise predictions.

c. **Lack of Diversity in Development Teams**: Homogeneous teams are less likely to have members who can watch out for bias and veto it when designing AI systems. Bias and blind spots can be experienced when members from specific groups are not visible or are excluded.

11.4.1.2 Risks of AI Bias in Legal Systems

The negative consequences of such bias in legal systems are numerous, and the dangers are not to be underestimated. Biased algorithms in the implementation of forensic technologies, such as bail decisions, sentencing, or determinations on parole, can lead to discrimination against certain groups. For instance, an AI algorithm trained using historical records that have racism in policing and sentencing will have a worse outcome for those from a specific race compared to the previous one. Likewise, tools employed for civil legal actions, including child custody or disability pensions, may also influence prejudice if not implemented securely. Prejudiced outcomes in these domains affect people's lives and cast aspersions on equal justice and the administration of the law.

11.4.2 PRIVACY AND DATA PROTECTION

As a result, constant vigilance is necessary to ensure that legal systems become safer and more equitable in response to AI advancement. Many apprehensions are being raised regarding privacy and data protection, particularly as AI and blockchain technology are incorporated into legal systems. Although human legal professionals are employing AI in processes such as the analysis of documents and cases, and the evaluation of cases and contracts, it is evident that the confidentiality of both persons and sensitive information needs to be guarded. The ethical and legal considerations of data privacy in the context of AI and blockchain in the legal context are discussed in this chapter.

a. **Privacy Risks in AI-Driven Legal Systems**: AI systems require a large amount of private data, including identification numbers, medical records, and credit card information. Another limitation that emanates from the use of big data is that many AI applications rely on large datasets, thus presenting a privacy concern. For instance, the GDPR in the European Union has specific regulations on how people's personal information is used and allows the use of such data only if the people involved give their consent, and if necessary, the use should be minimized. Litigation and transactional lawyers are at risk of falling foul of these regulations, which can lead to severe penalties, together with the loss of client trust. Furthermore, the factor that strategically complicates the determination of the definitive accounting treatment is the application of blockchain. Although the transactional transparency provided by blockchain improves data trustworthiness, it complicates the GDPR right to erasure. It is indicated that once data is entered on the blockchain, it cannot be erased or changed, which violates the privacy of individuals. Consequently, it is possible to observe that legal actions should adapt to these contradictions because it is also important to provide privacy to users in the context of Open Science based on distributed networks.

b. **Ethical Considerations**: However, the ethical issues related to the use of AI in the legal decision-making process are not restricted to compliance with rules and legal standards only. Lawyers need to defend their client's interests and ensure that the AI system does not reveal protected data on its own. This responsibility covers essential security features like encryption and access controls of data throughout the data lifecycle. Further, legal practitioners need to be watchful about the consequences of sharing data with third-party AI supplier firms so that legally binding contracts may be developed to uphold data confidentiality and security.

With the increased adoption of AI and blockchain in reforming the legal system, privacy and data protection issues need to be considered. Legal professionals must evaluate the ethical implications of their employment, put in place significant protections, and retain humans in the loop to ensure that these technologies will work to advance the missions of legal systems while respecting and protecting the individual rights of citizens. Implementation of AI and blockchain can help stakeholders control the positive outcomes of AI in legal proceedings as much as possible while adhering to the policies and rules of privacy and data protection.

11.4.3 TRANSPARENCY AND ACCOUNTABILITY

AI in legal systems can enhance the effectiveness, accuracy, and accessibility of legal systems. However, the rather swift integration of AI in the legal sector entails elaborate procedures to monitor its efficiency and ensure that it is both transparent and accountable. In utilizing and progressing toward the idea of developing more autonomous AI systems, it is crucial to establish a robust and well-defined framework to ensure that the incorporation of AI is open, efficient, and responsible.

a. **Importance of Transparency**: Explaining how particular AI approaches are utilized in a specific decision (accountability of the AI system and use of AI in the legal system) and how the AI models are trained or the data utilized in the model. The support of performance evaluations with explanations enables legal professionals and the public to determine whether the AI-based decision is reasonable. This, in turn, enhances confidence in the use of AI systems, especially in areas like law, where the consequences of the systems can adversely affect individuals or organizations. Additionally, transparency fosters the identification of bias in the algorithms and models used in AI systems. If left unmanaged, biases are often manifested as discriminatory actions against specific groups or individuals bearing certain attributes. Knowledge of these AI systems can assist the stakeholders in determining any bias and its remediation to achieve some measure of fairness in legal judgments.

b. **Ensuring Accountability**: Responsibility is also referred to as another essential aspect of the correct functioning of AI in the legal environment. AI must involve a clear line of responsibility for the results it delivers and the appropriate steps to be taken when the AI makes a wrong/biased decision. This accountability should extend to all the legal persons in AI software developers, legal advisors, policymakers, among others. Supervision also plays a vital role in the whole process to make the process accountable. Even though AI can work wonders in terms of speed and precision, actual legal judgments cannot be made by computers; they have to be provided by legal experts. Lawyers need to be able to decode, critique, and debate AI-generated results, with an emphasis on respecting the law and advancing AI as a tool that enhances but does not replace human discretion.

11.5 CASE STUDIES AND BEST PRACTICES

AI and blockchain technologies hold a future in enhancing legal systems in a way that they could be made more efficient and easily accessible than before. Real-life examples and best practices of such technologies need to be critically analyzed as they progress further, so that the opportunities and risks can be observed and estimated.

Case Study 1: AI-Powered Contract Management at Deloitte: Deloitte, a global professional services network, has implemented an effective AI contract management system for its legal team. The system, called "Contract Haste," employs natural language processing (NLP) and machine learning techniques to detect and extract terms, clauses, and provisions of the contracts. After processing large amounts of contracts, including papers that have been signed and those that are still drafts, the system flags possible dangers and deviations from internal standards and creates contracts according to offered templates and the individual requirements of the client. This automation has resulted in tremendous gains in time and costs, with a cut of reduction of half the time spent on reviewing contracts and about a third of the time spent in contract negotiation.

- Develop reliable AI that meets the eligibility requirements for the successful analysis of legal documents.
- Integrate with other contract management systems that your organization has in place.
- Provide ongoing training and updates to AI models to ensure they reflect the twin parameters of accuracy and recency.

Case Study 2: Blockchain-Based Land Registry in Sweden: The Swedish Land Registry has been experimenting with integrating blockchain into its land registration processes in partnership with ChromaWay. Using distributed ledger technology, which holds all property and transaction data, the system aims to increase transparency, minimize paperwork, and eradicate fraud. The pilot project has indicated that blockchain can offer a secure, electronic, and decentralized register with an unalterable record of land ownership, thereby reducing the need for third parties and paperwork.

- Blockchain can solve issues in land registration where property rights and cases are ambiguous or prone to fraud.
- Innovation in legal processes can be fostered through collaboration between government agencies and technology startups.
- Pilot projects are important as they demonstrate the applicability of blockchain solutions and help determine their viability for a large-scale application.

Case Study 3: AI-Powered Litigation Analytics at Premonition: A legal analytics company Premonition has created an AI tool that uses litigation information to rate judges and attorneys. Analyzing hundreds of thousands of court cases, the system recognizes patterns and tendencies in case resolutions, judges' decisions, and attorneys' performance. The information improves the decision-making process of legal practitioners regarding the approaches to presenting a case, the choice of jurisdictions, and the selection of lawyers. Many clients, such as those in the healthcare, finance, and insurance industries, have adopted Premonition's platform to manage their legal expenses and enhance their performance in litigation.

- It can thus help find useful information within large data sets so that new legal decisions can be based on comprehensive analysis.
- Litigation analytics can be used by legal practitioners to determine the right approach and resources to use when handling certain cases.
- It is important that extra attention be paid to legal issues, including data protection and other ethical issues, concerning the application of AI in the analysis of litigation.

Here are several notable examples from various jurisdictions and organizations that have successfully integrated blockchain:

a. **Estonia's e-Residency Program**: Estonia has been at the forefront of implementing blockchain in government services. Its e-Residency enlists a virtual persona to enable the global population to access Estonian solutions such as starting or running an enterprise online. This is partly done using blockchain, which preserves the authenticity and sanctity of digital identity, thereby increasing transparency in governmental affairs.

b. **Georgia's Land Registry**: A pilot project of blockchain record-keeping has been launched in the country of Georgia to tackle problems such as numerous corruption schemes and to organize faster and more efficient property sales with less possibility of scams. The government, using blockchain, has recorded title deeds, providing clear and transparent records of ownership and hence reducing conflicts over land ownership.

c. **UAE's Ministry of Economy**: The United Arab Emirates is also already seeking blockchain use across numerous sectors, such as the Ministry of Economy which is now planning to obtain licenses and business registrations on a blockchain. This move has been made to promote efficiency, check and curb fraud, simplify processes, and bring efficiency to business operations within the region.

d. **Supply Chain Management in Food Safety**: Some popular industries such as Walmart are employing the use of blockchain technology to track food chains from the farm to the consumer. Through the implementation of IBM's Food Trust blockchain, Walmart is able to respond to contamination sources in the food chain system and hold them accountable.

e. **Smart Contracts in Real Estate**: In real estate, existing companies such as Propy are using smart contracts to conduct property sales. Promoting decentralized ownership transfer as soon as payment conditions are fulfilled, Propy saves effort and expenses usually spent on intricate procedures by buyers and sellers.

f. **COVID-19 Vaccination Tracking in Lesotho**: The Lesotho government was able to track COVID-19 vaccinations through the use of blockchain technology. Extra effort was made here as a measure to ensure that people have faith in the different vaccines that were being administered.

11.5.1 PRACTICES FOR INTEGRATING AI AND BLOCKCHAIN IN LEGAL SYSTEMS

This chapter submits that the incorporation of AI and blockchain technology as integral service components in legal systems means that the evolution of the latter has leaped to a new paradigm that makes it more efficient, transparent, and accessible. Here, these technologies not only correct the imperfections of the legal process but also enhance the egalitarian delivery of justice to marginalized groups through efficient automation of tasks, improved data analysis, and secure record-keeping. By following the approach described in this chapter, which identifies co-solutions associated with AI and blockchain, these can transform legal provisions and service delivery to create a fair and efficient legal solution system. From the case analysis and the incorporation of general IT trends, the following best practices are identified for applying AI and blockchain in legal systems.

a. **Prioritize Data Quality and Governance**: Ensure that the information fed to AI models and records kept on the blockchain is reliable, comprehensive, and well-processed. Set guidelines for the ownership, structure, and control of the data to ensure that it is accurate.

b. **Foster Interdisciplinary Collaboration**: Organize legal counsel, IT specialists, and specialists in a particular field to design and implement AI and blockchain tools. Promote knowledge exchange and cross-departmental learning to foster creativity.

c. **Implement Robust Security and Privacy Measures**: In managing its model clients and clientele, the company should prioritize on data security and confidentiality as well as comply with data protection legislation. Apply encryption, access controls, and other security measures to prevent data loss of data.

d. **Ensure Transparency and Explainability**: Pursue accountability in AI-powered decisions and the operations of blockchain solutions. Particularly, the performance of AI-generated results must come with clear explanations and allow stakeholders to scrutinize the systems.

e. **Continuously Monitor and Refine**: Continuously measure and assess the effectiveness and utility of AI and blockchain. This involves engaging users, reviewing feedback to identify biases or errors, and making corrections when necessary to ensure the system remains effective and up to date.

f. **Provide Training and Support**: Provide regular educational services to legal professionals to enhance their knowledge and understanding of AI and blockchain solutions. Enable them to use these technologies optimally while remaining ethical and responsible.

g. **Stay Informed and Adaptable**: Diligently maintain awareness of progress in AI and blockchain technology, as well as changes in law and legal frameworks. It is essential to be prepared to adapt legal practices to fully take advantage of these technologies where necessary, while minimizing their drawbacks.

11.5.1.1 Practical Recommendations for Integrating AI and Blockchain in Legal Systems

To effectively address the ethical issues associated with the integration of AI and blockchain technology in legal systems, legal practitioners can adopt the following practical recommendations:

a. **Implement Transparency Protocols**: Everyone, including legal practitioners, should champion the improvement of AI systems to explain the reasoning behind their decisions. This may be done by engaging with developers of AI to design models that are explainable so that all stakeholders can understand how results are obtained.

b. **Conduct Bias Audits**: More frequently, they should also check the AI algorithms they use to detect bias in the data used for training. Counselors should collaborate with big data experts to ensure that a range of data sets is employed in building the algorithms and then check fairness by evaluating the effectiveness of the algorithms across different categories of people.

c. **Establish Data Privacy Policies**: Introduce elaborate data protection provisions, particularly concerning the GDPR, to use blockchain technology in the storage of highly sensitive legal records. Ensure that the confidentiality necessary to protect some data is balanced by sufficient openness for authorized personnel to access the required information.

d. **Advocate for Regulatory Frameworks**: Interact with active stakeholders and act as a channel through which governments are encouraged to formulate laws regarding the application of AI and blockchain in the legal industry. This entails the endorsement of guidelines on ethical objectives, the extent of accountability, and the safeguarding of personal liberties.

e. **Foster Continuous Education**: Promote continuous professional development of present and future lawyers regarding the application of AI and the use of blockchain technology. This will enable practitioners to contribute to the improvement of ethical standards among practitioners through their employers. When operationalized, these recommendations assist legal practitioners in positioning themselves ethically with emerging technologies and ensuring that justice prevails in practice.

11.5.2   AI IMPROVES ACCESS TO JUSTICE IN DECENTRALIZED LEGAL SYSTEMS

It also means that AI can and should be used to improve access to justice in jurisdictions where the legal systems are decentralized, resource-constrained, or simply too expensive.

a. **Automating Legal Tasks**: In areas of legal practice where many documents must be reviewed or facts researched, the automation of these tasks can be done by an AI package. Through natural language processing and machine learning, AI can quickly analyze huge amounts of information within a short time, filter out pertinent data, and highlight the results. This automation saves time and effort on such tasks, allowing the key professional service providers in law to work more strategically and attend to their clients.

b. **Simplifying Legal Processes**: Thus, AI is useful for breaking down intricate legal papers and processes into forms that normal people can comprehend. Through directed prompts and filtering out possible mistakes, AI-based applications enable people to complete legal tasks on their own. It is particularly handy in environments where people might not have adequate legal advice.

c. **Enhancing Legal Analytics**: The use of AI can yield substantial analysis-oriented benefits to the legal decision-making process. Through case analysis, legal reasoning, and previous findings, AI systems may understand and recognize patterns, probable solutions, and possible references. This approach assists legal experts in improving their decision-making and enhancing strategies based on available data to provide the best results.

d. **Expanding Access to Legal Services**: Moreover, one of the primary benefits of AI is its ability to lower the costs of legal services and increase access to justice for the public that requires it most. Since it can perform tasks and optimize workflows, AI can minimize the expenses generated by legal services. This makes it possible for legal practitioners to provide their services at relatively lower prices, thus increasing the accessibility of legal aid and enabling more pro bono work.

11.6   CONCLUSION AND FUTURE DIRECTIONS

The incorporation of AI and blockchain technology in legal systems marks a major shift in delivering and accessing legal services. These technologies remain promising in increasing efficiency, openness, and justice as they continue to develop. Nevertheless, unlocking their full potential becomes an important issue that depends on the ability to address the ethical, legal, and regulatory aspects of using smart technologies.

a. **Enhancing Access to Justice**: AI can also be used to bring fairness in providing legal services to less fortunate individuals through advanced technology. Using AI to perform tasks such as document review, legal research, and contract analysis, to name a few, already has the propensity of lowering the cost at which legal services can be provided to members of society who cannot afford an attorney. Furthermore, AI products like chatbots and virtual legal assistants can give instant legal advice, which means that people can get legal support even if they do not have access to an attorney. This is further supported by blockchain technology, which provides efficient, secure, and unalterable records of legal transactions. This can enhance services such as land registration, contract formation, and dispute administration, resulting in reduced time taken to address legal issues. Thus, using blockchain can make these processes faster and more efficient, reducing the load on overburdened legal systems and improving people's access to justice.

b. **Addressing Ethical and Legal Challenges**: Nonetheless, several ethical and legal factors related to AI and blockchain technology need to be considered. This has been a major issue as it raises the question of how the use of AI could help improve the situation when the algorithm itself is flawed and reflects biases that already exist in the legal system. Promising and fair decision-making by intelligent systems is key to guaranteeing public uptake and acceptance of the technologies.

Lawyers, engineers, and ethicists must work together to come up with rules and regulations that will support the use of AI while avoiding bias. Another consideration is data privacy and security, especially since legal documents often contain confidential information. In legal systems, there is a need for institutional measures to protect the rights of people over their data and meet legal requirements such as those of the GDPR. This entails having protocols for handling, storing, and sharing data, with individuals having rights over their information.

c. **Regulatory Frameworks and Collaboration**: Due to the emerging development of both AI and blockchain solutions, it is becoming increasingly critical to establish extensive legislation that specifically aims to meet the requirements and specify the solutions of these two progressive technologies. It is now up to policymakers to collaborate with members of the legal profession and technologists to devise policies that address the ethical use of AI while encouraging technological advancement. These frameworks should also incorporate principles of accountability, transparency, and fairness so that the use of these technologies is consistent with the core values of the legal profession. Additionally, cross-sector collaboration is critical when addressing the challenges arising from the application of AI and blockchain in the legal sphere. On the one hand, legal professionals must communicate and interact with technologists to learn about what these technologies can and cannot do, and the reverse is true as well, in that technologists should be aware of the legal and judicial guidelines governing their work. This cooperative approach will assist in guaranteeing that both technologies are implemented appropriately in the legal sphere.

11.6.1 CALL TO ACTION FOR LEGAL PROFESSIONALS

1. **Engage with Technology**: Legal professionals should go out of their way to understand more about blockchain and AI technologies. Knowledge of these tools will assist lawyers and legal scholars in helping their clients, writing policies, and engaging in discussions on existing and desirable legal frameworks.

2. **Consider Policy Implications**: The impact of these technologies on legal practice requires stakeholders to engage with policymakers. This refers to supporting forms of consumer protection while encouraging innovation. Policies related to the legal profession can be molded legally, practically, and ethically through the participation of legal professionals.

3. **Promote Equitable Access**: The legal community can harness blockchain and AI technologies to improve accessibility to justice. Practical implementation of this could need the creation of legal aid services, case tracking mechanisms, or in general, better exposition of the legal process. These technologies, therefore, help stakeholders devise strategies for eliminating barriers to practices that discriminate against those on the periphery.

4. **Collaborate Across Disciplines**: It has been recommended that technologists, ethicists, and those in the legal profession engage in finding new ideas on how the blockchain and AI work and can be used to solve problems arising from their execution. Such collaborations would enable the identification of a range of benchmarks for the acceptable usage of technology in fulfilling legal tasks.

5. **Advocate for Education and Training**: Law schools should also ensure they teach lawyers about blockchain and AI. In this way, the legal profession can guarantee a better-equipped workforce of future lawyers, who will be aware of these technologies and their influence on society and will be ready to face new challenges.

11.6.2   DIVERSE PERSPECTIVES ON BLOCKCHAIN AND AI REGULATION

A. Legal Scholars

Legal scholars offer conceptual perspectives for understanding one of law's theoretical frameworks about technology. In their research, they tend to look for the interaction between the current spread of technologies and legal systems, ethical issues, and prospects for change.

- **Regulatory Theory**: Lawrence Lessig provides opinions stating that behavior is shaped by law, norms, and architecture, with architecture here referring to technology. Understanding this synergy is paramount to the regulation of blockchain and AI systems.
- **Privacy and Data Protection**: Scholars like Paul M Schwartz explore how technologies disrupt privacy and data security trends, especially within the scope of GDPR and comparable rules.

B. Practitioners

Legal professionals present the operational experience in the conversation, focusing on the problems and prospects of using blockchain or AI technology in law. Their perspectives can include:

- **Compliance Challenges**: It remains challenging for practitioners to address the current and evolving state of restraints. Recommendations from legal professionals who practice in the technology law field may help organizations adopt the most accurate strategies concerning compliance with new legislation.

- **Client Advisory**: Insurance companies' legal counselors, providing the company with recommendations on the utilization of technologies, may provide substantial insights into how blockchain and AI support the optimization of contract processing while remaining legal.

C. **Technologists**

The technologists, therefore, offer a vital view of what is possible and what is not within the context of blockchain and AI technologies. Their experience can help legal stakeholders make the right decisions on implementation and regulation.

- **Innovation Insights**: The technologists also highlight how they are already working with the simplest type of blockchain technology to increase transparency in legal actions and show how AI can help with case administration and legal information searches.
- **Ethical Considerations**: It is, therefore, important to continue engaging in discussions on the ethical application of AI in legal practice. Professionals such as Kate Crawford are concerned with the social aspects of AI, and the adaptation must be made responsibly.

11.6.3 FUTURE DIRECTIONS

Legal systems seem to have a bright future when it comes to AI and blockchain technology, or at least, it will remain a promising field that will need constant focus and updates. As these technologies continue to emerge and advance, legal professionals cannot afford to be uninformed or unaware of these trends. This is about focusing on the trends, practices, and risks of AI and blockchain technologies. Educational institutions also have the responsibility of training the next generation of legal practitioners to operate in this environment. AI and blockchain technologies must be included in the training curriculum of law schools to ensure that students are well-prepared to work with these technologies in the future. Moreover, as AI and blockchain technologies play a larger role in legal procedures, there will be a constant need for further research and assessment. Legal academics and practitioners should conduct research to evaluate the effects of these technologies on access to justice, legal decisions, and the operations of legal systems. The findings of this study shall go a long way in helping policymakers and stakeholders in the legal profession to make informed decisions and chart a more appropriate course in the development of legal applications of AI and blockchain technology. AI and blockchain, coupled with the increasing adoption of technology in the delivery of legal services, stand the chance of improving access to justice. Nevertheless, there is significant potential to derive this value when the proper initiative is placed into realizing it, accompanied by a proper address of the ethical, legal, and regulatory implications that come with these technologies. Through collaboration, increasing transparency, and acting in fairness, stakeholders can achieve social impact based on these innovative technologies to change the existing legal system to provide equal, effective, and public access to justice for everyone. As we expand, it remains vital that innovation continues, maintaining justice and the rule of law, guaranteeing that society can access these technologies for the benefit of all.

REFERENCES

Artzt, M., & Richter, T. (Eds.). (2020). *Handbook of Blockchain Law: A Guide to Understanding and Resolving the Legal Challenges of Blockchain Technology*. Kluwer Law International BV, Alphen aan den Rijn, Netherlands.

Centobelli, P., et al. (2021). Surfing blockchain wave, or drowning? Shaping the future of distributed ledgers and decentralized technologies. *Technological Forecasting and Social Change*, 165, 120463.

Corea, F. (2019). *Applied Artificial Intelligence: Where AI can be used in Business* (Vol. 1). Springer International Publishing, Singapore.

Course, L. L. M. (2022). *Blockchain and Smart Contracts: Main Issues Arising from the Conclusion, Interpretation, and Performance of Smart Contracts*. www.eiopa.europa.eu/sites/default/files/publications/consultations/eiopa-discussion-paper-on-blockchain-29-04-2021.pdf accessed 16 November 2022.

Darwish, D. (2023). Blockchain and artificial intelligence for business transformation toward sustainability. In *Blockchain and Its Applications in Industry 4.0*. Springer Nature, Singapore, pp. 211–255.

Dimitropoulos, G. (2020). The law of blockchain. *Washington Law Review*, 95, 1117.

Florescu, C. I. (2024). The interaction between AI (Artificial Intelligence) and IA (International Arbitration): Technology as the new partner of arbitration. *Romanian Arbitration Journal*, 18, 42.

Gürkaynak, G., et al. (2018). Intellectual property law and practice in the blockchain realm. *Computer Law & Security Review*, 34(4), 847–862.

Haque, M., Hossain, M. H. S., & Hossain, M. A. (2022). A comprehensive review and architecture of a decentralized automated direct government system using artificial intelligence and blockchain. *International Journal of Scientific & Engineering Research*, 13, 1.

Magnusson Sjöberg, C. (2019). Legal automation: AI and law revisited. In *Legal Tech, Smart Contracts and Blockchain*. Springer International Publishing, New York, pp. 173–187.

Pagallo, U., et al. (2015). Introduction: Legal and ethical dimensions of AI, NorMAS, and the web of data. In *AI Approaches to the Complexity of Legal Systems*. Springer International Publishing, New York, pp. 1–15.

Ramos, S., & Ellul, J. (2024). Blockchain for artificial intelligence (AI): Enhancing compliance with the EU AI Act through distributed ledger technology. *International Cybersecurity Law Review*, 5(1), 1–20.

Rhim, Y.-Y., & Park, K. (2023). The artificial intelligence in international law. In *Revolutionary Approach to International Law: The Role of International Lawyer in Asia*. Springer Nature, Singapore, pp. 215–237.

Sabharwal, S. M., Chhabra, S., & Aiden, M. K. (2024). AI and blockchain for secure data analytics. In *Next-Generation Cybersecurity: AI, ML, and Blockchain*. Springer Nature, Singapore, pp. 39–81.

Sansone, C., & Sperlí, G. (2022). Legal information retrieval systems: State-of-the-art and open issues. *Information Systems*, 106, 101967.

Tan, E. (2022). The role of big data, AI, and blockchain technology in digital public governance. In *The New Digital Era Governance: How New Digital Technologies are Shaping Public Governance*. Wageningen Academic Publishers, Wageningen, Netherlands, pp. 193–204.

Zekos, G. I. (2021). AI and legal issues. In *Economics and Law of Artificial Intelligence: Finance, Economic Impacts, Risk Management and Governance*. Springer, Cham, pp. 401–460.

12 Ethical and Legal Implications for Artificial Intelligence in Law

Hysmir Idrizi

12.1 THE CONSEQUENTIALIST AND CATEGORICAL ETHICAL THEORIES IN THE AGE OF ARTIFICIAL INTELLIGENCE

12.1.1 INTRODUCTION

This part considers two important theories of ethics: consequentialism and categorical ethical theory models, and their relation to artificial intelligence (AI). The section discusses consequentialism as a theory focused on outcomes. It then discusses Kant's deontological ethics, which is concerned with obligations and moral principles regardless of the results. Moreover, it evaluates AI as a decision-maker and examines the problems of self-regulatory AI within a legal framework. It provides an understanding of the ethical aspects that accompany AI-based systems to support more advanced discussions on AI in the scope of legal reasoning, justice, and responsibility.

The topic here is centered on how the utilitarian ethics proposed by Jeremy Bentham and John Stuart Mill can be incorporated into AI systems. Furthermore, it assesses the dangers that can arise from this, particularly the fact that in AI, reasoning focuses on achieving an outcome may lead to the infringement of individual rights to benefit the majority. It also considers real cases to demonstrate the complications involved in the practical application of utilitarian ethics to AI and law. In this section, the discussion focuses on Kant's deontological ethics, which relates to moral obligations and duties, and the free will of moral agents. Additionally, this section critically evaluates whether AI can fulfill the Kantian requirement of being a moral agent, particularly considering that AI is programmed and does not have free will.

12.1.2 CONSEQUENTIALIST MORAL REASONING AND AI: THE IMPLEMENTATION OF AI BASED ON THE OUTCOME

Consequentialism prioritizes the consequences of actions, emphasizing that the morality of an action is determined by its outcome. Utilitarianism, associated with Jeremy Bentham, seeks to maximize pleasure as its goal (Sinnott-Armstrong et al., 2023). The foundation of Bentham's theory of utilitarianism derives from the perspective that "humans are equipped by nature by two 'sovereign masters': pain and

DOI: 10.1201/9781003541899-12

pleasure. These two masters govern one's life" (Stumpf, 2015, p. 285). Bentham went further by saying that "actions are only justified if they have a clear and discernible effect on the welfare of the people involved" (Sinnott-Armstrong et al., 2023). In other words, utilitarianism is often expressed as the "greatest benefit (pleasure/happiness/welfare) for the largest number of people" (Sinnott-Armstrong et al., 2023). Nevertheless, utilitarianism is criticized by many opponents because it fails to respect individual rights (Sandel, 2010). This is the weakness of utilitarianism: justifying the maximization of pleasure for the largest number of people may, on many occasions, violate individual rights (Sandel, 2010).

Utilitarianism uses the logic of "cost-benefit" to measure pleasure and as a methodology for solutions to different and complex social issues (Sandel, 2010). Sandel, in his book *Justice: What's the Right Thing to Do?* presents a real-life example to help develop a critical view of the methodology of utilitarianism for the measurement of pleasure or welfare (Sandel, 2010). Sandel uses the case of a tobacco company run by Philip Morris. The relationship between the state of the Czech Republic and the tobacco company went through a cost-benefit analysis commissioned by Philip Morris to measure the effects on the national budget (Fairclough, 2011). The government, on the other hand, decided to increase taxes because of the cost of smoking-related health care. The study discovered that the government earned more than it lost because of the shortened lives of taxpayers due to smoking of cigarettes. This earning was estimated to be $147 million per year (Sandel, 2010). Despite the profits to the national budget of the Czech Republic, it was publicly assumed that this was not a desirable form of financial welfare since it violated human rights. Later, the chief executive of Philip Morris apologized and said that the study was "a complete and unacceptable disregard of fundamental human rights" (Fairclough, 2011). This study reveals the weakness of the "cost-benefit" methodology since it focuses on the consequence rather than the cause (Sandel, 2010).

Nevertheless, Jeremy Bentham was not the only utilitarian. John Stuart Mill made a very influential contribution to the theory of utilitarianism. Mill, in contrast with Bentham, put human dignity at the center of utilitarianism (Sandel, 2010). Mill defended the idea of individual freedom. He went on to emphasize that everybody is "free to do whatever they want to do, provided they do not harm others" (Sandel, 2010, p. 47). Mill said the only actions that can be subject to government intervention are those that harm others. He argued that "independence is, of right, absolute. Over himself, over his own body and mind, the individual is sovereign" (Miller, 2007, p. 20). Mill linked individual liberty with the prosperity of society in the long run. He argued that respecting individual freedom will benefit society in numerous ways because only by respecting the freedom of the individual can society make progress. He opposed the idea that an individual should be forced to live based on the customs or prevailing opinions of the majority (Sandel, 2010). Mill reasoned that violating individual freedom prevents humans from achieving the highest purpose of life: the full and free development of their human attributes (Sandel, 2010). Mill is in line with the idea of Kant. He claimed that actions and consequences are not that important, but what is important is character (Mill, 1859). Thus, Mill supported the idea of individual freedom and consciousness. In addition, Mill challenged the idea of pleasure in a comparative approach. He proposed a test for identifying higher pleasures.

This test was expressed as follows: "Of two pleasures, if there be one to which all or almost all who have experience of both give a decided preference, irrespective of any feeling or moral obligation to prefer it, that is the more desirable pleasure" (Mill, 1859). Nonetheless, pleasure itself is a very relative concept, e.g., one might prefer reading Plato instead of attending an opera, and vice versa.

Consequentialism represents a theory providing a conceivable ground for setting a code of ethics for AI (Della Foresta, 2020). Consequentialism is composed of two theses: a) rights and values are independent of one another, and b) a priori explanation of values. The first thesis emphasizes that regardless of the morality of the action, what's important is the consequence (McGee, 2024). The second thesis is a critical assessment of the quality of the action, determining whether it is wrong or right. Moreover, consequentialism, as a normative ethical theory, is teleological, maximizing, and impartial (Della Foresta, 2020). For instance, if an individual has A, B, C, and D as options to bring about the best outcome, it will be determined that only the action that could bring the best outcome will be qualified as the right action (Kim & Schonecker, 2022). This approach defines consequentialism as maximizing outcomes. However, consequentialist normative theory installed on robots or machines can produce analyses to maximize opportunities but cannot resolve moral conflicts.

12.1.3 CATEGORICAL MORAL REASONING AND AI: THE CONCEPT OF DUTY, AUTONOMY, AND MORAL AGENCY

This section explores how Immanuel Kant's categorical moral reasoning applies to AI, considering whether robots using machine learning can be moral agents with consciousness and awareness or simply serve as tools to achieve certain goals. The idea that robots are not able to fulfill the requirements of Kant's philosophy is related to the human-centered approach, which holds that personality/personhood is a human attribute (De Lucia Dahlbeck, 2022). The terminology 'robot-ethics' sounds paradoxical at first, because ethics is related to morality, and robots are programmed tools that are predetermined, meaning they differ from humans in terms of subjectivity and personality (De Lucia Dahlbeck, 2022). Considering the above, robotics seeks to mimic human behavior and is equipped with a code of ethics.

Kant considers that moral agency contains two components (a) moral law and (b) autonomous will. In Kant's theory, meeting the criterion of "moral law" is crucial for determining whether an action is morally justifiable. This criterion is the 'universal law,' implying that an action is morally justifiable if it could be willed as a universal law. In other words, the action is qualified as morally right if it can be implemented universally (Kim & Schonecker, 2022). It is difficult to say that robots meet this criterion because they lack free will. Even though they can act autonomously, they are algorithmically (pre)determined. Kant aligns with Aristotle, who argued that humans have two distinct kinds of decision-making systems: (a) an irrational and (b) a rational system (Aristotle, 2020). The first is based on the emotional part, which is fast, intuitive, and mostly unconscious. The second is based on the rational part, which imagines the possible outcome of a particular action and chooses the one that is morally justifiable. Nevertheless, this approach is not without opponents. Compatibilists oppose this consideration because they view free will because of a chain of events and not the cause itself. The first system is rooted in the emotional realm, characterized by fast, intuitive, and unconscious reactions. The second is grounded in the rational mind, envisioning potential outcomes of a specific action and selecting the morally justifiable choice.

Now let us put this criterion in the context of AI. The concept was first introduced by McCarthy "to find how to make machines use language, form abstractions and concepts, solve kinds of problems now reserved for humans, and improve themselves." In other words, machines that can enhance their capabilities meet the criteria for AI as they can operate autonomously. Nonetheless, this autonomy does not equate to free will, as it is confined within algorithms. As such, these machines cannot be held morally responsible because of their (pre)determined algorithmic nature. Autonomy is the component that determines a machine as a product of AI. This autonomy is understood as freedom under Kant's "Metaphysics of Morality" (Denis, 2010). Kant defines freedom in terms of "the ability of pure reason to be of itself practical" or in terms of "the internal lawgiving of reason" (Kim & Schonecker, 2022). When Kant refers to freedom, he refers to transcendental freedom, implying that freedom should not be a result of any external causes, but should legitimize itself.

Another key point emphasized by Kant is the criterion that determines whether humans act morally or not. This criterion requires humans to act based on duty rather than merely in compliance with duty (Boddington, 2017). This implies that humans are obliged to know what duty is, e.g., what is wrong and why it is wrong. This requires humans to increase their knowledge and not just execute orders for the sake of duty. Furthermore, Kant emphasized the intellectual attributes of humans, the lack of which leads to destruction. Therefore, it can be predicted that AI emerges from the creativity of human, and it is the understanding of the consequences and functions of such tools that defines whether they benefit mankind or a curse.

12.1.4 CONCLUSION

To sum up, the study of moral reasoning related to AI is extremely difficult because it incorporates both consequentialist and deontological systems, generating one of the most serious ethical issues in the moral integration of AI systems into society. At the same time, it is important to understand that AI, as a cognitive augment, will only be able to assume a consequentialist position and judgment. This means that AI will be logic- and reasoning-focused. On the other hand, the emphasis Kant places on ethical duty, moral agency, and autonomy raises questions about whether machines could be ethically considered moral agents as they are algorithmically controlled and lack free will.

The emergence and increasing integration of AI technologies into various spheres of social life raise several ethical issues that AI must actively tackle. In addition, it must strike a balance between respect for autonomy and ethical obligation. The possibility of machines operating and making decisions with no humans' intervention raises serious concerns about whether such machines ought to have the capacity to be moral agents. It suggests that if AI systems are to be given such responsibilities and powers, then vehicles, the healthcare system, and the legal system should have strong ethical measures that are clear and human-centered. The ongoing debate between consequentialist and deontological perspectives provides no easy resolution, but it sets the stage for the kind of critical discussion needed to address the ethical dilemmas created by AI in the future. In this context, as AI systems become more autonomous, the issue of ensuring dignity-respecting ethical AI systems design goes beyond technical competence to include human values.

The next struggle is how to infuse human values, which are often contradictory and do not always come to the surface, into unbending algorithms, all while AI keeps developing. As a result, the explanation does not involve AI perfection but other areas: the construction of ethics in technology should be goal-oriented while observing fundamental human rights. The future of AI will be defined by the dispute between efficiency and morality, between autonomy and control.

12.2 ARTIFICIAL INTELLIGENCE AND THE RULE OF LAW: TRANSPARENCY, ACCOUNTABILITY, AND DUE PROCESS IN AUTONOMOUS SYSTEMS

12.2.1 INTRODUCTION

AI's legal challenges are deeply connected to ethical concerns about its decision-making. Experts like Virginia Dignum, Nick Bostrom, and Joanna Bryson have explored how to manage AI responsibly. They stress the need for AI systems that prioritize human values and transparency, especially in legal settings where they can affect people's rights.

AI tools created to support values like accountability, transparency, and justice are used to actively implement the ethical norms set by academics and legislators in actual court systems. The U.S. Correctional Offender Management Profiling for Alternative Sanctions (COMPAS) system shows how AI can assist in risk assessment, while Singapore's SENTRA tool and Estonia's AI judge pilot program serve as examples of how AI may reduce human bias and improve efficiency in legal decision-making. These instances show how legal pragmatism and philosophical principles might be balanced to produce systems that function well while respecting moral principles. Global debates on ethics and the law have been sparked by the development of AI technology and its growing integration into legal frameworks. AI's impact on decision-making, bias reduction, and judicial transparency presents benefits and challenges as it continues to transform several legal procedures. This section examines how real-world legal structures and applications reflect moral issues in AI governance.

Considering global legal frameworks, such as (a) the European Commission's "Ethics Guidelines for a Trustworthy AI," the following section highlights the potential opportunities and challenges of integrating AI into legal systems and highlights accountability and transparency in AI-driven decision-making; (b) Regulation (EU) 2024-1689 of the European Parliament and of the Council of June 13, 2024, for the regulation of AI; and (c) the Council of Europe Framework Convention on Artificial Intelligence and Human Rights, Democracy, and the Rule of Law, the European Union's AI Act. To provide a more complete picture of global AI ethics and legislation, this chapter also examines recent developments in AI outside of Europe. One important U.S. advancement is the Algorithmic Accountability Act. Introduced in 2019, this law requires businesses to analyze the effects of their algorithms, especially regarding bias, privacy, and discrimination (Algorithmic Accountability Act of 2019, H.R.2231, 2019). By requiring regular checks and effect analyses, the Act highlights the importance of accountability and transparency in AI systems. By focusing on business responsibility in reducing algorithmic harm, rather than industry-wide regulation, this approach stands in contrast to European initiatives like the EU AI Act (Artificial Intelligence Act, Regulation (EU) 2024/1689).

Section 12.2.3 analyzes how AI can be used in criminal justice, with a focus on the principle of due process of law and the challenge of maintaining justice in court. It also examines the dangers AI poses to the integrity of the law, especially when AI-powered systems serve as tools in court rulings and investigations. Regarding AI's growing role in criminal justice, this section emphasizes the significance of maintaining human oversight and abiding by legal standards that protect individual rights.

12.2.2 ALGORITHMIC JUSTICE AND HUMAN RIGHTS: THE PRINCIPLE OF ACCOUNTABILITY, TRANSPARENCY, AND NON-DISCRIMINATION

A major difficulty in the legal domain is making sure AI systems do not promote pre-existing biases or create new kinds of discrimination. According to recent studies, AI systems have the potential to reinforce biases found in historical data if they are not appropriately regulated, which would defeat the goal of delivering justice. One study on algorithmic bias in facial recognition technology emphasizes the moral risks connected to AI systems that are trained on biased datasets. However, academics emphasize the significance of "algorithmic accountability," arguing that AI systems used in the legal industry need to be open and accountable. This makes it possible to examine and challenge AI judgments, especially when they have potentially life-altering outcomes like sentencing or bail decisions.

This section looks at how AI can minimize human error in legal settings while maintaining moral principles to guarantee decision-making that is transparent and accountable. AI has been shown to reduce cognitive overload, reduce biases, and improve decision-making accuracy by automating complex activities and offering data-driven insights. For example, the danger of human error in document analysis and case preparation has been reduced by the AI-powered legal research tool Research Operating System for Service Solutions (ROSS Intelligence). In the same way, New Jersey's Public Safety Assessment (PSA) methodology has reduced subjective biases and helped reduce inequalities in bail decisions, leading to more equitable outcomes. These examples underscore the significance of aligning AI's efficiency with the ethical principles of fairness and transparency discussed earlier. When utilized responsibly, AI can augment human judgment and reduce errors, but it must be accompanied by ongoing ethical oversight to prevent the emergence of new forms of injustice. The protection of human rights in the AI era represents legal challenges for all authorities. This issue becomes more important because human decision-making tends to be replaced by autonomous machines and robots. Nevertheless, AI cannot have legal subjectivity the same as humans (De Lucia Dahlbeck, 2022). For this reason, AI should be designed in detail to prevent any potential violation of human rights.

The rapid development of AI has been associated with an increasing debate about whether these machines will violate subjects' data protection and privacy rights. The interaction between AI and human rights is associated with a debate concerning data protection and privacy, non-discrimination, and human dignity (CETS 225 – Artificial Intelligence, 2024). AI systems can affect fundamental human rights underlined in the European Convention on Human Rights, the European Charter of Fundamental Rights, and other international human rights instruments. For the first time, the European Union, through Regulation (EU) 2024/1689 of the European Parliament (EU AI Act, 2024), has designed a regulatory framework focused on the regulation of the use and implementation of AI. These acts address issues related to the protection of health, safety, and fundamental rights (EU AI Act, 2024).

In Europe, the General Data Protection Regulation (GDPR) offers comprehensive safeguards against data misuse, granting individuals the right to access, correct, and delete their data. Nevertheless, the GDPR faces challenges in keeping up with the rapid advancement of AI, particularly in ensuring algorithmic transparency. It might be challenging for people to understand how their data is used or to challenge judgments made by AI-powered surveillance tools because AI systems usually function in mysterious ways. As AI systems evolve, concerns about privacy and data protection have emerged. AI systems are required by the General Data Protection Regulation (GDPR) to ensure their use conforms with laws and guidelines related to privacy and data protection. Article 11 of the Council of Europe Framework Convention on Artificial Intelligence and Human Rights, Democracy, and the Rule of Law (CETS 225 – Artificial Intelligence, 2024) also has this responsibility. Transparency and accountability are essential because the use of AI presents major risks to data privacy (Wachter et al., 2017). As previously noted, concerns about privacy violations have also been linked to the growing usage of AI. Many social media platforms, for example, can violate users' privacy by using "deep fake technology." These tools pose a significant risk of modifying photos and videos, making an artificial image of the person appear authentic (Custers & Fosch-Villaronga, 2022).

Another legal necessity is non-discrimination, since AI systems may give rise to prejudice and discriminatory actions (CETS 225 – Artificial Intelligence, 2024). Furthermore, Regulation (EU) 2024/1689 prohibits the use of AI for risk assessment of individuals based only on profiling or personal traits, acknowledging the risks such systems pose to equality. Barocas and Selbst discovered that algorithmic decision-making could lead to discriminatory practices, especially in fields like employment and criminal justice, making the fairness mechanism in AI systems mandatory (Barocas & Selbst, 2016).

As discussed in the previous section, human dignity is the end goal of the international law framework (CETS 225 – Artificial Intelligence, 2024). The protection of human dignity and individual autonomy is crucial in the implementation of AI technology. Article 7 of the Council of Europe Convention (CETS 225 – Artificial Intelligence, 2024) underlines the importance of respecting human dignity throughout the lifecycle of AI systems, aim to prevent systems that could undermine human autonomy (CETS 225 – Artificial Intelligence, 2024). Furthermore, to avoid dehumanization through automation, AI must operate in a way that respects human dignity by guaranteeing that people maintain control over AI systems that have an impact on their lives (Zuboff, 1988). The moral principles of respect for human autonomy, damage prevention, fairness, and explicability are thus essential in the implementation and progress of AI systems (European Commission: Directorate-General for Communications Networks, 2019). Additionally, the European Commission's "Ethics Guidelines for a Trustworthy AI" highlighted the significance of taking appropriate care of marginalized groups, children, and people with disabilities, as they may be unfairly excluded from the potential benefits of AI or subject to harmful actions by machines or robots (European Commission: Directorate-General for Communications Networks, 2019).

Meanwhile, nations like China, Japan, and Canada are all implementing different approaches to controlling AI, and the U.S. approach to ethics is part of a larger global trend. For example, Canada's Directive on Automated Decision-Making highlights the significance of ethical governance in public sector technology by emphasizing accountability and fairness in government AI applications. In the same way, Japan's AI policy covers privacy and security issues while promoting the creation of human-centered AI that enhances well-being (Fukuyama & Katsuno, 2020). China's AI Governance Initiative, on the other hand, addresses ethical concerns including privacy and surveillance while concentrating on enhancing economic growth, national security, and maintaining global leadership in AI innovation (Feng & Kreps, 2020). These methods demonstrate how regulation of AI is determined by a unique cultural, economic, and political setting.

In areas like employment, housing, healthcare, and criminal justice, AI systems have the potential to strengthen and intensify existing biases, disproportionately harming low-income people, women, and members of ethnic minorities. For instance, it has been argued that AI systems used in predictive policing unfairly target minority communities, leading to over-policing and perpetuating systemic injustices. Fairness and accountability in AI are the goals of international regulatory systems. Concerns remain, meanwhile, regarding how well they work to combat algorithmic prejudice. To lessen prejudice and promote equality in AI deployments, it is essential to ensure transparency in AI systems and to promote diverse AI development teams.

Automated hiring systems frequently use historical data to evaluate candidates, therefore repeating prior discriminatory practices. In one significant example, it was discovered that Amazon's AI hiring tool, which was trained on resumes submitted primarily by men, favored male candidates for technical roles. (These issues are tough for the American legal system to handle. Although Title VII of the Civil Rights Act forbids discrimination in the workplace based on race, sex, and other characteristics, it does not adequately address the complex nature of algorithmic prejudice. Because AI systems frequently operate as "black boxes," it might be challenging to identify the cause of discriminatory results and raise questions regarding responsibility. To reduce biases in AI systems, calls for stricter legal frameworks—such as the Algorithmic Accountability Act—emphasize the necessity of accountability, transparency, and inspection.

12.2.3   AI IN CRIMINAL JUSTICE: UPHOLDING DUE PROCESS OF LAW

The effort to govern AI is impacted by ethical issues and legal difficulties, creating a situation where accountability and creativity are linked. A global interest in developing legislative frameworks that strike a balance between innovation and ethical protections is shown in the European Union Artificial Intelligence Act, the United States Algorithmic Accountability Act, the OECD's AI Principles, and China's New Generation AI Development Plan. These frameworks address issues of accountability and fairness while promoting the responsible and transparent application of AI in crucial fields like justice and law enforcement. They are essential for influencing how AI is used in legal systems and are the result of in-depth philosophical debates over the ethical implications of AI in society, especially in high-risk areas like criminal justice. In the context of AI, this means that unexpected results should not affect AI design.

The significance of the "intended purpose" for the implementation of AI systems is stated in EU Regulation 2024/1689. In accordance with usage instructions, the "intended purpose" includes the particular context and usage conditions (Article 3(12)). EU Regulation 2024/1689 goes further and defines the cases that constitute "serious incidents" including (c) "the infringement of obligations under Union law intended to protect fundamental rights" (EU AI Act, 2024). The regulation introduces the concept of a "serious incident" referring to a situation where the consequences are rooted in the malfunctioning of an AI system, directly or indirectly leading to any of the following: (a) the death of a person or serious harm to a person's health, (b) a serious and irreversible disruption of the management or operation of critical infrastructure, (c) the violation of obligations under Union law designed to safeguard fundamental rights, and (d) serious harm to property or the environment (EU AI Act, 2024). Consequently, the intention and ability of the provider or deployer of the AI should have, before the deployment of AI, foreseen the potential harmful consequences of AI; otherwise, they will be held responsible if one of the "serious incidents" occurs. In accordance with the regulation, every deployer or provider of AI should design a risk-assessment mechanism that anticipates and manages potential risks that may occur as a result of AI implementation (EU AI Act, 2024).

EU Regulation 2024/1689 determines what constitutes a prohibited practice in criminal proceedings. According to the regulation, among the AI practices that should be prohibited is "the putting into service for a specific purpose, or the use of an AI system for making risk assessments of natural persons to assess or predict the risk of a natural person committing a criminal offense, based solely on the profiling of a natural person or on assessing their personality traits and characteristics." Nonetheless, this prohibition does not apply to AI systems used to "support the assessment on a suspected individual, based on clear and factual circumstances directly linked to criminal activity" (EU AI Act, 2024). The implementation of AI in criminal proceedings provides benefits in the context of preventive justice. Such prevention in the AI era can become easier because of the substantial amounts of data AI can analyze, through which it can produce improved results in terms of reducing recidivism (Custers & Fosch-Villaronga, 2022). These tools are known as evidence-based algorithmic profiling approaches because the data they process are related to personality traits and the circumstances in which the crime was committed, thereby helping courts and judges form evidence-based profiles of subjects. Such applications can be used in sanctions related to a particular group of crimes or a specific case (Custers & Fosch-Villaronga, 2022). This implies that by programming an AI tool with data related to circumstances, personality traits, and aggressiveness of subjects, it can help judges increase objectivity in their decisions. These applications are already in use in several countries. For instance, in the Netherlands, the government uses a system called REPRIS (Recidivism Prediction Instrument System), which publishes data on recidivism. This is a committee comprised of experts that evaluates the proposed programs based on their effectiveness and quality (Custers & Fosch-Villaronga, 2022). Additionally, through predictive analysis of data related to a certain location that, for instance, is identified as a high-intensity crime zone, these technologies can aid in improving the efficiency of criminal justice (Ferguson, 2019).

In order to predict crime trends and identify offenders, predictive policing uses AI algorithms to evaluate enormous volumes of data, including social media activity, historical crime records, and geographic data. Despite being regarded as a tool to improve the effectiveness of law enforcement, predictive policing has sparked concerns about inequality and bias. For example, the U.S. criminal justice system makes extensive use of the COMPAS technology. To assist judges in determining bail and sentencing, COMPAS aims to predict a defendant's probability of reoffending. However, studies have revealed that COMPAS frequently produces distorted findings, more frequently classifying Black defendants as high-risk in comparison to their white counterparts, even when their criminal histories are similar. The algorithm's training data, which often mirrors past injustices rooted in the criminal justice system, is the source of this bias. Predictive policing methods like COMPAS therefore carry the danger of escalating already-existing inequalities rather than reducing bias, which could result in over-policing in minority communities.

There are major ethical issues with AI in predictive policing. By depending on distorted historical data, AI systems face the risk of maintaining prejudices. Critics argue that algorithms' lack of transparency compromises the presumption of innocence by limiting accountability. There are significant concerns associated with using AI in sentencing. These systems have the potential to reinforce prejudices and restrict judicial discretion, despite their stated goal of ensuring uniformity and equity in judicial decision-making. Even if algorithmic recommendations are faulty or incorrect, judges may nonetheless follow them. A more inflexible and inhumane legal system may result from this reliance on AI since algorithmic predictions may take priority over unique situations. Legal issues are also raised by AI's "black-box" nature. Courts usually lack the expertise needed to evaluate AI-generated risk assessments carefully, and defendants have little power to challenge the fairness or accuracy of these technologies.

To guarantee that AI technologies do not violate civil freedoms, it is necessary to strengthen current legislative frameworks. This involves creating laws that particularly address how AI affects civil rights, privacy, and surveillance. To protect human freedom and dignity, AI systems also need to be made more transparent and accountable. Strong supervision procedures will safeguard public confidence in AI and ensure that these tools support a society that is more just and equal.

12.2.4 CONCLUSION

One of the most major areas of current legal research and practice is the combination of AI and law. AI systems highlight the shortcomings of existing legal frameworks and call for both innovation and discipline in their development as they progressively extend into fields like criminal justice and the protection of fundamental human rights, which have historically been subject to human decision-making. The principles of accountability, transparency, non-discrimination, and the preservation of human dignity are not merely abstract ideals; rather, they are the foundations that influence the future responsible use of AI systems.

In the future, bridging the gap between the slower evolution of legal systems and the faster progress of AI technology will be the main challenge facing legal systems around the world. In an increasingly digitally connected society, concerns about the responsibility of AI providers, the scope of human control, and the protection of data and privacy will become increasingly important. Early but vital steps in adjusting to this new reality are represented by legal frameworks like EU Regulation 2024/1689. However, as AI develops and is constantly integrated, these frameworks will need to evolve.

Looking ahead, interdisciplinary cooperation is necessary to address the interaction between AI and law. To create proactive ethical and regulatory frameworks that anticipate the potential and risks of AI, legal scholars, technologists, philosophers, and legislators must collaborate. For example, the application of AI in criminal justice focuses on reconsidering fundamental rights like due process, intention, and accountability. Although predictive justice may offer previously unheard-of chances to lower crime and criminal convictions, it also raises serious issues with bias, fairness, and the dehumanization of the judicial system. It will be crucial to preserve human beings at the center of legal decision-making as AI develops.

REFERENCES

Aristotle, R. H. (2020). *The Nicomachean Ethics* (A. Beresford, Trans.). Penguin Books, Westminster, London.

Barocas, S. & Selbst, A. D. (2016). Big data's disparate impact. *SSRN Electronic Journal, 104*, 671. https://doi.org/10.2139/ssrn.2477899

Boddington, P. (2017). *Artificial Intelligence: Foundations, Theory, and Algorithms: Towards a Code of Ethics for Artificial Intelligence*. Springer International Publishing, New York.

Council of Europe. (2024, September 5). *Framework Convention on Artificial Intelligence and Human Rights, Democracy, and the Rule of Law*. Council of Europe, France. https://www.coe.int/en/web/artificial-intelligence

Custers, B. H. M. & Fosch-Villaronga, E. (Eds.). (2022). *Law and Artificial Intelligence: Regulating AI and Applying AI in Legal Practice*. Asser Press, The Hague, Netherlands.

De Lucia Dahlbeck, M. (2022). *Spinoza, Legal Theory, and Artificial Intelligence: A Conceptual Analysis of Law and Technology* (Vol. 2, p. 18). Springer Nature, Switzerland. https://doi.org/10.1007/s43545-022-00458-w

Della Foresta, J. (2020). *Consequentialism and Machine Ethics – Towards a Foundational Machine Ethic to Ensure the Ethical Conduct of Artificial Moral Agents*. Montreal AI Ethics Institute, Montreal, Quebec. https://montrealethics.ai/consequential-ism-and-machine-ethics-towards-a-foundational-machine-ethic-to-ensure-the-ethical-conduct-of-artificial-moral-agents/

Denis, L. (2010). *Kant's Metaphysics of Morals: A Critical Guide.* Cambridge University Press, Cambridge, MA.

European Commission. (2019). *Ethics Guidelines for Trustworthy AI.* Publications Office, Luxembourg. https://doi.org/10.2759/346720

European Parliament & Council. (2024). *Artificial Intelligence Act (Regulation (EU) 2024/1689).* Publications Office, Luxembourg. https://artificialintelligenceact.eu/the-act/

Fairclough, G. (2011). Philip Morris notes cigarettes benefit for nation's finance. *The Wall Street Journal.*

Feng, E. & Kreps, S. (2020). AI and China's governance model: Implications for global ethics. *Journal of Contemporary China,* 29(123), 659–672. https://doi.org/10.1080/10670564.2020.1731068

Ferguson, A. G. (2019). *Predictive Policing Theory.* American University Washington College of Law, Washington, DC. https://papers.ssrn.com/sol3/papers.cfm?abstract_id=3516382

Fukuyama, M. & Katsuno, H. (2020). AI in Japanese society: Legal and ethical considerations for the future. *Asian Journal of Law and Society,* 7(1), 50–67. https://doi.org/10.1017/als.2020.7

Kim, H. & Schonecker, D. (Eds.). (2022). *Kant and Artificial Intelligence.* De Gruyter, Berlin.

McGee, R. W. (2024). *How Ethical is Utilitarian Ethics? A Study in Artificial Intelligence.* Working Paper. https://doi.org/10.13140/RG.2.2.26675.60969

Mill, J. S. (1859). *On Liberty.* John W. Parker and Son, London.

Miller, D. (2007). *National Responsibility and Global Justice* (1st ed.). Oxford University Press, Oxford.

National Institute of Standards and Technology (NIST). (2021). *AI Risk Management Framework.* https://doi.org/10.6028/NIST.AI.RMF.001

Sandel, M. J. (2010). *Justice: What is the Right Thing to Do?* Penguin Books, Westminster, London.

Sinnott-Armstrong, W., Zalta, N. E., & Nodelman, U. (2023). *Consequentialism.* (Winter 2023 Edition). Metaphysics Research Lab, Stanford University, Stanford, CA. https://plato.stanford.edu/archives/win2023/entries/consequentialism/

Stumpf, S. E. (2015). *Philosophy: A Historical Survey with Essential Readings* (9th ed.). McGraw-Hill Education, New York.

Wachter, S., Mittelstadt, B., & Russell, C. (2017). Counterfactual explanations without opening the black box: Automated decisions and the GDPR. *Harvard Journal of Law & Technology,* 31(2), 841–887. https://doi.org/10.48550/ARXIV.1711.00399

Zuboff, S. (1988). *In the Age of the Smart Machine: The Future of Work and Power.* Basic Books, New York.

13 Democratizing Legal Aid
The Role of AI in Providing Affordable Justice

Shashwata Sahu, Navonita Mallick,
and Sanghamitra Patnaik

13.1 INTRODUCTION

The access to justice policy is still a looming challenge for marginalized communities, given the enormous barriers that underserved populations confront when seeking justice for their legal problems. High legal fees, limited financial means, and geographical constraints only heighten the unmanageable disparities, making legal aid the only available means to attain justice (MacDowell, 2015). Yet, as it is, legal aid services fall short of the current demand and remain limited in the scope of their service delivery. Accordingly, there is a pressing need to facilitate the availability and affordability of these services. Artificial intelligence (AI) is now spreading to many sectors to diminish an overreliance on human labor. The legal industry is no exception to this trend (Feijóo et al., 2020). Legal services become more prompt and less expensive by using AI in the form of chatbots, predictive analytics, and automated document generation. Instant help, prompt operating time, and help in analyzing a case constitute only a minor advantage of increased reliance on AI for overburdened legal aid (Andrew Perlman, 2023). On the other hand, AI warrants increased reliance on the part of those who need its assistance to the greatest extent, thereby balancing the scales and giving their users a fighting chance. Importantly, AI can mitigate costs, making legal services affordable to humanity. On the other hand, however, AI needs to be regulated by a series of ethical and practical considerations, such as algorithmic bias or data management issues (Simshaw, 2022). Considering the above, the future of legal aid depends on a wise combination of AI and ethics. Properly regulated, it could make justice a right rather than a privilege.

13.2 RESEARCH OBJECTIVES

This chapter aims to inquire how AI could democratize legal aid, breaking the socioeconomic barriers that deprive disadvantaged groups in their pursuit of justice. The objectives of this research include examining the applied side of AI in legal assistance, such as chatbots or document creation, and its analysis to determine whether the costs of the tools could be reduced and their efficiency and, as a result, accessibility, increased. Another goal is to study the ethical issues associated with using AI in this aspect, which entails discussing fairness, transparency, and the protection of user's personal data.

DOI: 10.1201/9781003541899-13

13.3   RESEARCH METHODOLOGY

This research used a doctrinal method to observe and apply how the law works or, in this context, the rules. It relies on a literature review of the available legal doctrines rather than conceptual approaches. Researchers have used several legal cases and doctrines to determine how AI technologies can help people access the law more effectively by providing appropriate assistance. One advantage of this approach is that it is possible to detect problems and improvements at the same time.

13.4   CONCEPTUALIZATION

Artificial intelligence and its use in legal aid provide an invaluable opportunity to improve justice for underserved groups. Implementing chatbots, predictive analytics, and robotic process automation to complete and submit legal paperwork may help fill the gaps in providing personalized legal services (Greggwirth, 2023). First, AI-powered chatbots with natural language processing can provide useful legal advice and help instantly, making such basic legal services less costly for low-income people. Second, predictive analytics may help to forecast legal outcomes and can be used to manage cases and allocate resources. Third, robotic process automation may significantly benefit major law firms and their clients by saving time and money in preparing legal documents (Chakraborty et al., 2023).

The key structural elements of legal services can help ensure justice for different marginalized communities. Indeed, from legal aid to mediation and victim compensation, legal aid can be seen as the sum of its parts. Legal systems can meet various needs, resolve disagreements quickly, and aid those who might face challenges in terms of justice by utilizing these services. It is also possible to improve these services by using AI technologies. In this way, justice can be democratized.

Affordability and justice can be facilitated using AI. Since AI decreases the human factor in ordinary legal services, it becomes less expensive for marginalized regions. AI accelerates legal services, thus enabling more people to have timely justice. When legal aid is not an unachievable service for low-income citizens, they can defend their rights more efficiently, demanding democracy in this sphere (Lee et al., 2024). However, this type of AI application cannot be considered indefinite and may cause ethical issues. AI algorithms can be biased if careful measures are not taken, meaning that AI tools in legal services will not bring fair results. At the same time, the data used to produce these algorithms can be stolen, which is unacceptable for legal matters. On the one hand, the discussed applications of AI cannot be deemed ethical without addressing the issues of fairness and privacy (Alvarez et al., 2024). Since AI tools can contribute to solving such noble issues, their controlled use is reasonable.

13.5   THEORETICAL FRAMEWORK

Legal theories regulate the incorporation of AI into legal systems for use in any justice system. Integrating AI into justice presupposes that it will make justice fairer and more accessible. However, as AI becomes more prevalent in legal services, it is crucial to maintain equity, due process, and fairness. This chapter aims to provide the theoretical foundation for AI systems to support legal practitioners without seeking to replace human judgment by maximizing efficiency and accuracy. It will explore the concept of AI efficiency balanced by legal ethics and legal aid, which helps achieve justice, equality, and the rule of law while saving money. First, it helps to promote equality before the law and judicial impartiality due to the provision of legal representation for the poor and marginalized. Another factor is that it cuts the cost of seeking justice. Overall, legal aid is indispensable to achieving justice.

AI's use in the justice system is controlled by several legal frameworks to ensure that it complies with the law and with ethics. For example, the GDPR in Europe and HIPAA in the United States are data protection laws that control how AI is implemented and what it can and cannot do with sensitive legal data. They ensure that the personal and confidential information processed by AI in legal services is protected (EU AI Act, 2023). Emerging AI governance models also provide standards of transparency, accountability, and fairness for AI systems. They argue for AI developers and legal workers to coordinate to ensure that these systems meet data protection, transparency, and bias prevention standards expected by law or ethics. When thinking about AI in legal services, it is important to keep justice and fairness in mind. AI systems are naturally based on data-trained algorithms (Camilleri, 2024). If the data sets used to train them contain bias, the choices of AI may also contain or amplify this bias, leading to unfair outcomes. AI use raises concerns for equity and non-discrimination. It is necessary to create and manage AI systems so they do not unfairly disadvantage marginalized or vulnerable populations. This requires constant oversight of the datasets used by AI systems and the application of measures to prevent bias. Justice in AI-aided court decisions is also crucial for maintaining public trust in the legal system (Dankwa-Mullan, 2024). If court AI decisions are viewed as unfair, the use of AI could destroy public trust in legal aid and in the judicial system. The use of AI in legal services should only be ethical and should ensure fairness. Accountability structures for biased AI systems are also necessary.

13.6 CASE STUDIES ON AI-POWERED LEGAL AID

AI is changing how legal aid is provided, and poor people and underprivileged groups have the most to gain from applying AI technologies in the legal field. AI chatbots enable interaction between AI and humans, predictive analytics for evaluating data and making predictions, as well as automated legal paperwork are a few examples of how AI use promotes cost-effective, efficient, and accessible legal services (Libai et al., 2020). Below are a few examples of how AI technologies are improving legal aid for poor and marginalized groups as well as overburdened legal systems.

13.6.1 AI Chatbots in Legal Aid

Artificial intelligence chatbots and other legal aid tools are most popular on the "DoNotPay" platform. It is a "robot lawyer" on whose creation its creator, Joshua

Browder from London, spent six days (Fernando et al., 2023). It initially helped people challenge parking charges, but later, Browder improved the program. The chatbot offers basic legal advice on landlord-tenant, contract, and consumer rights issues. The chatbot uses natural language processing to understand the user's question and guide them to their desired legal result. For example, DoNotPay can help a tenant appeal an unfair eviction by generating supporting legal documents and providing advice. Thus, the biggest result of the development of this AI tool is that AI chatbots can help poor communities with no access to legal services. Around 99 percent of DoNotPay users cannot pay for a human lawyer. This is why not all people can afford professional legal advice, and for many of these communities, DoNotPay helps them get justice quickly and for free. This tool shows that AI-powered legal aid technologies can offer quick, cost-efficient alternatives for justice delivery, which can change the way justice is delivered (Khawaja & Bélisle-Pipon, 2023). The Australian AI chatbot Ailira also offers support in tax laws and small businesses. Ailira guides users through lengthy tax laws and the correct corporate structure to meet their needs. Like DoNotPay, the Ailira AI bot also uses natural language processing. It proves that AI can also offer cost-efficient solutions for providing advice on tax law.

13.6.2   PREDICTIVE ANALYTICS IN LEGAL AID SERVICES

Low-cost legal aid organizations are using AI's predictive abilities to improve case success rates and streamline legal work. A non-profit housing dispute legal aid organization, HUMANITAS, uses predictive analytics. With past case data, HUMANITAS can estimate the probability of winning a legal case relative to the type of dispute, the parties engaged, and judicial trends. As a result, the company can focus on high-probability cases and spend more resources on them. Legal aid organizations can inform clients ahead of time with predictive analytics (Chien & Kim, 2024). For example, AI could assist tenants in learning their probability of winning a ruling in an eviction case based on history. For this cause, legal aid institutions would be able to provide tenants with more useful suggestions, which is vital due to resource scarcity. Predictive analytics can also estimate a case's likelihood of winning and help allocate time and resources to more clients in a legal aid firm (Ford, 2023). Public defenders use predictive analytics to determine plea agreements and court case tactics in the criminal justice system. The AI undertook risk evaluation for pending trial defendants of recidivism in the "COMPAS system" (Garrett & Rudin, 2023). Even though it has been accused of algorithmic prejudice, COMPAS demonstrates how lawyers can be assisted in making data-based decisions. Predictive analytics could aid public defenders and low-income defendants ethically and effectively if supervised.

13.6.3   AUTOMATED LEGAL DOCUMENTATION

The aspect of legal aid transformed by AI is legal documentation automation. Due to their overwhelming caseload, legal aid organizations always find themselves short on time. However, AI-powered systems that automate regular legal documentation help free the lawyers' time and mind space by performing menial tasks

(Kruszynska, 2024). For example, ROSS Intelligence, an AI-supported research assistant, helps lawyers draft legal documents by instantly researching case law and precedents. It draws on the full set of legal databases using natural language processing and machine learning to quickly and precisely draft legal documents. According to the provider, the system helps legal aid organizations draft a brief or a contract up to a hundred times faster than an average lawyer, boosting the efficiency of legal aid and, therefore, lowering the cost of legal aid for the clients (Collenette et al., 2023). In turn, luminance also helps low-income legal aid providers to assess legal contracts and documents instantly. To do this, Luminance relies on the same technology of machine learning. When applied to legal documents, these algorithms can help quickly and precisely assess key clauses, discrepancies, or legal compliance of a document, contributing to slimmer timelines for resolving housing disputes or signing employment contracts or immigration documents. Thus, with these tools, organizations can serve more clients without compromising the quality or accuracy of the work (Zakir et al., 2024). Finally, LawGeex uses AI to help legal aid clients quickly and precisely assess and approve incoming legal contracts. The system draws on the company's legal policies and compares them to the content of the incoming contract, highlighting issues and making recommendations for improvement. In such a way, the AI removes the need for most contract redlining activity and provides clients with instant and accurate advice from legal aid.

13.7 CHALLENGES AND ETHICAL CONSIDERATIONS

Although AI offers benefits, its implementation also introduces ethical and practical problems. These problems must be solved to provide important levels of access to justice with AI systems. This section will cover the subjects of AI prejudice, data security, and challenges in implementing AI in legal aid.

13.7.1 BIAS IN AI ALGORITHMS

One of the most critical ethical issues concerning AI-powered judicial systems is algorithmic prejudice. AI systems, particularly those that assist in the legal field, are trained on huge datasets to predict or make determinations. If these datasets perpetuate societal biases, such as racial or gender biases, the algorithm may further support these biases (Javed & Li, 2024). As an example, an AI system trained on historical data from a court system that disproportionately incarcerates certain races may continue to target those races unfairly. These races may also be the most disadvantaged and least able to obtain an effective defense due to systemic justice barriers, making these prejudices even more dangerous. Additionally, an AI system trained on biased data may incorrectly predict undesirable litigation outcomes, thereby increasing disparities that AI should ideally be used to decrease (Javed & Li, 2024). This is especially the case with respect to biased risk assessment algorithms that overestimate minority bail or sentences within the criminal justice system. As such, biased AI poses a danger to all domains of justice rather than being a tool of equal opportunity. AI development safeguards and governance must be embraced to handle algorithmic bias. Data scientists and attorneys must work to guarantee no bias in the datasets on which they base their AI training (Edenberg & Wood, 2023). AI systems should be audited regularly to identify and address biases. Transparency is also required to detect AI decision-making biases. Without these protections, AI would exacerbate the current inequalities in legal practice rather than provide everyone with equal access.

13.7.2   DATA PRIVACY CONCERNS

In addition to this problem, using AI in the legal sector raises some legal issues concerning data security. It is important to note that courts work with personal, financial, medical, and other privileged information. AI systems containing this information must comply with strong data protection standards. Otherwise, such data might face disclosure, access, or alteration by unauthorized agents (Laptev & Feyzrakhmanova, 2024). At the same time, AI needs large groups of data to function. That is, using this technology in the legal area can also negatively influence a human's privacy. The existing legal regulations on data protection may partially address these concerns. For example, the Personal Data Protection Law 2020 in many countries, including Ukraine, the EU GDPR, US HIPAA, and similar laws, specify how personal data should be protected. According to these laws, the organization must store all classified information in encrypted form and restrict access to this data. The main problem is that these measures are usually extremely expensive and complex (Securiti Research Team, 2024). Moreover, criminal charges can be brought against the employees and directors if the organization does not follow the law. Additionally, as this technology is used, all data is stored and processed on some cloud platform. While cloud servers offer high speed, storage capacity, and cost-effectiveness, they pose a serious threat regarding data storage and access. For example, third-party access is illegal under most countries' laws. Additionally, virtual reign also poses a problem. In either case, AI for legal aid is not free. This makes clients often wonder what happens to their data in computers operated by third parties or when they are restricted in transfer.

13.7.3   PRACTICAL CHALLENGES

AI in legal aid has both ethical and practical issues, especially in the context of limited resources. Primarily, a lack of infrastructure is impeding AI implementation. It is possible that legal aid organizations, especially those that work with low-income or rural populations, do not have access to the internet, high-performance computing technology, and cloud storage (Karan Singh Chouhan, 2019). As a result, AI legal services will not be available to many marginalized, poor, and vulnerable people, thus increasing the justice gap. Secondly, limited funds complicate the issue. For small and new legal aid companies, AI development and maintenance are too expensive. Both the AI software itself and the requisite information storage and security might prove very costly. Furthermore, the expenses of AI professional instruction for legal practitioners could be prohibitive. The third practical issue is the legal profession's general hostility to AI. Some lawyers may be unwilling to use AI features, particularly due to concerns over job insecurity and overreliance on AI technology. Moreover, legal services with an AI platform will be scrutinized for reliability and precision due to the previously stated risks. As a result, despite the system's usefulness, it is possible that it is not being used in practice (Hacker, 2021). To address those practical issues, a multilateral approach is required. Authorities and legal establishments should provide financial support to supply AI to non-internet and other inadequate populations. Legal aid organizations might be provided with grants to help them reform and adopt AI. To help lawyers rethink and understand the need for legal assistance, legal practitioners should conduct several coaching sessions on the benefits and ethical concerns surrounding legal aid AI (Table 13.1).

The table above shows how AI is shaping the provision of legal aid. While these technologies can transform legal access, efficiency, and affordability, they also pose some challenges. Ethical concerns include AI being biased, unfair, lacking data privacy, and lacking human oversight. Moreover, responses to these challenges are central to promoting AI-facilitated legal solutions and avoiding the perpetuation of injustices prevalent in the legal system.

TABLE 13.1

AI Applications in Legal Aid – Benefits and Challenges

AI Application	Potential Benefits	Challenges
AI Chatbots	• Provides instant legal advice • Reduces the cost of legal consultations • Accessible 24/7	• Limited in handling complex legal issues • Risk of biased advice
Predictive Analytics	• Helps forecast legal outcomes • Assists in resource allocation • Improves case management	• Risk of biased algorithms • Ethical concerns regarding fairness
Automated Legal Documentation	• Reduces time for preparing legal documents • Increases efficiency • Reduces human errors	• Privacy risks with sensitive data • Limited flexibility for unique cases
AI in Legal Research	• Speeds up case law and precedent searches • Increases the accuracy of research	• Requires access to vast legal databases • Potential bias in data sources
AI-Powered Decision-Making	• Reduces case backlog in courts • Provides more consistent rulings	• Algorithmic transparency issues • Potential loss of human judgment in critical cases

13.8 REGULATORY FRAMEWORK AND POLICY RECOMMENDATIONS

AI in legal aid services is both beneficial and alarming, requiring a comprehensive regulatory framework. AI may facilitate access to legal aid and make this service more affordable and expeditious. At the same time, AI raises a host of ethical and legal concerns, demanding regulatory instruments to ensure fair justice, transparency, accountability, and the protection of fundamental rights (Table 13.2).

This table lists the main ethical and legal challenges with AI in legal aid services and their remedies. By establishing strict control, transparency, and privacy measures, stakeholders may reduce AI risks and maximize its potential to improve justice. Ensuring accountability and human oversight in essential judgments is crucial to the ethical use of AI in law.

TABLE 13.2
Ethical and Legal Concerns in AI-Powered Legal Aid – Issues and Solutions

Ethical/Legal Concern	Description	Potential Solutions
Algorithmic Bias	AI systems may perpetuate biases from the data they are trained on, leading to unfair outcomes.	• Regular audits of AI algorithms • Diverse and representative training datasets
Data Privacy and Confidentiality	Legal cases involve sensitive personal data, and AI systems could expose this data to risks.	• Implementation of strict data protection protocols (e.g., encryption) • Use of privacy-enhancing technologies like blockchain
Transparency in Decision-Making	AI algorithms are often opaque, making it difficult to understand how decisions are made.	• Mandating explainable AI systems • Clear documentation of AI decision processes
Accountability in AI Use	Lack of clarity on who is accountable when AI makes incorrect or biased decisions.	• Establishing legal frameworks for AI liability • Clear guidelines for AI oversight and accountability
Ethical Use of AI in Legal Services	Ethical concerns over whether AI should replace human judgment in critical legal decisions.	• Limit AI use to assistive roles, ensuring human oversight • Implement ethical guidelines for AI deployment in legal contexts

13.8.1 NEED FOR REGULATION

An AI-driven approach to legal aid should be regulated effectively to prevent bias, privacy violations, and the exploitation of legal data. Without clear laws, AI can exacerbate inequities in the sphere of justice and harm underrepresented people. Biased AI algorithms employed in decision-making can unfairly decide the outcomes of legal aid provisions by attorneys to clients. Furthermore, poor data protection can result in clients' sensitive information being leaked to the public or compromising an individual in front of the authorities (Belenguer, 2022). Regulatory frameworks help to mitigate these risks and offer guidance for the ethical employment of AI in the provision of legal aid. In doing so, such legislation would clearly outline the rules for the development and employment of AI tools for lawyers. This would increase the transparency of legal professionals' ethical uses of AI. Rules and legislation would also raise public trust in responsible legal aid powered by artificial technologies (Lohr et al., 2019). Overall, the ordered balance between innovation and human rights requires legal and regulatory professionals, AI developers, and the appropriate legislative bodies to work in unison.

13.8.2 GLOBAL STANDARDS

There is an opportunity to use the governance of AI provided in the most important global AI targeting rules called the "European Union's AI Act." In 2021, the EU enacted the AI Act to direct the creation and use of AI technology according to risk. AI programs have four threat grades: prohibited, hard, controlled, and small. The utmost danger AI programs, executed in sectors such as healthcare and employment by police and justice operations, will provide more strict regulation accords. More severe standards will be set to protect people's rights in this matter by ensuring that AI is open, liable, and just (Arcila, 2024). The application of the Act will be appropriate to ministers of investment and ethics according to current dangers. More stringent audits will be processed, accords will be of a superior degree of openness, and the entity will be highly accountable. Since the use of AI will be restricted, global and regulatory standards for technological assistance in law may protect the legal provisions' compliance with legal protection and equitable prevention despite distant AI applications. There are global AI parameters that the "OECD AI Principles" and the EU AI Act have set up to guide the latest responsible AI creation (Comunale, 2024). Law will ensure that all AI technologies are steady, open, responsible, and efficient and promote widespread growth. Reserves can ensure the fostering of those technologies by accords on which legal advice creating justice can be done without exceptions.

13.8.3 RECOMMENDATIONS FOR AI GOVERNANCE

To manage risks and maximize the benefits of AI in improving legal aid services, the following policy recommendations can be made:

1. **Ethical Guidelines for AI in Legal Aid**: Governments and legal institutions must establish AI ethics for legal aid. These standards will focus on eliminating algorithmic bias, maintaining data privacy, and ensuring AI accountability. AI systems must be fair and egalitarian to avoid disproportionately affecting marginalized people. Also, professionals and AI developers should be trained in using ethical AI in law.

2. **Transparency and Accountability Policy**: Decisions made by legal aid AI technologies must be explained to ensure clients and legal practitioners understand how they work, including their data and algorithms. For example, a client can appeal when they are dissatisfied with the decision given by an AI. There is also a need for accountability measures to ensure that AI developers and legal experts do not use biased or unethical AI systems.

3. **Audits and Oversight**: Legal aid AI systems should be audited regularly to determine if they are operating ethically and legally. These audits will help discover and fix algorithmic bias, protect data, and ensure fair AI decisions. In addition, independent bodies are needed to oversee legal AI systems and resolve complaints from client and legal professional.

4. **Access to AI-Powered Legal Aid**: Policymakers should invest in infrastructure to deploy AI tools for justice in poor communities. Legal aid organizations should be funded to use AI systems to improve justice. This policy will also help increase internet access in rural and low-income areas. The government should also sponsor research into AI-driven legal aid tools to benefit marginalized people.

5. **Data Protection Regulations**: Legal aid AI systems must comply with high data privacy standards. AI developers and legal experts must encrypt their clients' data and use other security measures. In addition, governments should fund the development of privacy-enhancing technologies, such as blockchain, to secure legal data.

13.9 PROSPECTS OF AI IN LEGAL AID

The emerging AI technology will have substantial impacts on legal aid delivery. The rise of AI legal research assistants seems promising. These AI modalities can process significant legal material and help lawyers identify case law and precedents. In many cases, the legal research time and cost will be reduced, making legal research more accessible to those who could least afford it (Zeleznikow, 2023). Moreover, intelligent contract analysis is already on the rise in the context of commercial legal advice. Introduced at the beginning of the text, "intelligent contract analysis" uses AI to study, create, and analyze contracts accurately and eliminate human error. These AI modalities influence people's lives in terms of time and money, as AI technology shall make legal aid more affordable. This type of AI shall make legal aid delivery more affordable as low-income individuals and small entrepreneurs can access services previously affordable only to the absolute elite. Moreover, AI implementation will allow lawyers to dedicate more time to difficult cases rather than routine paperwork (Forbes, 2024). This shall improve efficiency within the context of any legal aid organization. Truly more democratic than hitherto seen, AI might do justice by making the system fairer, quicker, and cheaper. However, AI must be regulated and supervised, as on its own, AI could perpetuate existing biases or further widen the digital divide. Policymakers and lawyers should use AI to improve justice, not to make society and the economy even more inequitable. AI presents new opportunities to judicial systems, but ethical and societal concerns cannot be ignored.

13.10 CONCLUSION

This study illustrates the changing conceptions of legal aid facilitated by AI, which can make services more accessible to a variety of people while simultaneously making them more affordable and efficient. Assistant features, such as chatbots, predictive analytics, and automatic documentation tools, can facilitate fairer and more responsive justice for marginalized populations (Alessa, 2022). However, it is crucial for appropriate legislation and monitoring to prevent algorithmic biases, protect customers' data security and ensure that services may be trusted in practice. To achieve this end, policymakers, legal experts, and AI developers must cooperate to facilitate the best possible use of AI for legal aid. Such a collaborative effort should result in the determination of the standards that AI services should follow and the implementation of measures to ensure that appropriate methods are used, and systems are accountable (Stahl et al., 2021). In turn, such programs can be funded by public authorities and coordinated to ensure that all people in need can take advantage of AI-based legal aid. Overall, AI's incorporation into judicial systems should be guided by the principles of justice and fairness, which is possible if such tenets are followed.

REFERENCES

Alessa, H. (2022). The role of artificial intelligence in online dispute resolution: A brief and critical overview. *Information & Communications Technology Law, 31*, 319–342. https://doi.org/10.1080/13600834.2022.2088060

Alvarez, J. M., Colmenarejo, A. B., Elobaid, A., Fabbrizzi, S., Fahimi, M., Ferrara, A., Ghodsi, S., & Mougan, C. (2024). Policy advice and best practices on bias and fairness in AI. *Ethics and Information Technology, 26*, 31. https://doi.org/10.1007/s10676-024-09746-w

Arcila, B. B. (2024). AI liability in Europe: How does it complement risk regulation and deal with the problem of human oversight? *Computer Law & Security Review, 54*, 106012. https://www.sciencedirect.com/science/article/pii/S0267364924000797

Belenguer, L. (2022). AI bias: Exploring discriminatory algorithmic decision-making models and the application of possible machine-centric solutions adapted from the pharmaceutical industry. *AI and Ethics, 2*, 771–787. https://doi.org/10.1007/s43681-022-00138-8

Camilleri, M. A. (2024). Artificial intelligence governance: Ethical considerations and implications for social responsibility. *Expert Systems, 41*(7), e13406. https://doi.org/10.1111/exsy.13406

Chakraborty, C., Pal, S., Bhattacharya, M., Dash, S., & Lee, S.-S. (2023). Overview of Chatbots with special emphasis on artificial intelligence-enabled ChatGPT in medical science. *Frontiers in Artificial Intelligence, 6*, 1237704. https://doi.org/10.3389/frai.2023.1237704

Chien, C. V. & Kim, M. (2024). *Generative AI and Legal Aid: Results from a Field Study and 100 Use Cases to Bridge the Access to Justice Gap by Colleen V. Chien, Miriam Kim: SSRN.* https://papers.ssrn.com/sol3/papers.cfm?abstract_id=4733061

Chouhan, K. S. (2019). Role of an AI in legal aid and access to criminal justice. *International Journal of Legal Research, 6,* 2. https://papers.ssrn.com/sol3/papers.cfm?abstract_id=3536194

Collenette, J., Atkinson, K., & Bench-Capon, T. (2023). Explainable AI tools for legal reasoning about cases: A study on the European court of human rights. *Artificial Intelligence, 317,* 103861. https://doi.org/10.1016/j.artint.2023.103861

Comunale, M. (2024). The economic impacts and the regulation of AI: A review of academic literature and policy actions. *IMF Working Papers, 2024*(065), 1. https://doi.org/10.5089/9798400268588.001

Dankwa-Mullan, I. (2024). Health equity and ethical considerations in using artificial intelligence in public health and medicine. *Preventing Chronic Disease, 21,* E64. https://doi.org/10.5888/pcd21.240245

Edenberg, E. & Wood, A. (2023). Disambiguating algorithmic bias: From neutrality to justice. In *Proceedings of the 2023 AAAI/ACM Conference on AI, Ethics, and Society,* vol. 81, pp. 691–704. https://doi.org/10.1145/3600211.3604695

EU AI Act: First regulation on artificial intelligence. (2023). *Topics.* European Parliament. https://www.europarl.europa.eu/topics/en/article/20230601STO93804/eu-ai-act-first-regulation-on-artificial-intelligence

Feijóo, C., Kwon, Y., Bauer, J. M., Bohlin, E., Howell, B., Jain, R., Potgieter, P., Vu, K., Whalley, J., & Xia, J. (2020). Harnessing artificial intelligence (AI) to increase well-being for all: The case for modern technology diplomacy. *Telecommunications Policy, 44*(6), 101988. https://doi.org/10.1016/j.telpol.2020.101988

Fernando, Z. J., Kristanto, K., Anditya, A. W., Hartati, S. Y., & Baskara, A. (2023). Robot lawyer in Indonesian criminal justice system: Problems and challenges for future law enforcement. *Lex Scientia Law Review, 7*(2), 489–528. https://doi.org/10.15294/lesrev.v7i2.69423

Forbes. (2024). *AI Legal Services: How AI Is Providing Small Businesses with Affordable Legal Help.* https://www.forbes.com/sites/allbusiness/2024/01/18/ai-legal-services-how-ai-is-providing-small-businesses-with-affordable-legal-help/

Ford, J. (2023). *Artificial Intelligence Models Aim to Forecast Eviction, Promote Renter Rights.* Penn State University. https://www.psu.edu/news/information-sciences-and-technology/story/artificial-intelligence-models-aim-forecast-eviction

Garrett, B. L. & Rudin, C. (2023). Interpretable algorithmic forensics. *Proceedings of the National Academy of Sciences of the United States of America, 120,* e2301842120. https://www.pnas.org/doi/full/10.1073/pnas.2301842120

Greggwirth. (2023, May 25). *Forum: There's Potential for AI Chatbots to Increase Access to Justice.* Thomson Reuters Institute, New York. https://www.thomsonreuters.com/en-us/posts/legal/forum-spring-2023-ai-chatbots/

Hacker, P. (2021). The European AI liability directives – Critique of a half-hearted approach and lessons for the future. *Computer Law & Security Review, 51,* 105871.

Javed, K. & Li, J. (2024). Artificial intelligence in judicial adjudication: Semantic biasness classification and identification in legal judgement (SBCILJ). *Heliyon, 10,* e30184. https://www.sciencedirect.com/science/article/pii/S2405844024062157

Khawaja, Z. & Bélisle-Pipon, J.-C. (2023). Your robot therapist is not your therapist: Understanding the role of AI-powered mental health chatbots. *Frontiers in Digital Health, 5,* 1278186. https://doi.org/10.3389/fdgth.2023.1278186

Kruszynska, M. (2024). *AI in the Legal Sector: How Can Legal Professionals Use AI & Automation?* Spyrosoft. https://spyro-soft.com/blog/legal-tech/ai-in-the-legal-sector-how-can-legal-professionals-use-ai-automation

Laptev, V. A. & Feyzrakhmanova, D. R. (2024). Application of artificial intelligence in justice: Current trends and future prospects. *Human-Centric Intelligent Systems, 4*, 394–405. https://doi.org/10.1007/s44230-024-00074-2

Lee, D., Arnold, M., Srivastava, A., Plastow, K., Strelan, P., Ploeckl, F., Lekkas, D., & Palmer, E. (2024). The impact of generative AI on higher education learning and teaching: A study of educators' perspectives. *Computers and Education: Artificial Intelligence, 6*, 100221. https://doi.org/10.1016/j.caeai.2024.100221

Libai, B., Bart, Y., Gensler, S., Hofacker, C. F., Kaplan, A., Kötterheinrich, K., & Kroll, E. B. (2020). Brave new world? On AI and the management of customer relationships. *Journal of Interactive Marketing, 51*, 44–56. https://doi.org/10.1016/j.intmar.2020.04.002

Lohr, J. D., Maxwell, W. J., & Watts, P. (2019). Legal practitioners' approach to regulating AI risks. In K. Yeung & M. Lodge (Eds.), *Algorithmic Regulation*. Oxford University Press, Oxford. https://doi.org/10.1093/oso/9780198838494.003.0010

MacDowell, E. L. (2015). Reimagining access to justice in the poor people's courts. *Georgetown Journal on Poverty Law & Policy, 22*, 3.

Perlman, A. (2023). *The Implications of ChatGPT for Legal Services and Society*. Harvard Law School Center on the Legal Profession. https://clp.law.harvard.edu/article/the-implications-of-chatgpt-for-legal-services-and-society/

Securiti Research Team. (2024). *Data Privacy Laws and Regulations around the World*. Securiti. https://securiti.ai/privacy-laws/

Simshaw, D. (2022). Access to A.I. justice: Avoiding an inequitable two-tiered system of legal services. *Yale Journal of Law & Technology, 24*, 150.

Stahl, B. C., Andreou, A., Brey, P., Hatzakis, T., Kirichenko, A., Macnish, K., Laulhé Shaelou, S., Patel, A., Ryan, M., & Wright, D. (2021). Artificial intelligence for human flourishing – Beyond principles for machine learning. *Journal of Business Research, 124*, 374–388. https://doi.org/10.1016/j.jbusres.2020.11.030

Zakir, M. H., Bashir, S., Ali, R. N., & Khan, S. H. (2024). Artificial intelligence and machine learning in legal research: A comprehensive analysis. *Qlantic Journal of Social Sciences, 5*(1), 307–317. https://doi.org/10.55737/qjss.203679344

Zeleznikow, J. (2023). The benefits and dangers of using machine learning to support making legal predictions. *WIREs Data Mining and Knowledge Discovery, 13*(4), e1505. https://doi.org/10.1002/widm.1505

Index

Note: **Bold** page numbers refer to tables and *italic* page numbers refer to figures.